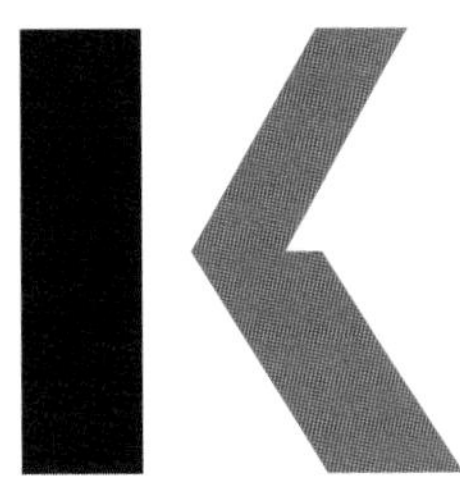

Kaplan Publishing are constantly finding new ways to make a difference to your studies and our exciting online resources really do offer something different to students looking for exam success.

...tes so that you can ...e is not sold ...arately and is included in the p... ...ok.

Having purchased this book, you have access to the follow...

CONTENT	AAT	
	Text	Kit
Electronic version of the book	✓	✓
Progress tests with instant answers	✓	
Mock assessments online	✓	✓
Material updates	✓	✓

How to access your online resources

Kaplan Financial students will already have a MyKaplan account and these extra resources will be available to you online. You do not need to register again, as this process was completed when you enrolled. If you are having problems accessing online materials, please ask your course administrator.

If you are not studying with Kaplan and did not purchase your book via a Kaplan website, to unlock your extra online resources please go to www.mykaplan.co.uk/addabook (even if you have set up an account and registered books previously). You will then need to enter the ISBN number (on the title page and back cover) and the unique pass key number contained in the scratch panel below to gain access. You will also be required to enter additional information during this process to set up or confirm your account details.

If you purchased through the Kaplan Publishing website you will automatically receive an e-mail invitation to MyKaplan. Please register your details using this email to gain access to your content. If you do not receive the e-mail or book content, please contact Kaplan Publishing.

Your Code and Information

This code can only be used once for the registration of one book online. This registration and your online content will expire when the final sittings for the examinations covered by this book have taken place. Please allow one hour from the time you submit your book details for us to process your request.

Please scratch the film to access your unique code.

Please be aware that this code is case-sensitive and you will need to include the dashes within the passcode, but not when entering the ISBN.

BOOKKEEPING TRANSACTIONS

STUDY TEXT

Qualifications and Credit Framework

AQ2016

This Study Text supports study for the following AAT qualifications:

AAT Foundation Certificate in Accounting – Level 2

AAT Foundation Diploma in Accounting and Business – Level 2

AAT Foundation Certificate in Bookkeeping – Level 2

AAT Foundation Award in Accounting Software – Level 2

AAT Level 2 Award in Accounting Skills to Run Your Business

AAT Foundation Certificate in Accounting at SCQF Level 5

British Library Cataloguing-in-Publication Data

A catalogue record for this book is available from the British Library.

Published by
Kaplan Publishing UK
Unit 2, The Business Centre
Molly Millars Lane
Wokingham
Berkshire
RG41 2QZ

ISBN: 978-1-78740-774-9

The text in this material and any others made available by any Kaplan Group company does not amount to advice on a particular matter and should not be taken as such. No reliance should be placed on the content as the basis for any investment or other decision or in connection with any advice given to third parties. Please consult your appropriate professional adviser as necessary. Kaplan Publishing Limited and all other Kaplan group companies expressly disclaim all liability to any person in respect of any losses or other claims, whether direct, indirect, incidental, consequential or otherwise arising in relation to the use of such materials.

Printed and bound in Great Britain.

CONTENTS

INTRODUCTION

HOW TO USE THESE MATERIALS

These Kaplan Publishing learning materials have been carefully designed to make your learning experience as easy as possible and to give you the best chance of success in your AAT assessments.

They contain a number of features to help you in the study process.

The sections on the Unit Guide, the Assessment and Study Skills should be read before you commence your studies.

They are designed to familiarise you with the nature and content of the assessment and to give you tips on how best to approach your studies.

STUDY TEXT

This study text has been specially prepared for the revised AAT qualification introduced in September 2016.

It is written in a practical and interactive style:

- key terms and concepts are clearly defined
- all topics are illustrated with practical examples with clearly worked solutions based on sample tasks provided by the AAT in the new examining style
- frequent activities throughout the chapters ensure that what you have learnt is regularly reinforced
- 'pitfalls' and 'examination tips' help you avoid commonly made mistakes and help you focus on what is required to perform well in your examination
- 'Test your understanding' activities are included within each chapter to apply your learning and develop your understanding.

ICONS

The chapters include the following icons throughout.

They are designed to assist you in your studies by identifying key definitions and the points at which you can test yourself on the knowledge gained.

Definition

These sections explain important areas of Knowledge which must be understood and reproduced in an assessment.

Example

The illustrative examples can be used to help develop an understanding of topics before attempting the activity exercises.

Test your understanding

These are exercises which give the opportunity to assess your understanding of all the assessment areas.

Quality and accuracy are of the utmost importance to us so if you spot an error in any of our products, please send an email to mykaplanreporting@kaplan.com with full details.

Our Quality Co-ordinator will work with our technical team to verify the error and take action to ensure it is corrected in future editions.

Progression

There are two elements of progression that we can measure: first how quickly students move through individual topics within a subject; and second how quickly they move from one course to the next. We know that there is an optimum for both, but it can vary from subject to subject and from student to student. However, using data and our experience of student performance over many years, we can make some generalisations.

A fixed period of study set out at the start of a course with key milestones is important. This can be within a subject, for example 'I will finish this topic by 30 June', or for overall achievement, such as 'I want to be qualified by the end of next year'.

Your qualification is cumulative, as earlier papers provide a foundation for your subsequent studies, so do not allow there to be too big a gap between one subject and another.

We know that exams encourage techniques that lead to some degree of short term retention, the result being that you will simply forget much of what you have already learned unless it is refreshed (look up Ebbinghaus Forgetting Curve for more details on this). This makes it more difficult as you move from one subject to another: not only will you have to learn the new subject, you will also have to relearn all the underpinning knowledge as well. This is very inefficient and slows down your overall progression which makes it more likely you may not succeed at all.

In addition, delaying your studies slows your path to qualification which can have negative impacts on your career, postponing the opportunity to apply for higher level positions and therefore higher pay.

You can use the following diagram showing the whole structure of your qualification to help you keep track of your progress.

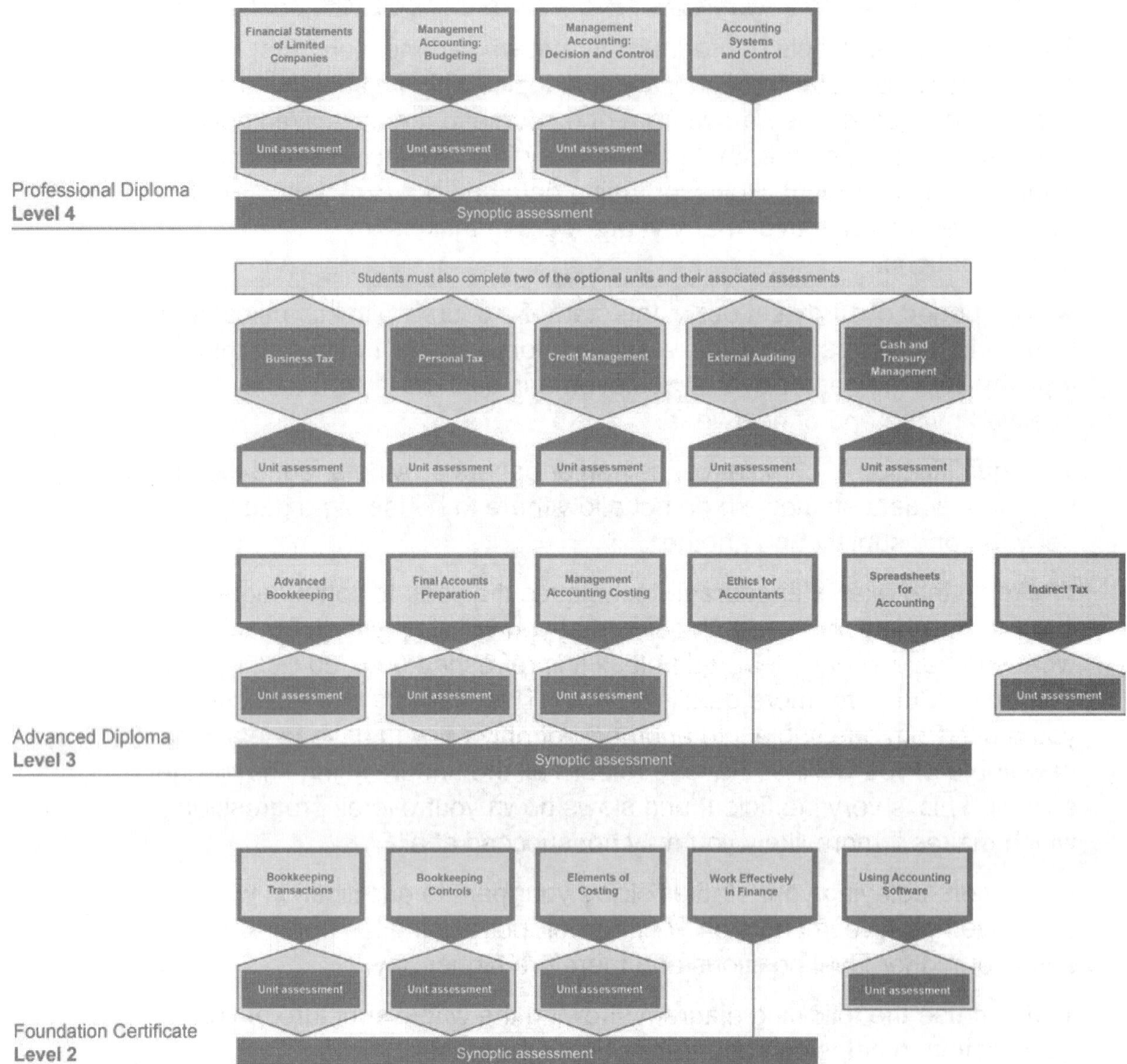
Financial Statements of Limited Companies
Management Accounting: Budgeting
Management Accounting: Decision and Control
Accounting Systems and Control
Unit assessment
Unit assessment
Unit assessment
Professional Diploma
Level 4
Synoptic assessment
Students must also complete two of the optional units and their associated assessments
Business Tax
Personal Tax
Credit Management
External Auditing
Cash and Treasury Management
Unit assessment
Unit assessment
Unit assessment
Unit assessment
Unit assessment
Advanced Bookkeeping
Final Accounts Preparation
Management Accounting Costing
Ethics for Accountants
Spreadsheets for Accounting
Indirect Tax
Unit assessment
Unit assessment
Unit assessment
Unit assessment
Advanced Diploma
Level 3
Synoptic assessment
Bookkeeping Transactions
Bookkeeping Controls
Elements of Costing
Work Effectively in Finance
Using Accounting Software
Unit assessment
Unit assessment
Unit assessment
Unit assessment
Foundation Certificate
Level 2
Synoptic assessment

UNIT GUIDE

Introduction

Bookkeeping Transactions introduces students to the double-entry bookkeeping system and the associated documents and processes. Students will reach the stage of extracting an initial trial balance, before any adjustments are made. This unit provides students with the skills necessary to operate a manual double-entry bookkeeping system and provides a strong foundation for progression to more advanced manual and computerised activities.

On completion of this unit, students will be able to check the accuracy of invoices, credit notes, remittance advices, statements of account and petty cash vouchers. They will know how to use these documents to make entries in sales and purchases daybooks, sales and purchases returns daybooks, and discounts allowed and received daybooks using account codes, as well as how to transfer those totals to the sales, purchases and general ledgers.

The UK government department responsible for collecting taxes (HMRC) offers more than one method of accounting treatment when prompt payment discount (PPD) is allowed and received. However, students at Foundation level are only required to use credit notes to adjust for PPD. Using this approach, credit notes are recorded in separate daybooks, a discounts allowed daybook and/or a discounts received daybook, removing the need for discount columns in the cash book. There is no requirement at this level for learners to understand how to account for PPD by any other method.

The cash book and petty cash book are also covered in this unit, including making entries into both and transferring totals to the ledgers. Students will make appropriate checks on the accuracy of supplier invoices and credit notes, reconcile supplier statements with the purchases ledger account and calculate payments due to suppliers. They will also calculate sales invoice and credit note amounts and check receipts from customers.

This unit refers to value added tax or VAT. This is an indirect tax operating in the UK but this type of tax may also operate and be known by another name in other countries.

Bookkeeping Transactions is a mandatory unit in this qualification.

Learning outcomes

On completion of this unit the learner will be able to:

- understand financial transactions within a bookkeeping system
- process customer transactions
- process supplier transactions
- process receipts and payments
- process transactions through the ledgers to the trial balance

Scope of content

To perform this unit effectively you will need to know and understand the following:

		Chapter
1	**Understand financial transactions within a bookkeeping system**	
1.1	**Indicate the purpose of business documents** Students need to know: • the purpose of business documents: petty cash voucher, invoice, credit note (including for PPD), remittance advice, statement of account.	1,8
1.2	**Distinguish between prompt payment, trade and bulk discounts** Students need to know: • the difference between discounts offered: prompt payment, trade and bulk • how discounts are shown on invoices: prompt payment, trade and bulk • how to use credit notes to adjust for PPD and how PPD is recorded once taken: discounts allowed or discounts received daybook, sales or purchases ledger account, general ledger discounts allowed or received account as income or expenditure, sales or purchases ledger control account, value added tax (VAT) account.	1, 5, 6, 8

		Chapter
1.3	**Demonstrate an understanding of a coding system** Students need to know: • the different types of code: customer account, supplier account, product • where to use codes: sales, sales returns and discounts allowed daybooks and purchases, purchase returns and discounts received daybooks, sales and purchases ledgers • how to create codes: alphabetical, numerical, alphanumerical.	1
1.4	**Demonstrate an understanding of the process of recording financial transactions** Students need to know: • the role of the books of prime entry: sales and sales returns daybooks, purchases and purchases returns daybooks, discounts allowed and discounts received daybooks • the role of the cash book and petty cash book: as a book of prime entry only, as a book of prime entry and as part of the double-entry bookkeeping system • the ledgers: sales, purchases and general • the accounting equation: calculation of assets, liabilities and capital, dual effect of transactions • the classification of items: assets and liabilities • the classification of income and expenditure: capital income, capital expenditure, revenue income, revenue expenditure • the purpose of the trial balance.	2, 3, 4, 5, 6, 7, 8,

		Chapter
2	**Process customer transactions**	
2.1	**Calculate invoice and credit note amounts** Students need to know: • the documents to be used: quotations, discount policy, customer order, delivery note, price list. Students need to be able to: • calculate invoice amounts: item price, net, VAT and total amounts, trade and bulk discounts • calculate credit note amounts: item price, net, VAT and total amounts, trade, bulk and prompt payment discounts.	1
2.2	**Enter sales invoices and credit notes into books of prime entry** Students need to know: • the books of prime entry: sales, sales returns and discounts allowed daybooks • the columns within books of prime entry: customer name, customer account code, total, VAT, net, analysis (including product codes). Students need to be able to: • calculate VAT amounts from net and total figures • calculate total and net amounts from the VAT figure • make entries in books of prime entry • total columns in books of prime entry.	2, 5

		Chapter
2.3	**Check the accuracy of receipts from customers** Students need to know: • the records and documents to use: sales ledger account, sales invoice, sales credit note, remittance advice, discount policy. Students need to be able to: • identify discrepancies: under- or over-payment, incorrect discount taken, incorrect amounts • calculate amounts due from customers, including PPD.	1, 5, 8
3	**Process supplier transactions**	
3.1	**Check the accuracy of supplier invoices and credit notes** Students need to know: • the documents to use: quotations including discounts, purchase orders, goods received notes, delivery notes, goods returned notes. Students need to be able to: • identify discrepancies that may be found: non-delivery of goods, incorrect type or quantity of goods, incorrect calculations, incorrect discounts (trade, bulk and prompt payment), date and terms of payment.	1, 6, 8

		Chapter
3.2	**Enter supplier invoices and credit notes into books of prime entry** Students need to know: • the books of prime entry: purchases, purchases returns and discounts received daybooks • the columns within books of prime entry: supplier name, supplier account code, total, VAT, net, analysis (including product code). Students need to be able to: • calculate VAT amounts from net and total figures • calculate total and net amounts from the VAT figure • make entries in books of prime entry • total columns in books of prime entry.	2, 6
3.3	**Prepare payments to suppliers** Students need to know: • the records and documents to use: purchases ledger account, invoices and credit notes (including discounts and VAT), statement of account • the information to take into account: agreed payment terms. Students need to be able to: • identify discrepancies between the supplier's statement of account and the purchases ledger account: timing differences, wrong amounts, missing transactions, duplicated transactions • calculate payments due to suppliers, including PPD.	6, 8

		Chapter
4	**Process receipts and payments**	
4.1	**Enter receipts and payments into a two column analysed cash book** Students need to know: • the format of the cash book: date, details, cash, bank, analysis columns (including VAT) • the documents to use: direct debit/standing order schedule, remittance advice (including BACS), paying in slip, cheque stub, cash receipt, receipts and payments listing. Students need to be able to: • calculate VAT amounts from net and total figures • make entries in the cash book.	2, 8
4.2	**Enter receipts and payments into an analysed petty cash book** Students need to know: • the format of the petty cash book: date, details, amount, analysis columns (including VAT) • the documents to use: cash receipt, petty cash voucher. Students need to be able to: • calculate VAT amounts from net and total figures • make entries in the petty cash book, including reimbursement, using the imprest and non-imprest systems.	2, 8
4.3	**Total and balance the cash book and petty cash book** Students need to be able to: • present totals and balances: column totals, balance carried down, balance brought down, debit balance, credit balance, date and details.	8

		Chapter
5	**Process transactions through the ledgers to the trial balance**	
5.1	**Transfer data from the books of prime entry to the ledgers** Students need to know: • the books of prime entry: sales and sales returns daybooks, purchases and purchases returns daybooks, discounts allowed and discounts received daybooks, cash book, petty cash book • the ledgers: sales, purchases, general • that the sales and purchases ledger control accounts are part of the double-entry system. Student need to be able to: • transfer data from books of prime entry to the relevant accounts in the ledgers.	5, 6, 7, 8
5.2	**Total and balance ledger accounts** Student need to be able to: • total and balance ledger accounts: balance carried down, balance brought down, debit balance, credit balance.	4
5.3	**Extract an initial trial balance** Students need to know: • to use the general ledger to extract balances • the column to use in the trial balance: debit, credit. Students need to be able to: • transfer balances to the initial trial balance • total and balance the initial trial balance.	4

Delivering this unit

Unit name	Content links	Suggested order of delivery
Bookkeeping Controls	Bookkeeping Transactions is the first of two bookkeeping units at Foundation level. With Bookkeeping Controls, it is the foundation for financial accounting at Advanced level.	It is recommended that Bookkeeping Transactions is delivered either before or at the same time as Bookkeeping Controls.
Elements of Costing	The use of codes in this unit links with Elements of Costing.	Elements of Costing might be delivered before, at the same time as or after Bookkeeping Controls.
Using Accounting Software	Bookkeeping Transactions gives students underlying knowledge that may support their study of Using Accounting Software.	It is recommended that Bookkeeping Transactions is delivered either before or at the same time as Using Accounting Software.

THE ASSESSMENT

Test specification for this unit assessment

Assessment type	Marking type	Duration of exam
Computer based assessment	Computer marked	1 hour and 30 minutes

The assessment for this unit consists of 10 compulsory, independent, tasks.

The competency level for AAT assessment is 70%.

Learning outcomes		Weighting
1	Understand financial transactions within a bookkeeping system	10%
2	Process customer transactions	10%
3	Process supplier transactions	15%
4	Process receipts and payments	25%
5	Process transactions through the ledgers to the trial balance	40%
Total		100%

UNIT LINK TO SYNOPTIC ASSESSMENT

AAT AQ16 introduced a Synoptic Assessment, which students must complete if they are to achieve the appropriate qualification upon completion of a qualification. In the case of the Foundation Certificate in Accounting, students must pass all of the mandatory assessments and the Synoptic Assessment to achieve the qualification.

As a Synoptic Assessment is attempted following completion of individual units, it draws upon knowledge and understanding from those units. It may be appropriate for students to retain their study materials for individual units until they have successfully completed the Synoptic Assessment for that qualification.

With specific reference to this unit, the following learning objectives are also relevant to the Foundation Certificate in Accounting Synoptic Assessment

LO1 Understand financial transactions within a bookkeeping system

LO2 Process customer transactions

LO3 Process supplier transactions

LO4 Process receipts and payments

LO5 Process transactions through the ledgers to the trial balance.

STUDY SKILLS

Preparing to study

Devise a study plan

Determine which times of the week you will study.

Split these times into sessions of at least one hour for study of new material. Any shorter periods could be used for revision or practice.

Put the times you plan to study onto a study plan for the weeks from now until the assessment and set yourself targets for each period of study – in your sessions make sure you cover the whole course, activities and the associated Test your understanding activities.

If you are studying more than one unit at a time, try to vary your subjects as this can help to keep you interested and see subjects as part of wider knowledge.

When working through your course, compare your progress with your plan and, if necessary, re-plan your work (perhaps including extra sessions) or, if you are ahead, do some extra revision/practice questions.

Effective studying

Active reading

You are not expected to learn the text by rote, rather, you must understand what you are reading and be able to use it to pass the assessment and develop good practice.

A good technique is to use SQ3Rs – Survey, Question, Read, Recall, Review:

1 **Survey the chapter**

Look at the headings and read the introduction, knowledge, skills and content, so as to get an overview of what the chapter deals with.

2 **Question**

Whilst undertaking the survey ask yourself the questions you hope the chapter will answer for you.

3 **Read**

Read through the chapter thoroughly working through the activities and, at the end, making sure that you can meet the learning objectives highlighted on the first page.

4 **Recall**

At the end of each section and at the end of the chapter, try to recall the main ideas of the section/chapter without referring to the text. This is best done after short break of a couple of minutes after the reading stage.

5 **Review**

Check that your recall notes are correct.

You may also find it helpful to re-read the chapter to try and see the topic(s) it deals with as a whole.

Note taking

Taking notes is a useful way of learning, but do not simply copy out the text.

The notes must:

- be in your own words
- be concise
- cover the key points
- be well organised
- be modified as you study further chapters in this text or in related ones.

Trying to summarise a chapter without referring to the text can be a useful way of determining which areas you know and which you don't.

Three ways of taking notes:

1 **Summarise the key points of a chapter**

2 **Make linear notes**

A list of headings, subdivided with sub-headings, listing the key points.

If you use linear notes, you can use different colours to highlight key points and keep topic areas together.

Use plenty of space to make your notes easy to use.

3 Try a diagrammatic form

The most common of which is a mind map.

To make a mind map, put the main heading in the centre of the paper and put a circle around it.

Draw lines radiating from this to the main sub-headings which again have circles around them.

Continue the process from the sub-headings to sub-sub-headings.

Annotating the text

You may find it useful to underline or highlight key points in your study text – but do be selective.

You may also wish to make notes in the margins.

Revision phase

Kaplan has produced material specifically designed for your final examination preparation for this unit.

These include pocket revision notes and an exam kit that includes a bank of revision questions specifically in the style of the new syllabus.

Further guidance on how to approach the final stage of your studies is given in these materials.

Further reading

In addition to this text, you should also read the 'Accounting Technician' magazine every month to keep abreast of any guidance from the examiners.

Business documents

1

Introduction

The purpose of accounting is to record and classify business transactions. There are many transactions that a business may undertake; credit sales, credit purchases, cash sales, cash purchases, other expenses either paid from the bank or by cash, paying cash into the bank, withdrawing cash from the bank and owner's drawings.

Various documents may be used when dealing with business transactions. This chapter reviews the flow of a transaction through the accounting system paying particular attention to the business documents involved.

The name of a transaction or document will depend on whether we are looking at it from the point of view of the seller or the purchaser. Thus an invoice may be called a 'sales invoice' for the seller but a 'purchase invoice' for the purchaser, it is the same invoice. Similarly, the seller makes a 'sale' and the purchaser makes a 'purchase', it is the same transaction.

ASSESSMENT CRITERIA

Indicate the purpose of business documents (1.1)

Distinguish between prompt payment, trade and bulk discounts (1.2)

Demonstrate an understanding of a coding system (1.3)

Calculate invoice and credit note amounts (2.1)

Check the accuracy of receipts from customers (2.3)

Check the accuracy of supplier invoices and credit notes (3.1)

CONTENTS

1 Business transactions

1.1 Introduction

Businesses may undertake many different financial transactions every day; credit sales, credit purchases, cash sales, cash purchases, other expenses either paid from the bank or by cash, paying cash into the bank, withdrawing cash from the bank and owner's drawings. These transactions are recorded on different business documents and are entered into an accounting system.

The Bookkeeping Transactions unit introduces the double-entry bookkeeping system and associated documents and processes.

1.2 Sales, purchases and expenses

Sales of goods or services and payment for purchases and expenses can be made on a cash or credit basis. Cash sales and purchases are relatively straightforward but credit sales and purchases require more accounting knowledge. Dependent upon whether we are the seller or the buyer dictates whether we view the transaction as a sale or purchase. The details of all aspects covered here will be dealt with in greater depth in later chapters.

1.3 Cash sales and purchases

A cash sale or purchase will normally be made in a retail environment. A customer will enter the shop, choose the goods they wish to buy then pay for them at the till or counter. The seller will tell the customer the price of the goods and the customer then offers payment for them, in the form of notes and coins. Alternatively, the customer may offer to pay for the goods by debit or credit card.

Finally, when the customer has paid for the goods, a receipt of some sort will be given to the customer. This may be printed automatically by the till or may be a handwritten receipt. The transaction is now complete.

1.4 Credit sales and purchases

The procedure for a sale or purchase on credit can be a bit more involved. The sale or purchase process will normally be initiated by a seller receiving an order from a customer. The purchase order from the customer may be in writing, over the telephone, by email, by fax or via a website. When your business receives the order, the first decision to be made is whether or not to allow the customer credit for this sale i.e. the period of time they can take before paying the invoice.

1.5 Offering credit

Selling goods on credit always involves an element of risk. The goods are taken away or delivered to the customer now with the promise of payment in the future. Therefore your business must be confident that the payment will be received. The decision process as to whether or not to make the sale on credit will be different depending upon whether this is a sale to an existing credit customer or a new customer.

1.6 Existing customers

If an existing credit customer wishes to make a further purchase on credit, it would be normal practice to carry out some basic checks. When the customer was originally accepted as a credit customer, a credit limit will have been set which should not be exceeded. Checks should be made to ensure that the new sale, when added to the amount currently owing, does not take the customer over their credit limit.

It would also be sensible to check that there have been no problems recently with receiving payment from this customer. If the checks are satisfactory then the credit sale can go ahead.

1.7 New customer

If a new customer asks for credit from your business then it would be normal practice to ask the customer to supply some trade references – names of other businesses that they trade with on credit that can vouch for their creditworthiness. Your business may also wish to check the customer's creditworthiness through an agency, or by asking for references from the customer's bank.

If the references and checks are satisfactory then a credit limit will be set for this customer and the sale can go ahead.

2 The accounting system

2.1 Introduction

A business may enter into a large number of transactions on a daily basis. It is quite clear that keeping track of all these transactions can be a detailed process.

To ensure that a business does keep track of all sales earned, purchases and expenses incurred, the transactions are recorded in an accounting system.

2.2 Overview of the accounting system

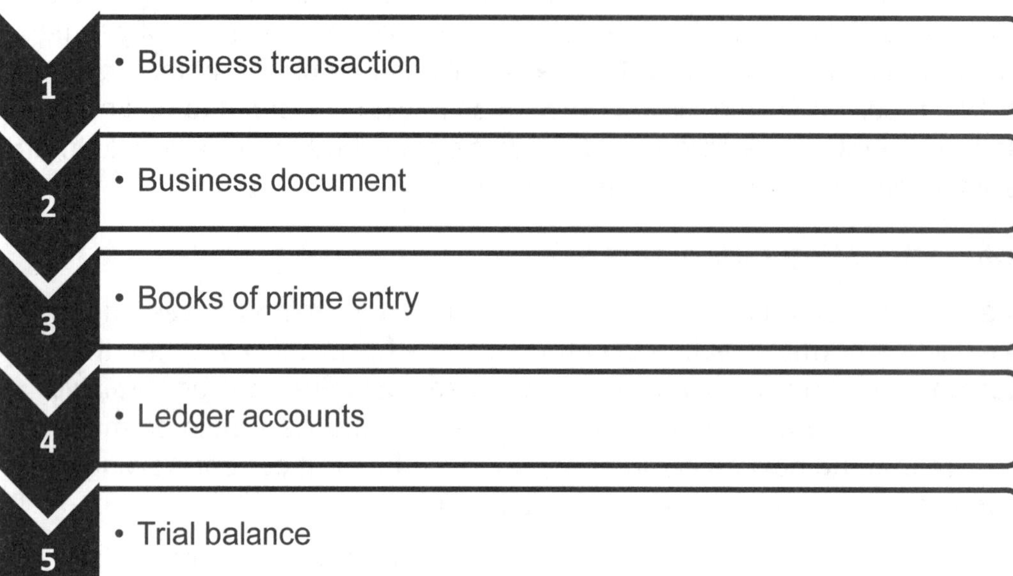

(1) Initially a **business transaction** will take place; a credit sale, a credit purchase, a cash sale, a cash purchase, another expense either paid from the bank or by cash, cash paid into the bank, withdrawal of cash from the bank and owner's drawings.

(2) A **business document** will be produced e.g. an invoice.

(3) The transaction and details from the business document will be entered into the **books of prime entry**. A book of prime entry is where a transaction is first recorded. There are several books of prime entry which may also be referred to as 'day books'. These are reviewed in chapter 2 of this text.

(4) The transactions that have been recorded in the books of prime entry are transferred into **ledger accounts** on a regular basis. Ledger accounts are used as part of the double entry accounting system. Double entry bookkeeping is introduced in chapter 3.

(5) A **trial balance** is a list of all of the ledger accounts in the accounting system and is used as a control to check that transactions have been recorded correctly in the double entry system prior to the preparation of the financial statements. The trial balance is studied as part of ledger accounting in chapter 4.

3 Business documents for a credit transaction

3.1 Overview

The main document flows for a credit transaction are illustrated below. The various documents are described in the sections that follow.

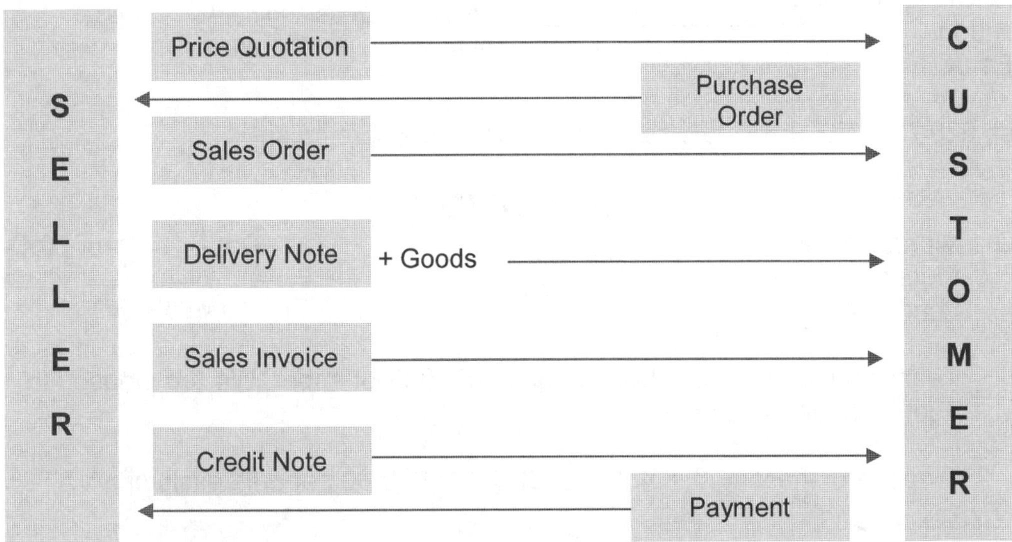

4 Quotation

4.1 Price enquiry

The first stage of the process for a credit sale may be the receipt of a price enquiry from a customer.

The price enquiry may be a formal written document, an email enquiry or a telephone call. When responding to a price enquiry it is important that you make sure that the price you quote is the correct one as if it is incorrect you may find that you are contracted to sell the goods at that price under contract law.

4.2 Price quotation

It is common practice to quote prices on a website if there is a standard price list from which there are no variations. However, some businesses will be prepared to offer certain customers goods at different prices or offer a discount. Therefore it is often the case that a price quotation is sent out to a customer showing the price at which the goods that they want can be bought.

Different types of discounts given or offered to customers will be considered in section 10 of this chapter.

A typical price quotation is shown:

City Woods Suppliers

192 Old Kent Road
London
SE1 8QT

Name, address and contact details of business quoting price

Tel: 020 7248 7009 – Email: sales@citywoodssuppliers.co.uk

QUOTATION

TO: Alpha Limited
Mountjoy Street
London W12 6RS

Name and address of customer

Date: 14 Sept 20X3

Today's date

Thank you for your telephone enquiry of 10 September. We are pleased to quote the following price:

Chipboard sheeting 6' × 4' Code CB0351 £23.00 per unit, excluding VAT

Details of goods

Price being quoted

J Kramer

Authorisation signature

Sales Manager

The price quotation is an important document as this is the price that your organisation is now contracted to sell the goods at. Therefore it is important that it is authorised by an appropriate person in the organisation.

5 Purchase order

5.1 The purchase order

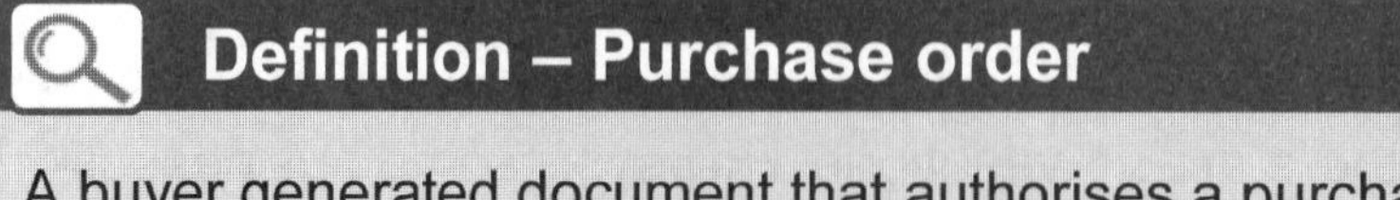

Definition – Purchase order

A buyer generated document that authorises a purchase transaction.

If the customer is happy with the price quotation that they have received from a business then they will place a firm order with the business. The order may be by telephone, email, fax or it may be in writing. Whichever method is used for the purchase order, it is important to check all of the details carefully.

- Does the price agree to what was quoted to the customer?
- Are the delivery terms acceptable?
- Are any discounts applicable?

A typical purchase order follows. Note that the purchase order has been authorised by an appropriate person in the customer's organisation.

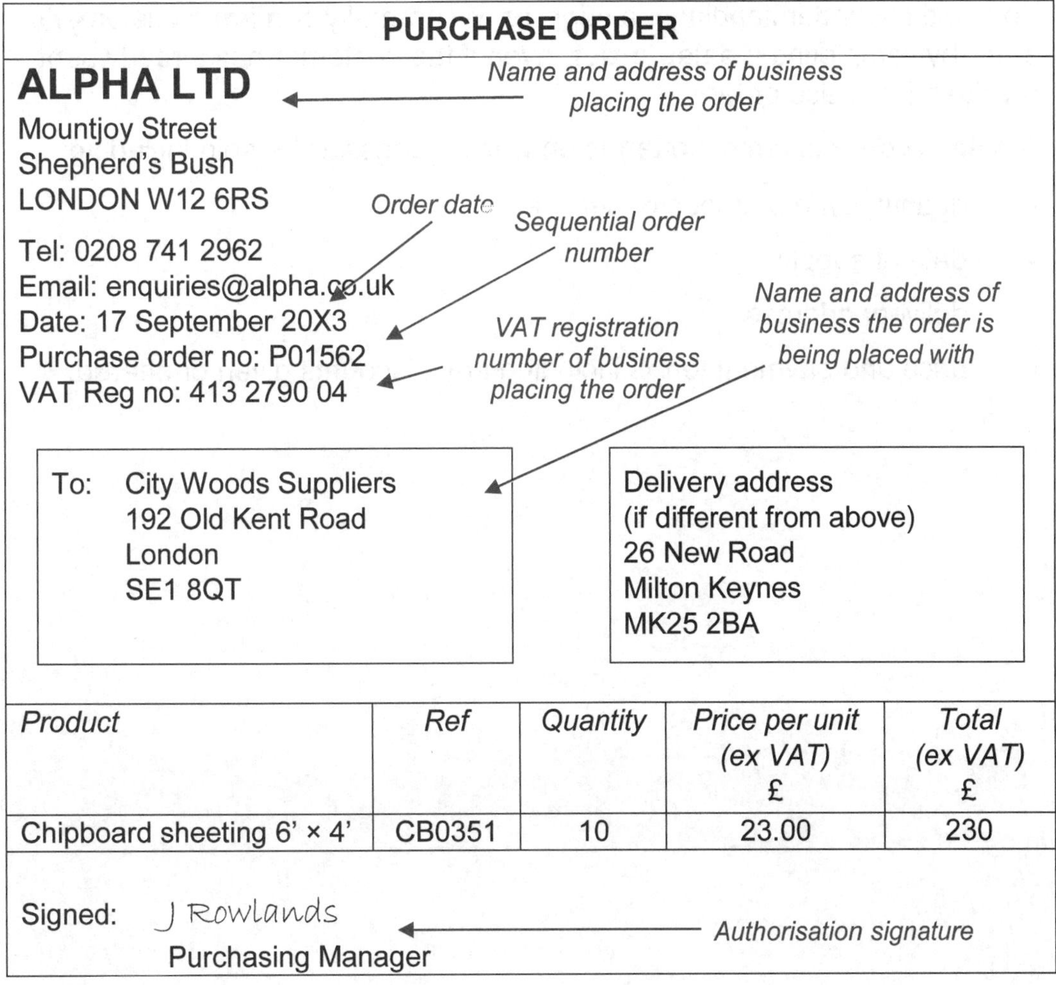

PURCHASE ORDER

ALPHA LTD
Mountjoy Street
Shepherd's Bush
LONDON W12 6RS

Tel: 0208 741 2962
Email: enquiries@alpha.co.uk
Date: 17 September 20X3
Purchase order no: P01562
VAT Reg no: 413 2790 04

To: City Woods Suppliers
192 Old Kent Road
London
SE1 8QT

Delivery address
(if different from above)
26 New Road
Milton Keynes
MK25 2BA

Product	*Ref*	*Quantity*	*Price per unit (ex VAT) £*	*Total (ex VAT) £*
Chipboard sheeting 6' × 4'	CB0351	10	23.00	230

Signed: J Rowlands
Purchasing Manager

6 Sales order

6.1 Confirming sales orders

Definition – Sales order

A seller generated document that authorises a sale to a customer, issued after the receipt of a purchase order.

To avoid misunderstandings, a supplier will normally confirm a customer's order by completing a **sales order**, even if the customer has already sent a written purchase order.

A **sales order** confirms the terms on which goods will be sold including:

- quantity/type of goods or service
- date of supply
- delivery address
- price and payment terms including any discounts given or offered.

City Woods Suppliers

192 Old Kent Road
London
SE1 8QT

Name and address of business making the sale

Delivery address and date

Tel: 020 7248 7009 – Email: sales@citywoodssuppliers.co.uk

SALES ORDER

To:	**Delivery:**	**Delivery date:**
Alpha Limited Mountjoy St London W12 6RS	26 New Road Milton Keynes MK25 2BA	25 September 20X3

Name and address of customer

Sales order number

Date: 20 September 20X3 **Sales order number:** 41161

We confirm the following order to be delivered as above.
Please note our credit terms are strictly 30 days net.

Code	Quantity	Description	Unit price (excl VAT)	Discount
CB0351	10	Chipboard sheeting 6' × 4'	£23.00	NIL

Details of goods *Price of goods*

Authorisation signature

Authorised: P. Anders Date: 20 September 20X3

7 Delivery note and goods received note

7.1 Introduction

When negotiations over the price and terms of the credit sale have been completed, then the goods will be delivered.

7.2 Delivery notes

Definition – Delivery note

A document accompanying goods despatched to a customer explaining what the delivery contains.

Delivery notes should have **sequential numbers** that are either pre-printed for a manual system or computer generated in a computer system, and should be used in order. Spoiled or scrapped delivery notes should be cancelled and retained.

There will normally be three parts to a delivery note:

Part one – This is kept by the **customer** in order to compare to the purchase order and then to the sales invoice.

Part two – This is signed and returned to the **supplier** of the goods as evidence that the goods have been received by the customer in good condition.

Part three – This is signed and kept by the **delivery organisation** such as a courier, as evidence that they have delivered the goods and that the customer has received them.

City Woods Suppliers
192 Old Kent Road
London
SE1 8QT

Tel: 020 7248 7009 – Email: sales@citywoodssuppliers.co.uk DN 005673

DELIVERY NOTE

To:	**Delivery:**	**Delivery date:**
Alpha Limited Mountjoy St London W12 6RS	26 New Road Milton Keynes MK25 2BA	25 September 20X3

Date: 25 September 20X3 **Sales order number:** 41161

We confirm the following order to be delivered as above.

Product	*Code*	*Quantity*
Chipboard 6' × 4'	CB0351	10

Received in good condition: *A Patel*

7.3 Goods received notes

Definition – Goods received note

A goods received note is an internal document completed by the purchaser that records the details of goods received and contains similar information to a delivery note.

The goods received note is often compared to the purchase order as part of a payment authorisation process. The information that a goods received note contains includes:

- supplier name
- quantity/type of goods or service
- the associated purchase order reference and delivery note number
- the name and reference of the carrier for delivery (if different from the supplier).

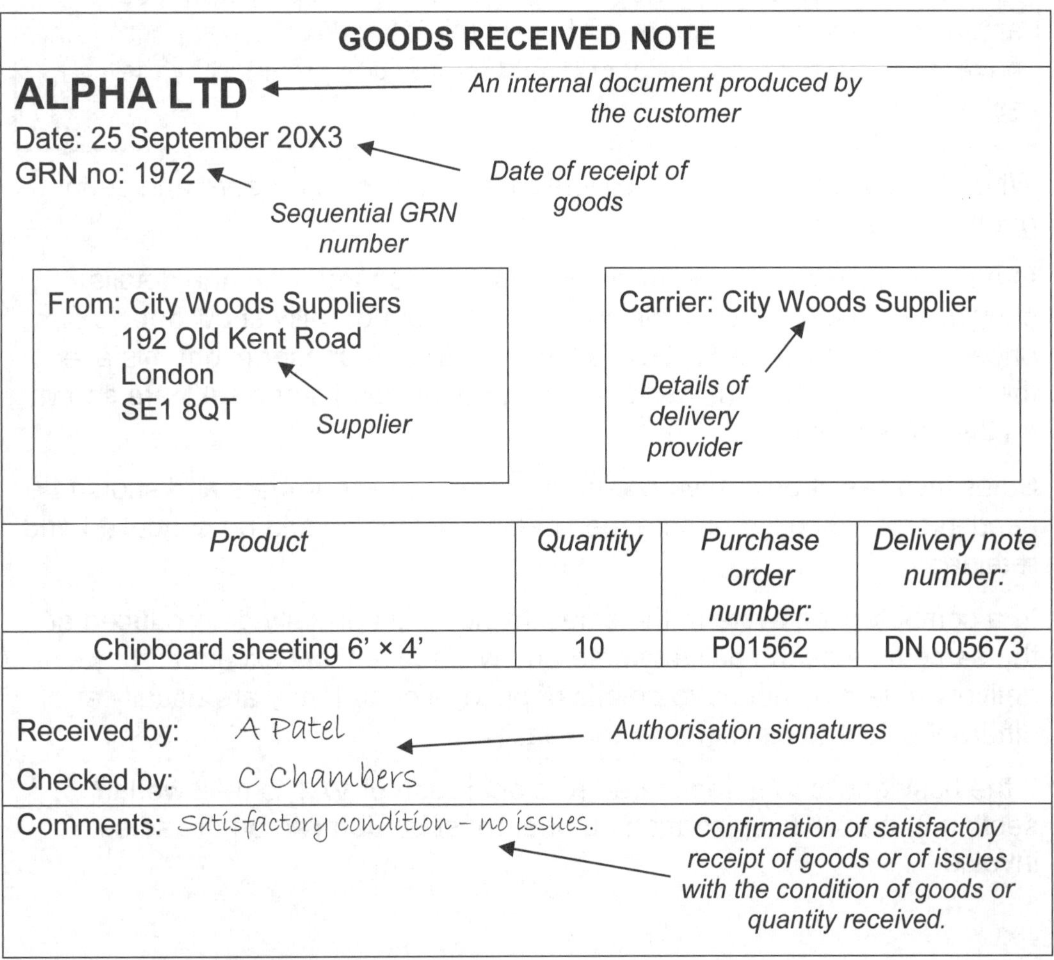

GOODS RECEIVED NOTE

ALPHA LTD ← *An internal document produced by the customer*

Date: 25 September 20X3 ← *Date of receipt of goods*

GRN no: 1972 ← *Sequential GRN number*

From: City Woods Suppliers
192 Old Kent Road
London
SE1 8QT ← *Supplier*

Carrier: City Woods Supplier ← *Details of delivery provider*

Product	*Quantity*	*Purchase order number:*	*Delivery note number:*
Chipboard sheeting 6' × 4'	10	P01562	DN 005673

Received by: A Patel

Checked by: C Chambers ← *Authorisation signatures*

Comments: Satisfactory condition – no issues. ← *Confirmation of satisfactory receipt of goods or of issues with the condition of goods or quantity received.*

8 Invoice

8.1 The sales invoice

Definition – Sales invoice

An invoice is a document that itemises a transaction between a buyer and a seller. A sales invoice can be simply defined as the request for the buyer to make payment for goods sold or services provided by the seller.

When the goods have been delivered the seller must prepare and send out the sales invoice.

In a manual system, sales invoices must be prepared from the details shown on delivery notes. Delivery notes do not normally show details of prices, discounts or VAT. (This is because the purchaser might mistake the delivery note for a sales invoice.) Price, discounts and VAT are shown on the sales invoice.

Sales invoices should have pre-printed sequential numbers and should be used in order. Spoiled or scrapped sales invoices should be cancelled and retained.

In a computerised system, the sales invoice will normally be produced at the same time as the delivery note and will be identical except that the delivery note may not have details of price, etc, and they are usually a different colour to distinguish them easily.

If the business is VAT registered (the operation of VAT is reviewed in section 9) the VAT registration number must be detailed on the sales invoice.

City Woods Suppliers

192 Old Kent Road
London
SE1 8QT

Tel: 020 7248 7009
Email: sales@citywoodssuppliers.co.uk

Invoice no: 1005673
Tax point: 25 September 20X3
VAT reg no: 618 2201 63
Delivery note: DN005673
Account no: AL6215

SALES INVOICE

To:
Alpha Limited
Mountjoy St
London W12 6RS

Delivery:
26 New Road
Milton Keynes
MK25 2BA

Delivery date:
25 September 20X3

Date: 25 September 20X3

Sales order number: 41161

We confirm the following order to be delivered as above.

Product	Code	Quantity	Price per unit £	Total £
Chipboard 6' × 4'	CB0351	10	23.00	230.00
			VAT (20%)	46.00
			Total	276.00

8.2 Pricing goods and services

Unit prices for goods or services are kept in master files which must be updated regularly. If a price quotation has been sent to a customer then this must be used to determine the price to use on the invoice.

Prices will normally be quoted exclusive of value added tax (VAT), as this is the true selling price to the business. We will now review the operation of VAT.

9 Operation of VAT

9.1 Introduction

Definition – VAT (sales tax)

VAT (sales tax) is a consumption tax added to a product's selling price. It represents a tax on the 'value added' to the product at each stage of a production or supply process.

Definitions – Output and input tax

VAT is charged on the **taxable supply of goods and services** in the United Kingdom by a **taxable person** in the course of a business carried on by him.

Output tax is the tax charged on the sale of goods and services

Input tax is the tax paid on the purchase of goods and services

Sales tax (VAT) is a tax levied on **consumer** expenditure. However the procedure is that it is collected at each stage in the production and distribution chain. Most businesses (being **taxable persons** as defined later) avoid having to treat VAT as an expense as they may deduct the VAT they have paid on their purchases **(input tax)** from the VAT they charge to customers on their sales **(output tax)** and pay only the net output tax to the tax authorities (HM Revenue and Customs).

9.2 How VAT works

Let us examine a simple illustration. We will assume a standard rate of 20%, and follow one article, a wooden table, through the production and distribution chain.

- A private individual cuts down a tree and sells it to a timber mill for £10. **Tax effect** – none. The individual is not a 'taxable person' in this case.
- The timber mill saws the log into planks and sells the timber to a furniture manufacturer for £100 + VAT.

Tax effect – Being a taxable person, the mill is obliged to charge its customers VAT at 20% on the selling price (output tax).There is no VAT paid on the purchase cost (input tax) available for offset.

Cash effect – The mill collected £120 from the customer (or has a receivable for this sum). Of this, £20 will be paid to HMRC and therefore only £100 would be recognised as sales.

- The manufacturer makes a table from the wood, and sells this to a retailer for £400 + VAT.

  Tax effect – The manufacturer is obliged to charge VAT at 20% on the selling price (i.e. £80), but in this instance would be allowed to reduce this amount by setting off the input tax of £20 charged on the purchase of wood from the mill.

  Cash effect – Tax of £60 is paid to the tax authorities (HM Revenue and Customs) (output less input tax = £80 - £20). £400 is recognised as sales and £100 as purchases in the accounts of the manufacturer.

- The retailer sells the table to a private customer for £1,000 plus VAT of £200. **Tax effect –** The retailer charges £200 of VAT to the customer but against this output tax may be set off the input tax of £80 charged on the purchase from the manufacturer.

  Cash effect – £120 (£200 – £80) is paid to HMRC. Purchases would be shown in the books at £400 and sales at £1,000.

- **The private customer –** VAT is a tax levied on consumer expenditure and the chain ends here. The customer is not a taxable person, and cannot recover the tax paid.

You will note that everybody else has passed the sales tax on and, though the customer has paid his £200 to the retailer, HMRC has received its tax by contributions from each link in the chain, as shown below:

	£
Timber mill	20.00
Manufacturer	60.00
Retailer	120.00
	200.00

9.3 Taxable supply of goods and services

Taxable supply is the supply of all items except those which are **exempt.** Examples of exempt items are as follows:

- certain land and buildings, where sold, leased or hired
- insurance
- Post Office postal services
- Admission charges to museums, art galleries etc.
- betting, gaming and lotteries.

Input tax cannot be reclaimed where the trader's supplies are all exempt.

9.4 Rates of VAT

In the UK, there are three rates of VAT on taxable supplies. Some items are 'zero-rated' (similar to exempt except that input tax can be reclaimed), there is a special rate of 5% for domestic fuel and power, and all other items are rated at the standard rate of 20%. Examples of 'zero-rated' supplies include:

- water and most types of food stuffs (i.e. not hot food and not eating in as service is also provided which is taxable)
- books and newspapers
- drugs and medicines
- children's clothing and footwear.

9.5 Non-deductible VAT

VAT on some items is non-deductible. This means that VAT on any purchases of these items can never be deducted from the amount of tax payable to HMRC. The business has to bear the VAT as an expense.

Non-deductible items include:

- motor cars
- business entertaining.

For our purposes you will normally be dealing with taxable supplies at the standard rate of 20%.

9.6 Taxable person

A taxable person is any individual, partnership, company, etc who intends to make taxable supplies and is liable to register.

A person is liable to register if the value of his taxable supplies exceeds a specified amount in a 12-month period. Most companies and partnerships and many sole traders are liable to register.

9.7 VAT exclusive amounts

Definition – Net of VAT

A net amount excludes VAT.

If you are given the net price of goods, the price excluding VAT, then the amount of VAT is 20/100 of this price.

Note: VAT is always rounded down to the nearest penny.

Example 1

A sale is made for £360.48 plus VAT. What is the amount of VAT to be charged on this sale?

Solution

VAT = £360.48 × 20/100 = £72.09

Remember to round down to the nearest penny.

An alternative way of calculating this would to be to multiply the net amount of £360.48 by 20%:

VAT = £360.48 × 20% = £72.09

9.8 VAT inclusive amounts

Definition – Gross of VAT

A gross amount includes VAT.

If a price is given that already includes the VAT then calculating the VAT requires an understanding of the price structure:

	%
Selling price incl. VAT (gross)	120
VAT	20
Selling price excl. VAT (net)	100

Example 2

Goods have a selling price of £3,000 inclusive of VAT. What is the VAT on the goods and the net price of these goods?

Solution

	£
Net price (£3,000 × 100/120)	2,500
VAT (£3,000 × 20/120)	500
Gross price (selling price)	3,000

Test your understanding 1

What is the amount of VAT on each of the following transactions?

(i) £100 net of VAT

(ii) £250 net of VAT

(iii) £480 including VAT (gross)

(iv) £600 including VAT (gross)

Test your understanding 2

Dora Ltd ordered some goods from Swipey Ltd, the purchase order and the sales invoice are provided below. You should review these documents and identify any discrepancies.

PURCHASE ORDER

Dora Ltd

Leek Lane
Northwich
Cheshire CW7 5HU
Tel: 01565 734 879
Email: enquiries@doraltd.co.uk

Date: 15 April 20X5
Purchase order no: P0987
VAT Reg no: 414 7985 05

To: Swipey Ltd, Keats Lane, Knutsford, Cheshire, WA16 7HT	**Delivery address** As above

Product	*Code*	*Quantity*	*Price per unit (ex VAT) £*	*Total (ex VAT) £*
Cream leather chairs	CL101	20	98.00	1,960.00

Signed: *Lee-Anne Rogers*
Purchasing Manager

Swipey Ltd

Keats Lane
Knutsford
Cheshire
WA16 7HT

Tel: 01565 879 852
Email: swipey@swipeyltd.co.uk

Invoice number: 15963
Invoice date: 20 April 20X5
VAT reg no: 687 2241 87
Delivery note: DN00154
Account no: DORA1

SALES INVOICE

To:
Dora Ltd
Leek Lane
Northwich
Cheshire
CW7 5HU

Delivery:
Leek Lane
Northwich
Cheshire
CW7 5HU

Delivery date:
20 April 20X5

Date: 20 April 20X5   **Sales order number:** 1569

We confirm the following order to be delivered as above.

Product	*Code*	*Quantity*	*Price per unit* £	*Total* £
Cream leather chairs	CL100	20	100.00	2,000.00
			VAT	400.00
			Total	2,400.00

10 Discounts

10.1 Introduction

A discount is a reduction to the price of the sales of goods or services. There are different types of discounts that may be given or offered for different reasons.

Trade discount

Bulk discount

Prompt payment discount

10.2 Trade discounts

Definition – Trade discount

A trade discount is a definite amount that is deducted from the list price of the goods for the supplies to some customers, with the intention of encouraging and rewarding customer loyalty.

A trade discount will appear on the invoice. It will be deducted from the list price of the goods before VAT is calculated.

The calculation of the trade discount on the face of the invoice should be checked and it should be agreed that the correct percentage of trade discount has been deducted.

10.3 Bulk discounts

Definition – Bulk discount

A bulk discount is similar to a trade discount in that it is deducted from the list price of the goods and disclosed on the invoice. However, a bulk discount is given by a supplier for sales orders above a certain quantity.

A bulk discount must be checked to the agreement between customer and supplier, to ensure that the correct discount has been deducted. The deduction of a bulk discount will appear on the invoice, deducted from the list price before VAT is calculated.

10.4 Prompt payment discount

Definition – Prompt payment discount

Prompt payment discounts (also known as settlement or cash discounts) are offered to customers in order to encourage early payment of invoices.

The details of the prompt payment discount will normally be shown at the bottom of the sales invoice and it is up to the customer to decide whether to pay the invoice early enough to benefit from the prompt payment discount or whether to delay payment and ignore the prompt payment discount. No deduction will occur for a prompt payment discount on the invoice, it will just be offered to the customer.

The agreement between the customer and supplier should be checked to confirm that the correct percentage of prompt payment discount according to the terms has been offered.

A trade discount or a bulk discount is a definite reduction in price from the list price whereas a prompt payment discount is only a reduction in price if the organisation decides to take advantage of it by making early payment.

10.5 VAT calculations and discounts

VAT is calculated after trade and bulk discounts have been deducted from the original list price.

Prompt payment discounts are only offered on an invoice so it does not impact the VAT calculation at the point of the invoice preparation.

If the customer goes on to take advantage of a prompt payment discount offered, the VAT amount is adjusted – this is looked at in more detail in chapter 5 of this text.

11 Preparing an invoice

11.1 Preparing a sales invoice

In order to prepare the sales invoice the customer master file must be found. This will show the details of any discounts given or offered to this customer.

Example 3

Preparing a sales invoice

Thelma Goody is the sales invoicing clerk for a VAT registered clothing wholesaler. Thelma prepares the sales invoices to be sent to the customer from the price list and a copy of the delivery note sent up to her by the sales department.

Today she has received the following delivery note from the sales department.

Delivery note: 2685

To: K Clothing Ltd
9 Port Street
MANCHESTER
M1 5EX

A B Fashions Ltd
3 Park Road
Parkway
Bristol
BR6 6SJ
Tel: 01272 695221
Fax: 01272 695222

Delivery date: 20 August 20X6

Quantity	**Code**	**DESCRIPTION**	**Colour**
90	SSB 330	Shawls (babies)	Assorted
30	CJA 991	Cashmere jumpers (adult)	Cream
30	GGC 442	Gloves (children)	Assorted

Received by: ....

Signature: .... Date: ....

Code	**Description**	**Colour**	**Unit price** £	**VAT rate**
SSG 001	Skirt (girls)	Black	13.50	Zero
SSW 002	Skirt (women)	Navy	15.90	Standard
TTW 037	Trousers (women)	Black	21.00	Standard
TTW 038	Trousers (women)	Navy	15.60	Standard
TTW 039	Trousers (women)	Red	15.60	Standard
SSB 330	Shawl (babies)	Assorted	11.50	Zero
SSB 331	Shawl (babies)	White	11.50	Zero
CJA 991	Cashmere jumper (adult)	Cream	65.00	Standard
CJA 992	Cashmere jumper (adult)	Pink	65.00	Standard
CJA 993	Cashmere jumper (adult)	Blue	65.00	Standard
CJA 994	Cashmere jumper (adult)	Camel	65.00	Standard
HHB 665	Hat (babies)	White	3.50	Zero
HHB 666	Hat (babies)	Blue	3.50	Zero
GGC 442	Gloves (children)	Assorted	6.20	Zero
GGC 443	Gloves (children)	White	6.50	Zero
GGC 444	Gloves (children)	Black	6.50	Zero

The customer master file identifies that K Clothing Ltd's account number is KC 0055 and that a trade discount of 10% is given to this customer.

Thelma must now prepare the sales invoice. Today's date is 22 August 20X6. The last invoice number used was 95123.

Solution

SALES INVOICE

Invoice to:
K Clothing Ltd
9 Port Street
MANCHESTER
M1 5EX

A B Fashions Ltd
3 Park Road
Parkway
Bristol
BR6 6SJ
Tel: 01272 695221
Fax: 01272 695222

Deliver to:

As above

Invoice no: 95124
Invoice date: 22 August 20X6
VAT reg no: 488 7922 26
Delivery note no: 2685
Account no: KC 0055

Code	*Description*	*Quantity*	*VAT rate*	*Unit price*	*Amount excl of VAT*
			%	£	£
SSB 330	Shawls (babies) assorted	90	0	11.50	1,035.00
CJA 991	Cashmere jumper (adult) cream	30	20	65.00	1,950.00
GGC 442	Gloves (children) assorted	30	0	6.20	186.00
					3,171.00
Trade discount 10%					(317.10)
					2,853.90
VAT					351.00
Total amount payable					3,204.90

Step 1 Enter today's date on the invoice and the invoice number which should be the next number after the last sales invoice number used.

Step 2 Enter the customer details – name, address and account number.

Step 3 Refer now to the delivery note copy and enter the delivery note number and the quantities, codes and descriptions of the goods.

Step 4 Refer to the price list and enter the unit prices of the goods and the rate of VAT (note that the VAT rate for children's clothes is zero).

Step 5 Now for the calculations – firstly multiply the number of each item by the unit price to find the VAT exclusive price – then total these total prices – finally calculate the trade discount as 10% of this total, £3,171 × 10% = £317.10 and deduct it.

Step 6 Calculate the VAT – in this case there is only standard rate VAT on the cashmere jumpers but you must remember to deduct the trade discount (£1,950 – £195) before calculating the VAT amount £1,755 × 20% = £351 – add the VAT to the invoice total after deducting the trade discount.

Test your understanding 3

You are an accounts assistant for Smith Fashions. You are required to prepare a sales invoice to be sent to a customer, Bella Boutique. You have been provided with the delivery note and an extract of Smith Fashions' price list.

Delivery note: 165

To: Bella Boutique
10 Main Street
Prestwick
South Ayrshire
KA9 4BB

Smith Fashions

4 Booth Road
Newton Mearns
G2 1PW
Tel: 0141 333 989
Email: admin@smithfashions.co.uk

Delivery date: 20 September 20X6

Quantity	**Code**	**DESCRIPTION**	**Colour**
20	SAZT01	Aztec embellished mini skirt	Assorted
20	TLIV02	Live, Laugh, Love slogan top	Grey
20	TMES03	Mesh stripe top	Black

Received by: ....

Signature: .... Date: ....

Extract of price list:

Code	Description	Colour	Unit price £	VAT rate
SAZT01	Aztec embellished mini skirt	Assorted	25.00	Standard
TLIV02	Live, Laugh, Love slogan top	Grey	12.50	Standard
TMES03	Mesh stripe top	Black	20.00	Standard

The customer file shows that Bella Boutique's account number is BB01 and that a trade discount of 10% is offered to this customer.

You must now prepare the sales invoice. Today's date is 22 September 20X6. The last invoice number was 1586.

SALES INVOICE

Invoice to:
Bella Boutique
10 Main Street
Prestwick
South Ayrshire
KA9 4BB

Deliver to:

As above

Smith Fashions
4 Booth Road
Newton Mearns
G2 1PW
Tel: 0141 333 989
Email: admin@smithfashions.co.uk

Invoice no:
Tax point: 22 September 20X6
VAT reg no: 488 7922 26
Delivery note no:
Account no:

Code	*Description*	*Quantity*	*VAT rate*	*Unit price*	*Total*
			%	£	£
Net amount of goods					
Trade discount @ 10%					
Net amount of goods after discount					
VAT					
Total amount payable					

11.2 The purchase invoice

Definition – Purchase invoice

An invoice is a document that itemises a transaction between a buyer and a seller. We now consider the situation from the customer perspective, what we previously regarded as a sales invoice, to the customer it is a purchase invoice.

When the customer receives their purchase invoice from the seller, a number of checks need to be made before it can be passed for payment.

11.3 Order and receipt of goods

The purchase invoice received must be agreed to the purchase order, the delivery note and goods received note. This is to ensure that not only is this an invoice for goods that were ordered but also for goods that were received. In particular check the description and the quantity of the goods per the invoice against the purchase order and delivery note.

For example, suppose that the purchase order for goods shows that 100 packs were ordered and the delivery note shows that 100 packs were received. If when the invoice arrives it is for 120 packs then the supplier should be politely informed of the error and a credit note requested to rectify the discrepancy.

11.4 Calculations

All of the calculations on the invoice should also be checked to ensure that they are correct. This will include the following:

- all pricing calculations
- any trade discount or bulk discount calculations
- the VAT calculations
- the total addition of the invoice.

11.5 Other terms found on invoices

You may also find other terms and conditions shown on invoices or other documents. Here are some of the more common:

E & OE – Errors and omissions excepted. The seller is claiming the right to correct any genuine errors on the invoice (e.g. prices) at a later date.

Carriage paid – The invoice value includes delivery of the goods to the customer's premises.

Ex works – Prices quoted do not include delivery to the customer's premises. The customer must organise and pay for the delivery of the goods.

Cash on delivery – The customer is expected to pay for the goods when they are delivered.

12 Credit note

12.1 Introduction

Definition – Credit note

Document issued by a supplier to a customer cancelling part or all of a sales invoice.

Businesses normally issue credit notes for any of the following reasons:

- when a customer has returned faulty or damaged goods
- when a customer has returned undamaged goods by agreement with the supplier for a refund
- to make a refund for short deliveries
- to settle a dispute with a customer
- to adjust an account after taking advantage of a prompt payment discount.

A credit note is the reversal of all or part of the earlier invoice value.

Credit notes are issued as documentary evidence that goods have been returned and that all or part of a previous sales invoice is cancelled. Therefore a business must keep strict control over the credit notes it raises and issues.

12.2 Return of goods

When a customer returns goods for any of the reasons mentioned previously, the return of goods will often be accompanied by a goods returned note.

Definition – Goods returned note

Document sent to the supplier by the customer detailing the goods returned and reason(s) for the return being made.

The contents of a goods returned note are similar to a goods received note but with the added detail of why a return is being made.

When a supplier receives returned goods they must be inspected, counted and recorded on receipt. They would normally be recorded on a returns inwards note.

From the perspective of a customer who is returning goods and consequently receives a credit note exactly the same checks should be made on credit notes as on invoices. The reason for the credit note and the amount that has been credited should be checked, along with all of the calculations and the VAT.

12.3 Authorising credit notes

All credit notes must be authorised by a supervisor prior to being issued to the customer.

Some credit notes may be issued without a returns inwards note. For example, an error may have been made in pricing on an invoice but the customer is satisfied with the goods and does not need to return them.

These credit notes must be issued only after written authorisation has been received from a supervisor or manager and must be reviewed and approved before being sent to the customer or recorded.

12.4 Preparing credit notes

A credit note is effectively the reverse of an invoice and therefore will tend to include all the details that would normally appear on a sales invoice.

Using the example of Alpha Limited from earlier in the chapter, if Alpha Limited returned two of the chipboard panels, the credit note would be as follows.

City Woods Suppliers

192 Old Kent Road
London
SE1 8QT

Name and address of issuer of credit note

Sequential credit note number

Tel: 020 7248 7009
Email: sales@citywoodssuppliers.co.uk

Credit note no: CN 02542
Tax point: 30 September 20X3
VAT reg no: 618 2201 63
Return inwards note no: 01531
Invoice no: 1005673
Account no: AL 6215

VAT registration number of supplier

Returns inwards note reference

Date of credit note

Customer's account code

CREDIT NOTE

Credit to:
Alpha Limited
Mountjoy St
London W12 6RS

Name and address of customer

Date: 30 September 20X3

Description	*Code*	*Quantity*	*VAT rate %*	*Unit price £*	*Amount exclusive of VAT £*
Chipboard 6' × 4'	CB0351	2	20	23.00	46.00
				Goods returned total	46.00
					46.00
VAT				*VAT charged*	9.20
				Total amount of credit	55.20

Rate of VAT on goods returned

13 Coding

13.1 Introduction

Definition – Code

A **code** is a system of numbers, letters and symbols designed to be applied to a classified set of items, to give a brief, accurate reference, which helps entry to the accounting records, collation and analysis.

Coding is used within an organisation to provide an efficient and accurate way of referencing customers, suppliers, products and other accounts within the accounting system.

Codes are used in accounting records and the accounting system; within day books, sales and purchases ledgers and other business documents.

Definitions

Ledger code is a unique reference given to different types of income, expenses, assets and liabilities. It may also be referred to as a general ledger (GL) or nominal code.

Customer account code is a unique reference given to each individual customer of an organisation.

Supplier account code is a unique reference given to each individual supplier of an organisation.

Product code is a unique reference given to each type of product of an organisation.

A code can be an alphabetical, numerical or alphanumeric identification system.

Definitions

Alphabetical codes consist of letters. If ordering alphabetically the order is a system whereby characters are placed in order of their position in the conventional ordering of an alphabet.

Numerical codes consist of numbers. If ordering numerically it can be ascending or descending.

Alphanumerical codes are a combination of alphabetic and numeric characters.

Customer files will normally be filed alphabetically by name or perhaps alphanumerically if part of the name is used within the code combined with a number allocation. Sales invoices tend to be filed in sequential order based upon invoice number.

Invoices should be coded to show:

- product group/type for analysis of sales/purchases
- customer/supplier account number.

There are several different systems of coding which can be used by a business.

13.2 Sequence codes

Allocate a number, or a letter, to items in a simple list.

For example:

Code	*Name*
01	ADAMS, Joan
02	AITKEN, James
03	ALCOCK, Freda
04	BROWN, Joe

13.3 Block codes

These allocate bands of numbers to particular categories.

For example, consider a furniture manufacturer who produces several types of tables, chairs and entertainment units. He could assign a code to each particular brand as follows:

Product type	*Block code*
Tables	01 – 19
Chairs	20 – 29
Entertainment units	30 – 39

13.4 Significant digit codes

These are a particular type of group classification code where individual digits and letters are used to represent features of the coded item. The example given is one used to describe different kinds of vehicle tyres sold by a garage.

Code	*Item*
TT67015B	Tube Tyre 670 × 15 Blackwall
LT67015W	Tubeless Tyre 670 × 15 Whitewall

13.5 Faceted codes

Faceted codes are another type of group classification code by which the digits of the code are divided into facets of several digits and each facet represents some attribute of the item being coded. These codes are similar to significant digit codes but are purely numerical.

Example: Faceted code for types of carpet.

Facet 1	=	type of weave (1 digit)	1	=	Cord
			2	=	Twist
			3	=	Short tufted, etc
Facet 2	=	material (1 digit)	1	=	All wool
			2	=	80% wool, 20% nylon
			3	=	50% wool, 50% nylon, etc
Facet 3	=	pattern (2 digits)	01	=	Self colour (plain)
			02	=	Self colour (embossed)
			03	=	Fig leaf, etc
Facet 4	=	colour (2 digits)	01	=	Off white
			02	=	Bright yellow
			03	=	Scarlet, etc

A typical code would be 2/2/03/02 representing a twist carpet in 80% wool, 20% nylon, pattern fig leaf and colour bright yellow.

Note that a two-digit facet allows up to 100 different codings (00 to 99).

13.6 Decimal codes (or hierarchical codes)

These are yet another form of a group classification code. The most obvious example of a decimal code is the Universal Decimal Code (UDC) devised by Dewey and widely used for the classification of books in libraries. UDC divides all human knowledge into more and more detailed categories as shown.

Code	*Item*
3	Social science
37	Education
372	Elementary
372.2	Kindergarten
372.21	Methods
372.215	Songs and games

Whatever the coding system used it is important for accounting purposes that the invoices and credit notes are coded according to type of sales and the particular customer.

You may be expected to code items such as sales invoices or credit notes according to a coding system that is given to you in an assessment.

Test your understanding 4

Is the cheque number used in a cheque book an example of a sequential code or a hierarchical code?

Test your understanding 5

ABC Ltd uses codes within the accounting system. An extract from the general ledger coding list is given below:

General ledger account	Code number
Equipment	10
Receivables	20
Electricity	30
Purchases	40
Sales	50

Required:

(a) Why are the general ledger codes numbered in steps of 10, rather than 1,2,3,4?

(b) Give 3 examples of the use of code numbers in an accounting system, other than general ledger accounts codes.

(c) Are the following statements true or false?

	TRUE/ FALSE
General ledger codes help when barcoding an item of inventory	
General ledger codes help when filing a financial document	
General ledger codes help trace relevant accounts quickly and easily	
General ledger codes help find the total amount owing to a supplier	

Test your understanding 6

Nethan Builders code all purchase invoices and credit notes with a supplier code and a general ledger code. Extracts of the codes used are as follows:

Supplier	Supplier account code
Haddow Bros	HAD29
AJ Broom & Company Ltd	AJB14
Jenson Ltd	JEN32
JM Bond & Co	JMB33

Item	General ledger code
Softwood	GL110
Hardwood	GL112
Sand	GL130
Steel	GL140
Brick	GL145

Required:

For each of the invoices and credit note shown below select the appropriate supplier account code and general ledger code to be used to code them.

SALES INVOICE

Haddow Bros

The White House, Standing Way, Manchester
M13 6FH
Tel: 0161 560 3140
Fax: 0161 560 5140

Invoice to:
Nethan Builders
Brecon House
Stamford Road
Manchester
M16 4PL

Deliver to:
As above

Invoice no: 033912
Tax point: 22 April 20X1
VAT reg no: 460 3559 71
Purchase order no:: 7166

Code	*Description*	*Quantity*	*VAT rate %*	*Unit price £*	*Amount excl of VAT £*
PLY8FE1	Plywood Hardwood 2440 × 1220 mm	12 sheets	20	17.80	213.60
					213.60
VAT at 20%					42.72
Total amount payable					256.32
Deduct discount of 2% if paid within 10 days					

SALES INVOICE

Invoice to:
Nethan Builders
Brecon House
Stamford Road
Manchester
M16 4PL

Deliver to:
As above

Jenson Ltd
30 Longfield Park, Kingsway, M45 2TP

Invoice no: 47792
Tax point: 22 April 20X1
VAT reg no: 641 3229 45
Purchase order no:: 7162

Code	*Description*	*Quantity*	*VAT rate %*	*Unit price £*	*Amount excl of VAT £*
PL432115	Steel rods 32 × 115 mm	14	20	30.25	423.50
PL432140	Steel rods 32 × 138 mm	8	20	33.15	265.20
					688.70
Trade discount 15%					103.30
					585.40
VAT at 20%					117.08
Total amount payable					702.48

Deduct discount of 3% if paid within 14 days

SALES INVOICE

Invoice to:
Nethan Builders
Brecon House
Stamford Road
Manchester
M16 4PL

Deliver to:
As above

A J Broom & Company Limited
59 Parkway, Manchester, M2 6EG
Tel: 0161 560 3392
Fax: 0161 560 5322

Invoice no: 046123
Tax point: 22 April 20X1
VAT reg no: 661 2359 07
Purchase order no: 7164

Code	*Description*	*Quantity*	*VAT rate %*	*Unit price £*	*Amount excl of VAT £*
DGS472	SDG Softwood	9.6 m	20	8.44	81.02
CIBF653	BIC Softwood	7	20	12.30	86.10
					167.12
Trade discount 10%					16.71
					150.41
VAT at 20%					30.08
Total amount payable					180.49

CREDIT NOTE

J M Bond & Co

North Park Industrial Estate, Manchester, M12 4TU
Tel: 0161 561 3214
Fax: 0161 561 3060

Credit note to:
Nethan Builders
Brecon House
Stamford Road
Manchester
M16 4PL

Credit note no: 06192
Tax point: 22 April 20X1
VAT no: 461 4367 91
Invoice no: 331624

Code	*Description*	*Quantity*	*VAT rate %*	*Unit price £*	*Amount excl of VAT £*
DGSS4163	Structural softwood untreated	6m	20	6.85	41.10
					41.10
Trade discount 20%					8.22
					32.88
VAT at 20%					6.57
Total amount of credit					39.45

14 Summary

In this chapter we have concentrated on the purpose and flow of a range of business documents. Before preparing an invoice it is necessary to ensure that this is for a valid sale by checking the order and delivery details. It is important that we understand the need to check business documents that are received and sent to ensure they agree to supporting documents, the calculations are correct in accordance with discounts and the treatment of VAT.

Test your understanding answers

Test your understanding 1

(i) £100.00 × 20/100 = £20.00

(ii) £250.00 × 20/100 = £50.00

(iii) £480.00 × 20/120 = £80.00

(iv) £600.00 × 20/120 = £100.00

Test your understanding 2

Discrepancies:

(1) incorrect product code

(2) incorrect price per unit (per chair)

Test your understanding 3

SALES INVOICE

Invoice to:
Bella Boutique
10 Main Street
Prestwick
South Ayrshire
KA9 4BB

Smith Fashions
4 Booth Road
Newton Mearns
G2 1PW
Tel: 0141 333 989
Email: admin@smithfashions.co.uk

Deliver to:

As above

Invoice no: **1587**
Tax point: 22 September 20X6
VAT reg no: 488 7922 26
Delivery note no: **165**
Account no: **BB01**

Code	*Description*	*Quantity*	*VAT rate*	*Unit price*	*Total*
			%	£	£
SAZT01	**Aztec embellished mini skirt**	**20**	**20**	**25.00**	**500.00**
TLIV02	**Live, Laugh, Love slogan top**	**20**	**20**	**12.50**	**250.00**
TMES03	**Mesh stripe top**	**20**	**20**	**20.00**	**400.00**
Net amount of goods					**1,150.00**
Trade discount @ 10%					**(115.00)**
Net amount of goods after discount					**1,035.00**
VAT					**207.00**
Total amount payable					**1,242.00**

Test your understanding 4

A sequential code (the numbers run in sequential order).

Test your understanding 5

(a) To allow for expansion of the number of accounts in the general (main) ledger

(b) Any three from:

- Customer account codes
- Supplier account codes
- Product codes
- Inventory codes
- VAT codes
- Department codes

(c)

	TRUE/ FALSE
General ledger codes help when barcoding an item of inventory	FALSE
General ledger codes help when filing a financial document	FALSE
General ledger codes help trace relevant accounts quickly and easily	TRUE
General ledger codes help find the total amount owing to a supplier	FALSE

Test your understanding 6

Invoice from:	Supplier account code	General ledger code
Haddow Bros	HAD29	GL112
Jenson Ltd	JEN32	GL140
AJ Broom & Company Ltd	AJB14	GL110
JM Bond & Co	JMB33	GL110

Books of prime entry

2

Introduction

In a typical business there will be a great number of transactions to be recorded on a daily basis. Transactions include credit sales and purchases, cash sales, purchases, expenses and other day-to-day transactions.

These transactions are initially recorded from their source document into the books of prime entry. Books of prime entry may also be referred to as 'day books'.

This chapter introduces the day books which will be used throughout the text.

ASSESSMENT CRITERIA

Demonstrate an understanding of the process of recording financial transactions (1.4)

Enter sales invoices and credit notes into books of prime entry (2.2)

Enter supplier invoices and credit notes into books of prime entry (3.2)

Enter receipts and payments into a two column analysed cash book (4.1)

Enter receipts and payments into an analysed petty cash book (4.2)

CONTENTS

1 Books of prime entry

1.1 Introduction

In a typical business there will be a great number of transactions to be recorded. If we were to record each transaction individually, the accounts would get cluttered.

In order to simplify the process (and exercise greater control) we divide the recording of the transactions into parts.

(a) The first part is entering the transaction into the appropriate book of prime entry (day book).

(b) The second part is recording the totals from the day books into the general ledger which contains many different ledger accounts. This is introduced in chapters 3 & 4.

(c) The third part is to ensure transactions are recorded in the subsidiary ledger which may also be referred to as a memorandum ledger. Recording transactions within subsidiary ledgers is reviewed in chapters 5, 6 & 7.

A book of prime entry is the place where the transaction (which is detailed on a business document) is first recorded in the books of the business. Whilst reviewing the day books take note of the use of codes throughout. There are several day books which will be reviewed in this chapter:

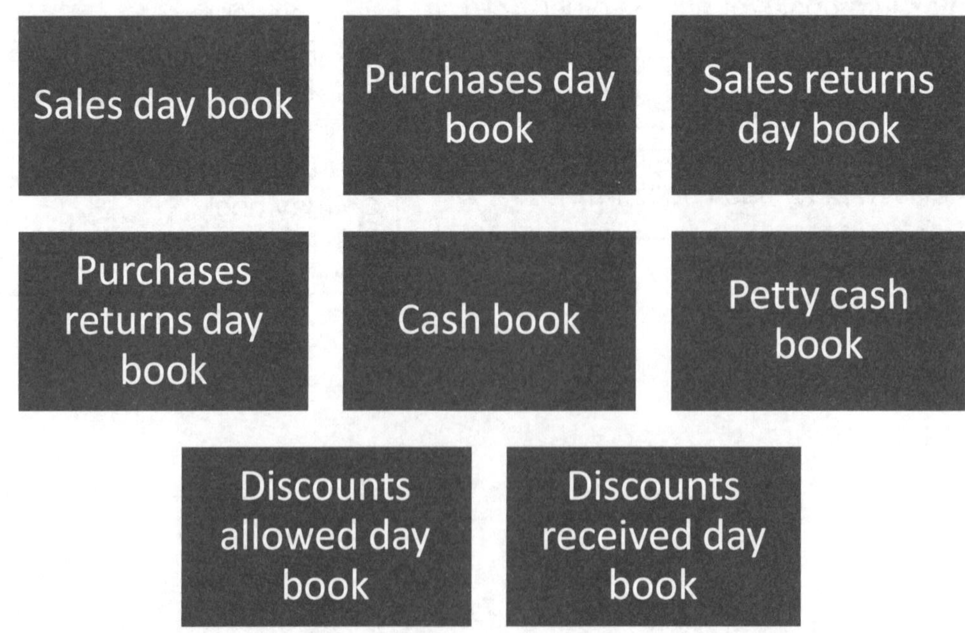

2 The sales day book

2.1 The sales day book (SDB)

In a typical business there will be numerous sales transactions to be recorded. Credit sales are recorded in the sales day book. We will review how cash sales are recorded when we study the cash book.

Definition – Sales day book

The sales day book is a list of the sales invoices that are to be processed for a given period (e.g. a week).

In its simplest form, the SDB will comprise just the names of the customers and the amount of the invoices issued in a particular week.

The SDB is a list, the totals of which are used to perform the accounting entry. Double entry bookkeeping is introduced in chapters 3 & 4.

An example of a SDB is shown below:

Week 1			
Customer	*Total* £	*VAT* £	*Net* £
X	1,200	200	1,000
Y	2,400	400	2,000
Z	3,600	600	3,000
Total	7,200	1,200	6,000

2.2 The analysed sales day book

The sales day book usually includes analysis columns showing how the total value of each customer's invoice is made up.

SALES DAY BOOK								
Date	*Customer*	*Reference*	*Invoice number*	*Total* £	*VAT* £	*Product 1* £	*Product 2* £	*Product 3* £
			TOTALS					

(a) The date column contains the date of the transaction

(b) The customer column contains the name of the customer

(c) The reference column may contain the code number of the customer's account

(d) The invoice number is the number of the invoice issued for this sale.

(e) The total column is the total value including VAT of the goods sold as shown on the invoice:

- after deducting any trade or bulk discounts that may have been given.

Example 1

An invoice to customer A is made up as follows:

	£
Sale of 50 units at £2 per unit	100.00
Less: 20% trade discount	(20.00)
	80.00
VAT (£80 × 20%)	16.00
Total invoice value	96.00

The £96 would be entered in the 'total' column.

(f) The VAT column – this column is the value of the VAT on the invoice – in this case (example 1) £16.00.

(g) Product 1, 2, etc. columns – these are columns that analyse the net sales value (i.e. the VAT exclusive amounts) into groupings that are of interest or use to the business. The columns may be categorised by product codes.

In this introductory section we shall not complicate things by considering more than one type of product so that there will only be one column for sales.

In this case (example 1) the entry in the sales column would be £80, the net amount after the deduction of the trade discount.

(h) The total boxes – at the end of a period (say a week or a month) the sales day book is totalled and the total values of each column are included in the total boxes. It is these totals which are used for the accounting entry.

The sales day book would look as follows for example 1:

SALES DAY BOOK

Date	*Customer*	*Reference*	*Invoice number*	*Total* £	*VAT* £	*Product 1* £	*Product 2* £	*Product 3* £
	A			*96*	*16*	*80*		
			TOTALS	96	16	80		

2.3 Casting and cross casting

Casting is the way we refer to adding a vertical column of figures and cross-casting is the way we refer to adding a horizontal row of figures.

It is worth very briefly doing a simple example of this just to show how a valuable check of the accuracy of your additions is provided by these two operations.

Example 2

The following table of numbers is similar to the contents of accounting records such as the 'sales day book' or the 'analysed cash book' which you will come across as part of your Bookkeeping Transactions studies.

This table might represent the sales of products A to E in three geographical areas.

You should calculate the totals yourself before looking at the solution.

	A	B	C	D	E	Total
UK	221,863	17,327	14,172	189,221	5,863	
USA	17,155	14,327	8,962	27,625	73,127	
Africa	18,627	33,563	62,815	1,003	57,100	
Total						

Solution

	A	B	C	D	E	Total
UK	221,863	17,327	14,172	189,221	5,863	**448,446**
USA	17,155	14,327	8,962	27,625	73,127	**141,196**
Africa	18,627	33,563	62,815	1,003	57,100	**173,108**
Total	**257,645**	**65,217**	**85,949**	**217,849**	**136,090**	**762,750**

3 The sales returns day book

3.1 The sales returns day book (SRDB)

Definition – Sales returns day book

The sales returns day book is a list of the credit notes that are to be processed for a given period (e.g. a week).

Sales returns are in practice entered in a 'sales returns day book'. This is similar to the sales day book, and the columns are used in the same way. The only difference is that instead of having a column for the invoice number, there is a column for the 'credit note number'. This is because when the goods are returned to the business it will issue a credit note to the customer.

SALES RETURNS DAY BOOK						
Date	*Customer*	*Reference*	*Credit note number*	*Total* £	*VAT* £	*Sales returns* £

3.2 Sales returns in sales day book

In some businesses the level of sales returns are fairly low and therefore it does not justify keeping a separate sales returns day book. In these cases any credit notes that are issued for sales returns are recorded as negative amounts in the sales day book.

Test your understanding 1

You work in the accounts department of D F Engineering and one of your tasks is to write up the day books. In your organisation there is no separate sales returns day book and therefore any credit notes are entered as negative amounts in the sales day book.

Given below are the details of the sales invoices and credit notes that have been issued this week. D F Engineering does not offer any discounts. The business is registered for VAT and all sales are for standard rated goods (at 20%).

Invoices sent out:

		Code	£	*Invoice number*
20X1				
1 May	Fraser & Co	SL14	128.68 plus VAT	03466
	Letterhead Ltd	SL03	257.90 plus VAT	03467
2 May	Jeliteen Traders	SL15	96.58 plus VAT	03468
3 May	Harper Bros	SL22	268.15 plus VAT	03469
	Juniper Ltd	SL17	105.38 plus VAT	03470
4 May	H G Frank	SL30	294.67 plus VAT	03471
5 May	Keller Assocs	SL07	110.58 plus VAT	03472

Credit notes sent out:

		Code	£	*Credit note number*
20X1				
2 May	Garner & Co	SL12	68.70 plus VAT	0746
4 May	Hill Traders	SL26	117.68 plus VAT	0747

Required:

Write up the sales day book given for the week ending 5 May 20X1 and total all of the columns.

Date	*Invoice no*	*Customer name*	*Code*	*Total* £	*VAT* £	*Net* £

4 The purchases day book

4.1 The purchases day book (PDB)

As seen earlier in the chapter, credit sales are recorded in the 'sales day book'. In the case of credit purchases, we have the 'purchases day book'.

Definition – Purchases day book

The purchases day book is a list of the purchases invoices that are to be processed for a given period (e.g. a week).

In its simplest form, the purchases day book will comprise just the names of the suppliers and the amount of the invoices received in the week.

The PDB is a list, the totals of which are used to perform the accounting entry. Double entry bookkeeping is studied later in this text.

A purchases day book will look something like this:

Week 1			
Supplier	*Total* £	*VAT* £	*Net* £
A	3,600	600	3,000
B	2,400	400	2,000
C	1,200	200	1,000
Total	7,200	1,200	6,000

4.2 The analysed purchases day book

The purchases day book usually includes 'analysis columns' showing how the total value of each supplier's invoice is made up.

PURCHASES DAY BOOK								
Date	*Supplier*	*Reference*	*Invoice number*	*Total* £	*VAT* £	*Product 1* £	*Product 2* £	*Product 3* £
			TOTALS					

(a) The date column contains the date of the transaction.

(b) The supplier column contains the name of the supplier.

(c) The reference column may contain the code number of the supplier's account.

(d) The invoice number is the number of the invoice from the supplier.

(e) The total column is the value of the goods purchased including VAT:

- after deducting any trade/bulk discount that may have been given.

(f) The VAT column – this column is the value of the VAT on the invoice.

(g) Product 1, 2, etc. columns – these are columns that analyse the net purchases value (i.e. the VAT exclusive amounts) into groupings that are of interest or use to the business. The columns may be categorised by product codes.

(h) The total boxes – at the end of a period (say a week or a month) the purchases day book is totalled and the total values of each column are included in the total boxes. It is these totals which are used for the accounting entry.

5 The purchases returns day book

5.1 The purchases returns day book (PRDB)

Definition – Purchases returns day book

The purchases returns day book is a list of the credit notes that have been received from suppliers for a given period (e.g. a week).

Purchases returns are in practice entered in a 'purchases returns day book'. This is similar to the purchases day book, and the columns are used in the same way. The only difference is that instead of having a column for the invoice number, there is a column for the 'credit note number'.

PURCHASES RETURNS DAY BOOK

Date	*Supplier*	*Reference*	*Credit note number*	*Total* £	*VAT* £	*Purchases returns* £

5.2 Purchases returns in purchases day book

In some businesses the level of purchases returns are fairly low and therefore it does not justify keeping a separate purchases returns day book. In these cases any credit notes that are received for purchases returns are recorded as negative amounts in the purchases day book. If this is the case then you will be told that this is the policy of the business. Care should be taken, however, when adding up the columns in the purchases day book as any credit notes must be deducted rather than added.

Test your understanding 2

Stevens Ltd operates an analysed purchases day book, analysing purchases by the geographical area from which the purchases are made. The areas concerned are:

Zone 1	London region
Zone 2	Scotland region
Zone 3	Other UK

The company is registered for VAT.

Today's date is 14 September 20X2. The company has received the following invoices from suppliers in the post today:

Supplier	*Region*	*Amount net of VAT* £	*VAT* £
Bradley Ltd	London	210.00	42.00
Hannah Ltd	Wales	470.20	94.04
Spearritt Ltd	London	402.00	80.40
Lee Ltd	Scotland	1,076.00	215.20
O'Meara Ltd	Northern Ireland	317.60	63.52
Cattermole Ltd	Scotland	62.44	12.48
Barrett Ltd	London	107.80	21.56

Required:

Write up the purchases day book given and total all of the columns.

Date	*Supplier*	*Total* £	*VAT* £	*Zone 1* £	*Zone 2* £	*Zone 3* £

6 The cash book

6.1 The cash book (CB)

Definition – Cash book

A cash book is a record of cash receipts and payments that can form part of the double entry bookkeeping system as well as being a book of prime entry.

There are various forms of cash book, a 'two-column' and a 'three-column' cash book. Bookkeeping Transactions requires you to be able to post transactions into a two-column analysed cash book. You may hear about a three-column cash book – this is not within the Bookkeeping Transactions assessment criteria.

The difference between a two-column cash book and a three-column cash book is that a three-column cash book incorporates discount columns. As part of Bookkeeping Transactions you deal with discounts in their own day books – the discounts allowed and discounts received day books, which are introduced later in this chapter.

6.2 Two column cash book

A proforma two column cash book is shown below.

CASH BOOK							
Date	*Narrative*	*Cash* £	*Bank* £	*Date*	*Narrative*	*Cash* £	*Bank* £

Notes:

(a) The left hand side of the cash book records money received.

(b) The right hand side of the cash book records money paid out.

(c) The date column contains the date of the transaction.

(d) The narrative column describes the transactions – typically the name of the customer who is paying or supplier who is receiving money. It would also contain the sales ledger or purchase ledger code of the credit customer (receivable) or credit supplier (payable).

(e) The cash column on the left hand side (debit side) represents cash received, whereas the cash column on the right hand side (credit side) represents cash paid.

(f) The bank column on the left hand side (debit side) represents money received (by cheque or other bank payment) whereas the bank column on the right hand side (credit side) represents money paid (by cheque or other bank payment).

A business may operate a bank current account as a means to settle business transactions. Receipts may be made automatically, in the form of a cheque or cash may be deposited into the current account. Payments may be made by drawing a cheque against the current account or by an automated payment.

To be able to record these bank specific transactions, a separate column must be introduced to the cash book to account for them. This is what leads to the use of a two-column cash book; a column for cash transactions and a column for transactions made through the bank current account. Each column represents a separate account, cash account and bank account, each with its own double entry as will be shown later in the text.

The cash book may be split into two separate books – the cash receipts book and the cash payments book. In addition to being aware of the use of separate cash receipts and cash payments books, you should also be aware that a cash book may have additional columns for the purpose of analysing the receipts and payments.

6.3 The analysed cash receipts book

Definition – Analysed cash book

An analysed cash book is a cash book with additional columns for analysing principal sources and payments for cash into types of income and expense.

A proforma analysed cash receipts book is shown below.

CASH RECEIPTS BOOK							
Date	*Narrative*	*Reference*	*Cash* £	*Bank* £	*VAT* £	*Receivables* £	*Cash sales* £
Totals							

Notes:

(a) The date column contains the date of the transaction.

(b) The narrative column describes the transactions – typically the name of the customer who is paying.

(c) The reference column contains any other information that may be helpful e.g. 'cash', 'cheque', 'BACS' or perhaps the customer's reference code.

(d) The cash receipts book may have a 'total' column which contains the total cash received (including VAT) – whether it is received through the bank, cheque or cash or it may have separate 'cash' and 'bank' columns to show the method of money received. A cash receipt would be recorded in the cash column whereas a cheque or other form of bank receipt would be recorded in the bank column.

(e) The VAT column contains the VAT on the transaction but not if the VAT has already been entered in the sales day book. When recording a receipt from a receivable, VAT was already considered in the sales day book. There is no requirement to analyse out the VAT from the receivable receipt – it has already been dealt with.

(f) The receivables column contains any cash received that has been received from a receivable (credit customer) in payment of an amount owed by the receivable.

(g) The cash sales will be the VAT exclusive amount otherwise known as the 'net' amount. A VAT registered business only recognises the net amount of the sale as income. The VAT collected is owed to HMRC.

Note: you may be told the total receipt of cash sales made – you should ensure you analyse this out to calculate the net and VAT amounts in order to enter these amounts into the correct columns.

 Test your understanding 3

You work in the accounts department of Solid Ltd. Given below is the cheque listing for the company showing all the cheques received from receivables in the week ended 14 February 20X8. You have also been told that there were cash sales totalling £480 including VAT, which is charged at 20% on all sales.

Cheques received:

Customer name	*Customer code*	*Cheque amount* £
D Asher	ASH01	74.62
L Maffiah	MAF03	193.75
G Mann	MAN04	107.64
A Burrell	BUR07	422.91
M Morgan	MOR09	60.36
D Skatt	SKA02	150.00

Required:

Write up the cash receipts book given for the week ended 14 February 20X8 and total all of the columns.

Date	*Customer name*	*Code*	*Total* £	*VAT* £	*Receivables* £	*Cash sales* £
TOTALS						

6.4 The analysed cash payments book

A proforma analysed cash payments book is shown below

CASH PAYMENTS BOOK								
Date	*Narrative*	*Reference*	*Cash* £	*Bank* £	*VAT* £	*Payables* £	*Cash purchases* £	*Admin* £
Totals								

Notes:

(a) The date column contains the date of the transaction.

(b) The narrative column describes the transactions. The reference column may include a reference to the source of the information or the code of a supplier being paid.

(c) The cash payments book may have a 'total' column which contains the total cash paid – whether it is paid through the bank, cheque or cash, or it may have separate 'cash' and 'bank' columns to show the method of money paid. A cash payment would be recorded in the cash column whereas a payment made by cheque or another form of payment via the bank would be recorded in the bank column.

(d) The VAT column contains the VAT on the transaction but not if the VAT has already been entered in the purchases day book.

(e) The payables column contains any cash paid that has been paid to a payable (credit supplier) in payment of an amount owed to the payable.

(f) The cash purchases column contains cash paid for purchases that are not bought on credit. This would be the VAT exclusive amount (net). The VAT element would be accounted for in the VAT column.

(g) We saw with the analysed cash receipts book that nearly all receipts come from receivables or cash sales. In the case of payments, there is a broader range of suppliers who are paid through the cash book – rent and rates, telephone, electricity, marketing, etc. The business will have a separate column for the categories of expense that it wishes to analyse.

Test your understanding 4

You are the accounts assistant at Brown Ltd, a small company which is not registered for VAT. Listed below are payments to credit suppliers on 31 May 20X2.

Supplier	*Payment* £	*Supplier code*
B Able	723.78	ABL02
Mann Ltd	556.98	MAN01
Sykes & Sons	689.00	SYK04
Dickens Ltd	879.95	DIC01
Barber & Co	364.84	BAR01
Ward & Ward	287.66	WAR02

Required:

You are required to enter the payments into the cash payments book and total all columns for the week ended 31 May.

Date	*Supplier*	*Supplier code*	*Total* £	*VAT* £	*Payables* £	*Other* £
TOTALS						

7 The discounts allowed day book

7.1 The discounts allowed day book

Definition – Discounts allowed day book

The discounts allowed day book is used to record the discounts that have not been deducted at the point of the invoice being recorded in the sales day book but instead were offered on a conditional basis i.e. prompt payment discounts allowed to credit customers.

The purpose of the discounts allowed day book is to record the credit notes that must be issued due to the customer taking advantage of a prompt payment discount that has been offered. The credit note deals with the reduction to the original goods value (net amount) and also the reduction in the VAT. The total (gross amount) is then deducted from the receivable's (credit customer's) balance.

The discounts allowed day book is a list, the totals of which are used to perform the accounting entry. Double entry bookkeeping is studied later in this text.

DISCOUNTS ALLOWED DAY BOOK					
Date	*Narrative*	*Reference*	*Total* £	*VAT* £	*Net* £
Totals					

Notes:

(a) The date column contains the date of the transaction.

(b) The narrative column provides details of the customer's name. The reference column may include a reference to the source of the information (the credit note) or the customer code the transaction relates to.

(c) The total column contains the total discount that has been allowed to the credit customer (including any VAT).

(d) The VAT column contains the VAT element of the transaction.

(e) The net column contains the amount of the discount excluding the VAT element.

The discounts allowed day book and associated accounting entries are studied in chapter 5.

8 The discounts received day book

8.1 The discounts received day book

Definition – Discounts received day book

The discounts received day book is used to record the discounts that have not been deducted at the point of the invoice being recorded in the purchases day book but instead were offered on a conditional basis i.e. prompt payment discounts received from credit suppliers.

The purpose of the discounts received day book is to record the credit notes that have been received due to the business taking advantage of a prompt payment discount that was offered. The credit note deals with the reduction to the original goods value (net amount) and also the reduction in the VAT. The total (gross amount) is then deducted from the payable's (credit supplier's) balance.

The discounts received day book is a list, the totals of which are used to perform the accounting entry. Double entry bookkeeping is studied later in this text.

DISCOUNTS RECEIVED DAY BOOK					
Date	*Narrative*	*Reference*	*Total* £	*VAT* £	*Net* £
Totals					

Notes:

(a) The date column contains the date of the transaction.

(b) The narrative column provides details of the supplier's name. The reference column may include a reference to the source of the information (the credit note) or the code of the supplier the transaction relates to.

(c) The total column contains the total discount that has been received from the supplier (including any VAT).

(d) The VAT column contains the VAT element of the transaction.

(e) The net column contains the amount of the discount excluding the VAT element.

The discounts received day book and associated accounting entries are studied in chapter 6.

9 The petty cash book

9.1 The petty cash book

Definition – Petty cash

Petty cash is the small amount of cash that most businesses hold in order to make small cash payments.

Definition – Petty cash book

A petty cash book is one in which all petty or small payments made through the petty cash fund are recorded systematically.

9.2 Layout of the petty cash book

A typical petty cash book is set out below. This is a typical petty cash book that is in the format of a ledger. A petty cash book that also forms part of the double entry bookkeeping system is studied in chapter 8.

Receipts			Payments								
Date	*Narrative*	*Total*	*Date*	*Narrative*	*Voucher no*	*Total*	*Postage*	*Cleaning*	*Tea & Coffee*	*Sundry*	*VAT*
		£				£	£	£	£	£	£
1 Nov	Bal b/f	35.50									
1 Nov	Cheque 394	114.50	1 Nov	ASDA	58	23.50			23.50		
			2 Nov	Post Office Ltd	59	29.50	29.50				
			2 Nov	Cleaning materials	60	15.07		12.56			2.51
			3 Nov	Postage	61	16.19	16.19				
			3 Nov	ASDA	62	10.57		8.81			1.76
			4 Nov	Newspapers	63	18.90				18.90	
			5 Nov	ASDA	64	12.10				10.09	2.01

9.3 Receipts side of the petty cash book

The receipts side (left hand side) of the petty cash book, only requires one column, as the only receipt into the petty cash box is the regular receipt into the petty cash box of cash withdrawn from the bank account.

Referring to the example of a typical petty cash book (above), we can see that the balance brought forward (representing the opening balance) was £35.50. The petty cash float has then been restored up to £150 by paying in an additional £114.50.

9.4 Payments side of the petty cash book

Payments out of the petty cash float will be for a variety of different types of expense and an analysis column is required for each type of expense in the same way as the cash payments book is analysed. The example above has analysed the expenses into postage, cleaning, tea & coffee and sundry expenses.

Note that a column is also required for VAT, as if a petty cash expense includes VAT this must also be separately analysed. In addition, it is important to remember that any VAT included in a petty cash expense must be shown separately on the petty cash voucher.

Any VAT shown on the petty cash voucher must be analysed into the VAT column and the net amount shown in the appropriate expense analysis column.

10 Summary

This session has introduced the different books of original entry (day books) that invoices, credit notes, discounts, receipts and payments are recorded in. It is from these day books that we then go on to post the transactions into the general and subsidiary ledgers. We will now study how to do this by introducing 'double entry bookkeeping' in chapters 3 and 4.

Test your understanding answers

Test your understanding 1

Sales day book

Date	Invoice no	Customer name	Code	Total £	VAT £	Net £
20X1						
1/5	03466	Fraser & Co	SL14	154.41	25.73	128.68
	03467	Letterhead Ltd	SL03	309.48	51.58	257.90
2/5	03468	Jeliteen Traders	SL15	115.89	19.31	96.58
	CN0746	Garner & Co	SL12	(82.44)	(13.74)	(68.70)
3/5	03469	Harper Bros	SL22	321.78	53.63	268.15
	03470	Juniper Ltd	SL17	126.45	21.07	105.38
4/5	03471	H G Frank	SL30	353.60	58.93	294.67
	CN0747	Hill Traders	SL26	(141.21)	(23.53)	(117.68)
5/5	03472	Keller Assocs	SL07	132.69	22.11	110.58
				1,290.65	215.09	1,075.56

Test your understanding 2

Date	Supplier	Total	VAT £	Zone 1 £	Zone 2 £	Zone 3 £
20X2						
14/9	Bradley Ltd	252.00	42.00	210.00		
	Hannah Ltd	564.24	94.04			470.20
	Spearritt Ltd	482.40	80.40	402.00		
	Lee Ltd	1,291.20	215.20		1,076.00	
	O'Meara Ltd	381.12	63.52			317.60
	Cattermole Ltd	74.92	12.48		62.44	
	Barrett Ltd	129.36	21.56	107.80		
		3,175.24	529.20	719.80	1,138.44	787.80

Test your understanding 3

Date	*Customer name*	*Code*	*Total* £	*VAT* £	*Receivables* £	*Cash sales* £
14/2/X8	D Asher	ASH01	74.62		74.62	
14/2/X8	L Maffiah	MAF03	193.75		193.75	
14/2/X8	G Mann	MAN04	107.64		107.64	
14/2/X8	A Burrell	BUR07	422.91		422.91	
14/2/X8	M Morgan	MOR09	60.36		60.36	
14/2/X8	D Skatt	SKA02	150.00		150.00	
14/2/X8	Cash sales		480.00	80.00		400.00
TOTALS			**1,489.28**	**80.00**	**1,009.28**	**400.00**

Test your understanding 4

Date	*Supplier*	*Supplier code*	*Total* £	*VAT* £	*Payables* £	*Other* £
31/5/X2	B Able	ABL02	723.78		723.78	
31/5/X2	Mann Ltd	MAN01	556.98		556.98	
31/5/X2	Sykes & Sons	SYK04	689.00		689.00	
31/5/X2	Dickens Ltd	DIC01	879.95		879.95	
31/5/X2	Barber & Co	BAR01	364.84		364.84	
31/5/X2	Ward & Ward	WAR02	287.66		287.66	
TOTALS			**3,502.21**		**3,502.21**	

Double entry bookkeeping – introduction

3

Introduction

We have reviewed the background to business transactions, looking at the different business documents we may encounter and how we record information from these source documents into the day books (books of prime entry).

This chapter introduces the different business organisations that we may encounter. We then study the basic concepts and rules of bookkeeping. In particular:

- the dual effect principle
- the separate entity principle, and
- the accounting equation.

Together these will show how the assets of a business will always equal its liabilities and pave the way for studying ledger accounting in the next chapter.

ASSESSMENT CRITERIA

Demonstrate an understanding of the process of recording financial transactions (1.4)

CONTENTS

1 Business organisations

1.1 Introduction

A business is an organisation that regularly enters into different transactions. There are three types of business organisations that you should have awareness of:

1.2 Sole traders

Definition – Sole trader

Organisations that are owned and operated by one person.

They tend to be small as they are constrained by the limited financial resources of their owner. Preparing final accounts for sole traders is assessed in the Advanced Diploma level's Final Accounts Preparation unit.

1.3 Partnerships

Definition – Partnership

These are organisations owned by two or more persons working in common with a view to making a profit.

The greater number of owners compared with a sole trader increases the availability of finance and this is often the reason for forming this structure. Producing accounts for partnerships is assessed in the Advanced Diploma level's Final Accounts Preparation unit.

1.4 Companies

Definition – Company

These are organisations recognised in law as 'persons' in their own right. A company may own assets and incur liabilities in its own name. The accounting of these organisations must meet certain minimum obligations imposed by legislation, for example, via company law and other regulations.

Drafting financial statements for a limited company is assessed in the Professional Diploma level's Financial Statements of Limited Companies unit.

2 Types of accounting

2.1 Management accounting and financial accounting

Depending on what purposes the statements are being produced for, the accounts can be referred to as being either **management accounts** or **financial accounts**.

Definition – Management accounts

These are usually prepared on a monthly basis to present timely financial and statistical information to business managers. This aids managers to run the business more effectively by making day-to-day and short-term decisions.

Definition – Financial accounts

These are prepared annually, mainly for the benefit of people outside the management of the business, such as the owners of the business (for example, shareholders who have appointed directors to run the business on their behalf), HM Revenue and Customs, banks, customers, suppliers and the government.

In Bookkeeping Transactions, we focus on financial accounting principles, though the majority of concepts we encounter also apply to management accounting.

2.2 The two main financial statements

The objective of financial accounting is to provide financial information about a business. This information is given in a set of financial statements (or accounts), which consists of two principal statements:

- The **statement of profit or loss.** This is a summary of the business's transactions (income and expense) for a given period.
- The **statement of financial position.** This is a statement of the assets and liabilities of the business at a given date. This date is the end of the period covered by the statement of profit or loss.

These financial statements are the final product of the accounting system of a business and it is useful to be aware of where all of the double entry bookkeeping that you will study in this chapter is leading. However, you do not need to know anything about the format or rules governing the preparation of the financial statements for this unit.

2.3 Statement of profit or loss – definitions

The following definitions will be used throughout your studies.

Definitions

- **Sales revenue** is income generated from the trading activities of the business.
- **Cost of sales** is the cost of buying or producing the goods for resale.
- **Gross profit** is the profit remaining, after the cost of sales have been deducted from sales revenue.
- **Sundry income** – other types of income that aren't generated by the primary trading activities of the business.
- **Expenses** are the day to day running costs of the business.
- **Net profit or loss** – the profit or loss remaining after expenses have been deducted.

2.4 Statement of financial position – definitions

The following definitions will be used throughout your studies.

Definitions

- An **asset** is something owned or controlled by a business, available for use in the business.
- **Non-current asset** – an asset which is to be used for the long term in the business and not resold as part of the trading activities, for example the purchase of a delivery van.
- **Current asset** – a short-term asset of the business which is to be used in the business in the near future i.e. cash or something that will soon be converted into cash.
- A **receivable** is an example of a current asset. A receivable is someone who owes the business money i.e. a credit customer.
- **Non-current liability** – an amount owed by the business and due to be paid in the longer term (after 12 months).
- A **liability** is an amount owed by the business, i.e. an obligation to pay money at some future date.
- A **payable** is an example of a liability. A payable is someone the business owes money to i.e. a credit supplier.
- **Capital** is the amount which the owner has invested in the business; this is owed back to the owner and is therefore a special liability of the business.
- **Drawings** are amounts withdrawn by the owner for their own personal use: drawings may be of cash or items of inventory.

A typical statement of profit or loss is shown below.

Statement of profit or loss for the year-ended 31 December 20X2

	£	£
Sales revenue		X
Less: Cost of sales		
Inventory on 1 January (opening inventory)	X	
Add: Purchases of goods	X	
	X	
Less: Inventory on 31 December (closing inventory)	(X)	
		(X)
Gross profit		X
Sundry income:		
Discounts received	X	
Commission received	X	
Rent received	X	
		X
		X
Less: Expenses:		
Rent	X	
Rates	X	
Lighting and heating	X	
Telephone	X	
Postage	X	
Insurance	X	
Stationery	X	
Payroll expenses	X	
Accountancy fees	X	
Bank charges and interest	X	
Irrecoverable debts	X	
Delivery costs	X	
Van running expenses	X	
Selling expenses	X	
Discounts allowed	X	
		(X)
Profit/(loss) for the year		X/(X)

An example of a typical sole trader's statement of financial position is given below:

Statement of financial position as at 31 December 20X2

	Cost	*Depreciation*	*CA*
	£	£	£
Non-current assets			
Freehold factory	X	X	X
Machinery	X	X	X
Motor vehicles	X	X	X
	X	X	X
Current assets			
Inventories		X	
Trade receivables		X	
Cash at bank		X	
Cash in hand		X	
		X	
Current liabilities			
Trade payables		(X)	
Net current assets			X
Total assets less current liabilities			X
Non-current liabilities			
Loan			(X)
Net assets			X
Capital at 1 January			X
Net profit for the year			X
			X
Less: Drawings			(X)
Proprietor's funds			X

2.5 The difference between 'cash' and 'bank'

A possible confusion in terminology is caused by the apparent interchangeable use of the words 'cash' and 'bank'.

The normal use of the words suggests that a bank account operates by paying money out of the account with a cheque and paying either cash or cheques into the account. In practice you cannot pay 'cash' out of a bank account.

However, accounting terminology does not stick to this distinction, and the terms cash and bank are for the most part, interchangeable. Thus the bank account is often referred to as the 'cash book'. Similarly we will often refer to someone 'taking cash out of the bank' or we will say things like 'John bought a car for £5,000 cash', whereas in reality John would have paid for the car using a cheque.

For the early part of your studies all movements of cash/cheques shall be made through the bank account and references to 'cash' or 'cheques' effectively mean the same thing.

2.6 Capital and revenue

You must also be able to define capital expenditure, revenue expenditure, capital income and revenue income.

Definitions

- **Capital expenditure** is the purchase of, or improvement of, non-current assets.
- **Revenue expenditure** is the day to day running costs of the business.
- **Capital income** is income from the sale of capital assets of the business.
- **Revenue income** is income generated from the sale of goods or services.

3 Basic principles of accounting

3.1 Introduction

Double entry bookkeeping is based upon three basic principles:

- the dual effect principle
- the separate entity principle
- the accounting equation.

3.2 The dual effect principle

This states that every transaction has two financial effects.

(a) If, for example, you spend £2,000 on a car and pay for it by a cheque, you will have £2,000 less money in the bank, but you will also have acquired an asset worth £2,000.

(b) Again, if you owe a payable £100 and send him a cheque for that amount, you will owe £100 less than before, but you will have £100 less money in the bank.

3.3 The separate entity principle

This states that the owner of a business is, for accounting purposes, a completely separate entity from the business itself. Therefore the money that the owner pays into the business as initial capital has to be accounted for as an amount that the business owes back to the owner. In just the same way, any money that the owner takes out of the business, known as 'drawings', is treated as a reduction of the initial capital that is owed back to the owner.

The dual effect principle works here as well. If the owner of the business pays £5,000 into his business, one effect is that the business has £5,000 more cash and the second effect is that the business has a £5,000 liability (called 'capital').

Note that we look at this from the **point of view of the business**, not from the owner's point of view. This is because when studying bookkeeping we are only interested in the business – we are not considering the owner's personal finances.

3.4 The accounting equation

At its simplest, the accounting equation simply says that:

Assets = Liabilities

If we treat the owner's capital as a special form of liability then the accounting equation is:

Assets = Liabilities + Capital

Or, rearranging:

Assets – Liabilities = Capital

Profit will increase the proprietor's capital and drawings will reduce it, so that we can write the equation as:

Assets – Liabilities = Capital + Profit – Drawings

Test your understanding 1

(a) State whether each of the following are classified as an asset or a liability:

(i) Funds in the business bank account

(ii) A payable

(iii) Inventory of goods for resale

(iv) A computer used in the accounts department

(v) A receivable

(vi) A salesman's car

(vii) An overdrawn balance on the business bank account.

(b) Name 3 different parties who would be interested in financial statements.

(c) Name the 3 basic principles of double entry bookkeeping and briefly describe each.

4 The accounting equation: examples

Example 1

John starts his business on 1 July and pays £2,000 into his business bank account.

(a) What is the dual effect of this transaction?

(b) What is the accounting equation after this transaction?

Solution

(a) **The dual effect**

The business bank account has increased by £2,000 (an asset). The business capital has increased by £2,000 (a liability).

(b) **The accounting equation**

Assets – Liabilities = Capital

£2,000 – £0 = £2,000

Example 2

Percy started business on 1 January by paying £20,000 into a business bank account. He then spent £500 on a second-hand van by cheque, £1,000 on purchases of inventory for cash, took £500 cash for his own use and bought goods on credit costing £400.

What are the two effects of each of these transactions?

What would the accounting equation look like after each of these transactions?

Solution

(a) **Percy pays £20,000 into a business bank account**

The bank balance increases from zero to £20,000 (an asset) and the business now has capital of £20,000 (a liability). Capital is the amount that is owed back to the owner of the business, Percy.

Accounting equation:

Assets – Liabilities = Capital

£20,000 – £0 = £20,000

(b) **Percy buys a second-hand van for £500 by cheque**

The bank balance decreases by £500 (a reduction of assets) but the business has acquired a new £500 asset, the van.

The van is a specific type of asset known as a non-current asset as it is for long-term use in the business rather than an asset that is likely to be sold in the trading activities of the business.

The assets of the business are now:

	£
Van	500
Bank (20,000 – 500)	19,500
	20,000

The liabilities and capital are unchanged.

Accounting equation:

Assets – Liabilities = Capital

£20,000 – £0 = £20,000

(c) **Percy spends £1,000 on purchases of goods for cash**

The bank balance goes down by £1,000 but the business has another asset, inventory of £1,000.

Inventory is a short-term asset as it is due to be sold to customers in the near future and is known as a current asset.

The assets of the business are now:

	£
Van	500
Inventory	1,000
Bank (19,500 – 1,000)	18,500
	20,000

Accounting equation:

Assets – Liabilities = Capital

£20,000 – £0 = £20,000

(d) **Percy took £500 of cash out of the business**

The bank balance has decreased by £500 and capital has also decreased as the owner has taken money out of the business – this is known as drawings.

Remember that the owner is a completely separate entity from the business itself and if he takes money out of the business in the form of drawings then this means that the business owes him less.

The assets of the business are now:

	£
Van	500
Inventory	1,000
Bank (18,500 – 500)	18,000
	19,500

The capital of the business is now £(20,000 – 500) = £19,500.

Accounting equation:

Assets – Liabilities = Capital

£19,500 – £0 = £19,500

(e) **Purchased goods on credit for £400**

The asset of inventory increases by £400 and the business now has a liability of £400, the amount that is owed to the credit supplier. A liability is an amount that is owed by the business.

The assets of the business are now:

	£
Van	500
Inventory (1,000 + 400)	1,400
Bank	18,000
	19,900

The liability of the business is £400. The capital is unchanged.

Accounting equation:

Assets – Liabilities = Capital

£19,900 – £400 = £19,500

General notes:

1 Each and every transaction that a business undertakes has two effects. The accounting equation reflects the two effects of each transaction and the accounting equation should always balance.

2 The owner is a completely separate entity from the business, any money the owner puts into the business is known as capital and any amounts taken out by the owner are known as drawings.

Test your understanding 2

Required:

Show the two effects of each of these transactions and what the accounting equation would look like after each of these transactions.

1 **Introduce capital**

Example 1

You win £10,000 and use it to create a retail business (called TLC) selling hearts and roses. What is the effect?

Answer 1

Dual effect

The business has cash of	£10,000	(asset)
The business owes you	£10,000	(capital)

TLC's position is:

Assets	*Capital*
£	£

(In this first example, we recorded the dual effect for you just to get you started. In later examples you will need to enter the dual effect yourself, as well as TLC's position after the transaction.)

2 **Buy inventory with cash**

Example 2

TLC buys 500 chocolate hearts. The cost of each heart is £5. What is the effect?

Answer 2

Dual effect

TLC's position is:

Assets	*Capital*
£	£

3 **Buy inventory on credit**

In reality a business will not always pay for its purchases with cash but is more likely to buy items on credit. When goods are bought on credit, a liability of the business called a **payable** is generated.

Example 3

TLC buys inventory of 200 red roses on credit. Each red rose costs £10. What is the effect?

Answer 3

Dual effect

TLC's position is:

Net assets	*Capital*
£	£

4 **Buy a delivery van**

The delivery van is bought for ongoing use within the business rather than for resale. Such assets are known as **non-current assets**.

Example 4

TLC buys a delivery van for £1,000 cash. What is the effect?

Answer 4

Dual effect

TLC's position is:

Net assets	*Capital*
£	£

5 **Sell inventory for profit**

Example 5

TLC sells 200 red roses for £15 cash each. What is the effect?

Answer 5

Dual effect

TLC's position is:

Net assets	*Capital*
£	£

6 **Sell inventory (on credit) for profit**

It is equally likely that a business will sell goods on credit. When goods are sold on credit, an asset of the business called a **receivable** is generated.

Example 6

TLC sells 400 chocolate hearts to Valentino for £12.50 each on credit. What is the effect?

Answer 6

Dual effect

TLC's position is:

Net assets	*Capital*
£	£

7 **Pay expenses**

Example 7

In reality, TLC will have been incurring expenses from its commencement. TLC received and paid a gas bill for £500. What is the effect?

Answer 7

Dual effect

TLC's position is:

Net assets	*Capital*
£	£

8 **Take out a loan**

In order to fund your future expansion plans for TLC, you persuade your Aunt to lend TLC £2,000.

Example 8

TLC is lent £2,000 cash by your Aunt. She expects to be repaid in two years' time. What is the effect?

Answer 8

Dual effect

TLC's position is:

Net assets	*Capital*
£	£

9 **Payment to payables for purchases**

Example 9

TLC pays cash of £1,500 towards the £2,000 owed to the supplier. What is the effect?

Answer 9

Dual effect

TLC's position is:

Net assets	*Capital*
£	£

10 **Receive cash from receivables**

Example 10

TLC's receivable sends a cheque for £3,000. What is the effect?

Answer 10

Dual effect

TLC's position is:

Net assets	*Capital*
£	£

11 **Drawings**

Example 11

You withdraw £750 from the business. Such a withdrawal is merely a repayment of the capital you introduced. Your withdrawal is called **drawings**. What is the effect?

Answer 11

Dual effect

TLC's position is:

Net assets	*Capital*
£	£

Test your understanding 3

Bertie Wooster started a business as an antique dealer on 1 July 20X9.

Required:

Show the accounting equation which results from each of the following transactions made during Bertie's first two weeks of trading.

(a) Started the business with £5,000 in cash as opening capital.

(b) Bought an Edwardian desk for £500 cash.

(c) Bought five art deco table lamps for £200 each, on credit from Roderick Spode.

(d) Sold the desk for £750 cash.

(e) Sold four of the table lamps for £300 each on credit to his Uncle Tom.

(f) Paid rent of £250 cash.

(g) Drew £100 in cash out of the business for living expenses.

(h) Earned £50 for writing a magazine article, but had not yet been paid for it.

(i) Paid Roderick Spode £500 on account.

(j) Received £1,200 from Uncle Tom in full settlement of the amount due.

(k) Bought a van for use in the business for £4,000 cash.

(l) Received a telephone bill for £150 but did not pay it yet.

Note: Each transaction follows on from the one before.

5 Summary

You must understand the basic definitions covered in this chapter. You must also understand the principles of dual effect and separate entity. The accounting equation underlies the whole of bookkeeping and it is imperative that you fully understand these foundations which will be built on further. Re-work the examples in this chapter if necessary.

Test your understanding answers

Test your understanding 1

(a) (i) Asset

(ii) Liability

(iii) Asset

(iv) Asset

(v) Asset

(vi) Asset

(vii) Liability

(b) Any 3 from the choice of:

- Shareholders (investors)
- Potential investors
- HMRC
- Banks
- Customers
- Suppliers
- Employees (of the business)
- Government

(c) 1 Dual effect – each transaction has two financial effects.

2 Separate entity – the owner of the business and the business are seen as two separate entities. All transactions are recorded in the point of view of the business.

3 Accounting equation –
Assets – Liabilities = Capital + Profit – Drawings

Test your understanding 2

Answer 1

	Assets		*Capital*
	£		£
Cash	10,000	Capital introduced	10,000

Answer 2

Dual effect

Increase inv.	£2,500	(↑ asset)
Decrease cash	£2,500	(↓ asset)

	Assets		*Capital*
	£		£
Inventory	2,500	Capital introduced	10,000
Cash	7,500		
	10,000		10,000

Answer 3

Dual effect

Increase inv.	£2,000	(↑ asset)
Increase payable	£2,000	(↑ liability)

	Net assets		*Capital*
	£		£
Inventory	4,500	Capital introduced	10,000
Cash	7,500		
	12,000		
Less: Payables	(2,000)		
	10,000		10,000

Answer 4

Dual effect

Increase NCA	£1,000	(↑ asset)
Decrease cash	£1,000	(↓ asset)

	Net assets		*Capital*
	£		£
Non-current asset	1,000	Capital introduced	10,000
Inventory	4,500		
Cash	6,500		
	12,000		
Less: Payables	(2,000)		
	10,000		10,000

Answer 5

Dual effect

Increase cash	£3,000	(↑ asset)
Decrease inv.	£2,000	(↓ asset)
Increase profit	£1,000	(↑ profit)

	Net assets		*Capital*
	£		£
Non-current asset	1,000	Capital introduced	10,000
Inventory	2,500	Profit	1,000
Cash	9,500		
	13,000		
Less: Payables	(2,000)		
	11,000		11,000

Answer 6

Dual effect

Inc. receivables	£5,000	(↑ asset)
Dec. inventory	£2,000	(↓. asset)
Increase profit	£3,000	(↑ profit)

	Net assets		*Capital*
	£		£
Non-current asset	1,000	Capital introduced	10,000
Inventory	500	Profit	4,000
Receivables	5,000		
Cash	9,500		
	16,000		
Less: Payables	(2,000)		
	14,000		14,000

Answer 7

Dual effect

Decrease cash	£500	(↓ asset)
Decrease profit	£500	(↓ profit)

	Net assets		*Capital*
	£		£
Non-current asset	1,000	Capital introduced	10,000
Inventory	500	Profit	3,500
Receivables	5,000		
Cash	9,000		
	15,500		
Less: Payables	(2,000)		
	13,500		13,500

Answer 8

Dual effect

Increase cash	£2,000	(↑ asset)
Increase loan	£2,000	(↑ liability)

	Net assets		*Capital*
	£		£
Non-current asset	1,000	Capital introduced	10,000
Inventory	500	Profit	3,500
Receivables	5,000		
Cash	11,000		
	17,500		
Less: Payables	(2,000)		
Loan	(2,000)		
	13,500		13,500

The loan will be shown separately from payables for purchases, which are known as trade payables.

Answer 9

Dual effect

Decrease cash	£1,500	(↓ asset)
Decrease payables	£1,500	(↓ liability)

	Net assets		*Capital*
	£		£
Non-current asset	1,000	Capital introduced	10,000
Inventory	500	Profit	3,500
Receivables	5,000		
Cash	9,500		
	16,000		
Less: Payables	(500)		
Loan	(2,000)		
	13,500		13,500

Answer 10

Dual effect

Dec. receivables	£3,000	(↓ asset)
Increase cash	£3,000	(↑ asset)

	Net assets		*Capital*
	£		£
Non-current asset	1,000	Capital introduced	10,000
Inventory	500	Profit	3,500
Receivables	2,000		
Cash	12,500		
	16,000		
Less: Payables	(500)		
Loan	(2,000)		
	13,500		13,500

Answer 11

Dual effect

Decrease cash	£750	(↓ asset)
Increase drawings	£750	(↓ capital)

	Net assets		*Capital*
	£		£
Non-current asset	1,000	Capital	10,000
Inventory	500	Profit	3,500
Receivables	2,000		
Cash	11,750		
	15,250		13,500
Less: Payables	(500)	Less: Drawings	(750)
Loan	(2,000)		
	12,750		12,750

We do not simply deduct drawings from profit as we want to show separately the profit or loss for the period before any drawings were made.

Test your understanding 3

(a) Opening capital

		£		£
Assets	Cash	5,000	Capital	5,000

(b) Cash purchase

		£		£
Assets	Inventory	500	Capital	5,000
	Cash (5,000 – 500)	4,500		
		5,000		5,000

(c) Credit purchase

		£		£
Assets	Inventory (500+(5×200))	1,500	Capital	5,000
	Cash	4,500		
		6,000		
Liabilities	Payables	(1,000)		
		5,000		5,000

(d) Cash sale

		£		£
Assets	Inventory (1,500 – 500)	1,000	Capital	5,000
	Cash (4,500 + 750)	5,250	Profit (750 – 500)	250
		6,250		
Liabilities	Payables	(1,000)		
		5,250		5,250

(e) Credit sale

		£		£
Assets	Inventory (1,000 – 800)	200	Capital	5,000
	Receivables	1,200	Profit (250 + 1,200 – 800)	650
	Cash	5,250		
		6,650		
Liabilities	Payables	(1,000)		
		5,650		5,650

(f) **Paid rent**

		£		£
Assets	Inventory	200	Capital	5,000
	Receivables	1,200	Profit (650 – 250)	400
	Cash (5,250 – 250)	5,000		
		6,400		
Liabilities	Payables	(1,000)		
		5,400		5,400

(g) **Drawings**

		£		£
Assets	Inventory	200	Capital	5,000
	Receivables	1,200	Profit	400
	Cash (5,000 – 100)	4,900		
		6,300	Drawings	(100)
Liabilities	Payables	(1,000)		
		5,300		5,300

(h) **Sundry income**

		£		£
Assets	Inventory	200	Capital	5,000
	Receivables(1,200+50)	1,250	Profit (400 + 50)	450
	Cash	4,900		
		6,350	Drawings	(100)
Liabilities	Payables	(1,000)		
		5,350		5,350

(i) **Payment to payable**

		£		£
Assets	Inventory	200	Capital	5,000
	Receivables	1,250	Profit	450
	Cash (4,900 – 500)	4,400		
		5,850	Drawings	(100)
Liabilities	Payables(1,000–500)	(500)		
		5,350		5,350

(j) **Receipt from receivable**

		£		£
Assets	Inventory	200	Capital	5,000
	Receivables(1,250–1,200)	50	Profit	450
	Cash (4,400 + 1,200)	5,600		
		5,850	Drawings	(100)
Liabilities	Payables	(500)		
		5,350		5,350

(k) **Purchase of van**

		£		£
Assets	Van	4,000	Capital	5,000
	Inventory	200	Profit	450
	Receivables	50		
	Cash (5,600 – 4,000)	1,600		5,450
			Drawings	(100)
		5,850		
Liabilities	Payables	(500)		
		5,350		5,350

(l) **Telephone bill**

		£		£
Assets	Van	4,000	Capital	5,000
	Inventory	200	Profit (450 – 150)	300
	Receivables	50		
	Cash	1,600		5,300
			Drawings	(100)
		5,850		
Liabilities	Payables (500 + 150)	(650)		
		5,200		5,200

Ledger accounting

Introduction

In the first two chapters of this text we looked at different business documents and how these documents are entered into the books of prime entry. In the third chapter we reviewed the basic concepts and principles underlying double entry bookkeeping.

Before we review how details from the books of prime entry are entered into the accounting system we shall introduce how to record basic transactions in a 'ledger account' as part of the 'general ledger'. We will review the procedure for balancing a ledger account and how those balances are brought together to prepare the trial balance.

ASSESSMENT CRITERIA

Demonstrate an understanding of the process of recording financial transactions (1.4)

Total and balance ledger accounts (5.2)

Extract an initial trial balance (5.3)

CONTENTS

1 Ledger accounting

1.1 Introduction

The accounting equation introduced in Chapter 3 has limitations. Although we are able to calculate a profit figure, we are unable to determine which part of the profit are sales and which part are expenses. To be able to make this determination, we will now account for the movement in sales and purchases, rather than simply the movement of inventory.

Another limitation of the accounting equation is that in practice it would be far too time consuming to write up the accounting equation each time that the business undertakes a transaction. Instead the two effects of each transaction are recorded in ledger accounts.

1.2 The ledger account

A typical ledger account is shown below:

Title of account							
DEBIT				CREDIT			
Date	*Details*	*Folio*	*Amount* £	*Date*	*Details*	*Folio*	*Amount* £

The important point to note is that it has two sides. The left hand side is known as the **debit** side **(Dr)** and the right hand side is known as the **credit** side **(Cr).**

- The date column contains the date of the transaction.
- The details column (can also be referred to as the narrative column) usually contains the title of the other account that holds the second part of the dual effect. It may also have a brief description of the nature of the entry (e.g. 'rent 1.1.X3 to 31.3.X3').

- The folio column contains a reference to the source of the information, for example, 'sales day book p17' or 'payroll month 6'. You may not always see the folio column being used within a ledger account.
- The amount column simply contains the monetary value of the transaction.
- The title of the account is a name that reflects the nature of the transaction ('van account', 'bank account', 'electricity account', etc).

The importance of completing the ledger account correctly, in terms of the presentation, should not be underestimated. Vital marks can be gained in the exam by ensuring all details, including the date and narrative are completed accurately.

1.3 Simplified account

The ledger account in 1.2 is very detailed and in much of this book we use a simpler form of the account. Part of the reason for this is that it is easier to 'see' the entries being made if there is less detail in the accounts. Thus, we sometimes do without the date or folio to keep things clear and simple.

For example, we will often use accounts which look like this:

Bank account

	£		£
		Van	500

Van account

	£		£
Bank	500		

1.4 The golden rule for making entries in the ledger accounts

The golden rule for making entries in ledger accounts is:

Every debit entry must have an equal and opposite credit entry.

This reflects the dual effect of each transaction and ensures the accounting equation always balances.

It is also why we refer to the process as 'double entry bookkeeping'.

1.5 Which accounts to debit and credit?

The mnemonic 'DEAD/CLIC' is a good way to help determine if an entry should be made on the debit side or on the credit side of a ledger account.

Ledger account	
Debits increase:	**Credits increase:**
Expenses	**L**iabilities
Assets	**I**ncome
Drawings	**C**apital

We need to appreciate the effect a debit or a credit entry will have.

Ledger account	
A **debit entry** represents:	A **credit entry** represents:
• An increase in the value of an asset	• A decrease in the value of an asset
• A decrease in the value of a liability	• An increase in the value of a liability
• An increase to an item of expenditure	• An increase to an item of income (revenue)
• A decrease to an item of income	• A decrease to an item of expense

1.6 What goes on the debit or credit side?

Example (part 1)

If John pays £2,000 into his business bank account as capital, we need to ask a number of questions to determine the double entry required.

(a) **Which** accounts are affected?

(b) What **type** of accounts are they i.e. asset/liability/income/expense?

(c) Is the transaction **increasing or decreasing** the account?

So let's consider these questions for John's investment of capital into his business.

(a) The accounts that are affected are the bank account and the capital account.

(b) The bank account is an asset whereas the capital is a special kind of liability.

(c) As we have paid money into the bank account, the asset is increasing – therefore a debit entry is required.

As John (the owner) has invested £2,000 into the business, the business owes him this amount back. This is an increase to a liability – therefore a credit entry is required.

To summarise:

Debit Bank account

Credit Capital account

Bank account

	£		£
Capital	2,000		

Capital account

	£		£
		Bank	2,000

Example (part 2)

If John's business now pays £1,000 out of the bank to buy a van, considering the questions again:

(a) The accounts that are affected are the bank account and the van account.

(b) The bank account is an asset and the van account is also an asset (a non-current asset).

(c) As we have paid money out of the bank account, the asset is decreasing – therefore a credit entry is required.

The business has acquired a van, which is a non-current asset, this is an increase to an asset – therefore a debit entry is required.

To summarise:

Debit Van account

Credit Bank account

Bank account

	£		£
Capital	2,000	Van	1,000

Capital account

	£		£
		Bank	2,000

Van account

	£		£
Bank	1,000		

2 Worked example

2.1 Introducing capital into the business – explanation

The owner of a business starts the business by paying money into the business bank account. This is the capital of the business. The business will need this money to 'get going'. It may need to pay rent, buy inventory for sale or pay wages to its staff before it has actually generated money itself through making sales.

Example 1

Frankie starts a business and pays £5,000 into the business bank account. What is the double entry for this transaction?

Solution

- £5,000 has been paid into the bank account.

  It represents an asset of the business.

  This is therefore a debit in the bank account.

- The business has a liability because it owes Frankie (the owner) £5,000.

  This liability will be a credit in the capital account.

Bank

Capital	£5,000		

Capital

		Bank	£5,000

2.2 Purchasing goods for resale

A business buys goods for resale to customers – that is how most businesses (e.g. shops) make their money. These goods (known as 'inventory') are assets which the business owns (until the inventory is sold). Buying inventory is referred to as making a 'purchase' which is a type of expense.

Example 2

Frankie buys £300 of chocolate bars for resale. He pays with a cheque to his supplier.

What is the double entry for this transaction?

Solution

- The business has paid £300 out of its bank account.

  Therefore, the £300 will be credited to the bank account.

- Buying the chocolate bars (inventory) is known as making a purchase (a type of expense).

  This expense will be debited to the purchases account.

Purchases

Bank	£300		

Bank

		Purchases	£300

2.3 Paying office rent

A business will typically rent premises in order to carry out its operations. It will pay rent to the landlord of the premises. Rent is an expense of the business.

Example 3

Frankie pays £1,000 per quarter for the rent of his offices. He pays with a cheque to the landlord.

What is the double entry for this transaction?

Solution

- The business has paid £1,000 out of its bank account.

  Therefore, the £1,000 will be credited to the bank account.

- The rent is an expense.

  This expense will be debited to the rent account.

Rent

Bank	£1,000		

Bank

		Rent	£1,000

2.4 Buying stationery

A business will buy stationery in order to be able to operate. The items of stationery (pens, paper, etc) are not for resale to customers but they tend to be used quickly after they are purchased. Therefore, stationery tends to be classified as an expense of the business, as opposed to an asset.

Example 4

Frankie pays £200 for items of stationery. He pays with a cheque to the supplier.

What is the double entry for this transaction?

Solution

- The business has paid £200 out of its bank account.

  Therefore, the £200 will be credited to the bank account.
- The stationery is an expense.

  This expense will be debited to the stationery account.

Stationery

Bank	£200		

Bank

		Stationery	£200

2.5 Buying a computer

A business will buy computers in order to streamline its operations. These computers are not bought with a view to re-sale and are to be used in the business for the long term. They are therefore a non-current asset of the business.

Example 5

Frankie pays £900 to purchase a computer. He pays with a cheque to the supplier.

What is the double entry for this transaction?

Solution

- Once again start with the bank account.

  The business has paid £900 out of its bank account.

  Therefore, the £900 will be credited to the bank account.
- The computer is a non-current asset.

  The £900 will be debited to the non-current asset computer account.

Computer

Bank	£900		

Bank

		Computer	£900

2.6 Receiving income from sales of goods

A business will sell the goods it has purchased for re-sale. This is income for the business and is referred to as 'sales'. You may also hear the terms 'revenue' or 'sales revenue'.

Example 6

Frankie sells goods for £1,500. The customer pays cash.

What is the double entry for this transaction?

Solution

- Once again start with the bank account.

  The business has received £1,500 into its bank account.

  Therefore, the £1,500 will be debited to the bank account.

- The cash received is income.

  This income will be credited to the sales account.

Sales

		Bank	£1,500

Bank

Sales	£1,500		

2.7 Receiving income for services provided

A business may provide services to its customers, e.g.it may provide consultancy advice. This is income for the business and will usually be referred to as 'sales'.

Example 7

Frankie provides consultancy services to a client who pays £2,000 in cash. What is the double entry for this transaction?

Solution

- Once again start with the bank account.

  The business has received £2,000 into its bank account.

  Therefore, the £2,000 will be debited to the bank account.

- The cash received is income.

  This income will be credited to the sales account.

Sales

		Bank	£2,000

Bank

Sales	£2,000		

3 Additional example

Example 8

Percy started business on 1 January and made the following transactions.

1 Paid £20,000 into a business bank account.

2 Spent £500 on a second-hand van.

3 Paid £1,000 on purchases of inventory.

4 Took £50 cash for his own personal use.

5 On 5 January bought goods for cash costing £500.

6 Made sales for cash of £2,000.

7 On 15 January paid £200 of rent.

Task 1

Show how the debit and credit entries for each transaction are determined.

Task 2

Enter the transactions into the relevant ledger accounts.

Solution

Task 1

(1) *Capital invested*

Percy has paid £20,000 into the bank account – therefore the bank account is debited.

Debit (Dr) Bank £20,000

The business now owes the owner £20,000. Capital is the amount owed by the business to its owner – this is a liability, therefore a credit entry is required in the capital account.

Credit (Cr) Capital £20,000

(2) *Purchase of van*

The business has paid £500 out of the bank account – therefore a credit entry in the bank account.

Cr	Bank	£500

The business now has a van costing £500 – this is an asset therefore a debit entry in the van account. This is a non-current asset of the business.

Dr	Van	£500

(3) *Purchase of inventory for cash*

The business has paid out £1,000 out of the bank account – therefore a credit to the bank account.

Cr	Bank	£1,000

The business has made purchases of inventory costing £1,000 – this is an item of expenditure therefore a debit entry in the purchases account. Note that the debit entry is to a purchases account not an inventory account. The inventory account is a different account altogether and inventory movements will be considered later.

Dr	Purchases	£1,000

(4) *Drawings*

The business has paid £50 out of the bank account – therefore credit the bank account.

Cr	Bank	£50

The proprietor has made drawings of £50 – this is a reduction of capital and therefore a debit entry to the drawings account.

Dr	Drawings	£50

Drawings should not be directly debited to the capital account. A separate drawings account should be used.

(5) *Purchase of goods for cash*

The business has paid out £500 – therefore credit the bank account.

Cr	Bank	£500

The business has made purchases of inventory costing £500 – an expense therefore debit the purchases account.

Dr	Purchases	£500

(6) *Sale for cash*

The business has paid £2,000 into the bank account – therefore a debit to the bank account.

Dr Bank £2,000

The business has made sales of £2,000 – this is income therefore a credit to the sales account.

Cr Sales £2,000

(7) *Payment of rent*

The business now paid £200 out of the bank account – therefore a credit to the bank account.

Cr Bank £200

The business has incurred an expense of rent – as an expense item the rent account must be debited.

Dr Rent £200

Task 2

Bank

Date			£	*Date*			£
1 Jan	Capital	(1)	20,000	1 Jan	Van	(2)	500
5 Jan	Sales	(6)	2,000		Purchases	(3)	1,000
					Drawings	(4)	50
				5 Jan	Purchases	(5)	500
				15 Jan	Rent	(7)	200

Capital

Date			£	*Date*			£
				1 Jan	Bank	(1)	20,000

Van

Date			£	*Date*			£
1 Jan	Bank	(2)	500				

Purchases

Date			£	Date			£
1 Jan	Bank	(3)	1,000				
5 Jan	Bank	(5)	500				

Drawings

Date			£	Date			£
1 Jan	Bank	(4)	50				

Sales

Date			£	Date			£
				5 Jan	Bank	(6)	2,000

Rent

Date			£	Date			£
15 Jan	Bank	(7)	200				

Test your understanding 1

Write up the following cash transactions in the ledger accounts.

Transaction	*Details*
1	Set up the business by introducing £150,000 in cash.
2	Purchase property costing £140,000. Pay in cash.
3	Purchase goods costing £5,000. Pay in cash.
4	Sell goods for £7,000. All cash sales.
5	Purchase goods costing £8,000. Pay in cash.
6	Pay a sundry expense of £100, by cheque.
7	Sell goods for £15,000. All cash sales.
8	Pay wages of £2,000 to an employee.
9	Pay postage costs of £100, by cheque.

4 Credit purchases

Definition – Cash purchase

A cash purchase occurs when goods are bought (or a service received) and the customer pays immediately using cash, cheques or credit cards. A receipt is issued for the amount of cash paid.

Definition – Credit purchase

A credit purchase occurs when goods are bought (or a service received) and the customer does not have to pay immediately but can pay after a specified number of days. An invoice is then issued to request that payment is made.

Example 9

We have already seen the double entry for a cash purchase and we shall now contrast this with the double entry for a credit purchase by means of an illustration.

John buys goods from Sam for £2,000.

(a) Record the double entry in John's books if John pays for the goods immediately with a cheque.

(b) Record the double entry in John's books if John buys the goods on credit and pays some time later.

Solution

(a) **Cash purchase**

The double entry is simply to:

Credit the bank account with £2,000 because £2,000 has been paid out.

Debit the purchases account with £2,000 because goods have been purchased with £2,000.

Bank

	£		£
		Purchases	2,000

Purchases

	£		£
Bank	2,000		

(b) **Credit purchase**

We have to record two transactions separately:

(i) *At the time the purchase is made*

At the time the purchase is made we debit £2,000 to the purchases account because a purchase has been made, but we do not make any entry in the bank account yet, because at that point, no cash has been paid. The other effect is that John has a liability, he owes £2,000 to the supplier, Sam, who we can refer to as a payable.

The double entry is:

Debit the purchases account with £2,000 because expenses have increased by £2,000.

Credit payables account with £2,000 (this is a liability of the business).

Purchases

	£		£
Payables	2,000		

Payables

	£		£
		Purchases	2,000

(ii) *When John pays the £2,000*

The double entry now will be:

Credit the bank account with £2,000 because £2,000 has been paid out.

Debit the payable account because John has paid and the payable has been reduced by £2,000.

Payables

	£		£
Bank	2,000	Purchases	2,000

Purchases

	£		£
Payables	2,000		

Bank

	£		£
		Payables	2,000

4.1 Summary

The net effect of the above credit purchase is that the payable has a nil balance because John has paid, and we are left with a debit in the purchases account and a credit in the cash book. This is exactly as for a cash purchase – we just had to go through the intermediate step of the payables account to get there.

5 Credit sales

Definition – Cash sale

A cash sale occurs when goods are sold (or a service provided) and the customer pays immediately with cash, cheque or credit card. A receipt is issued for the amount of cash received.

Definition – Credit sale

A credit sale occurs when goods are sold (or a service provided) and the customer does not have to pay immediately but can pay after a specified number of days. An invoice is issued to request that the balance owed is then paid.

Example 10

We have already seen the double entry for a cash sale and we shall now contrast this with the double entry for a credit sale by means of an illustration.

George sells goods to Harry for £1,000.

(a) Record the double entry in George's books if Harry pays for the goods immediately with a cheque.

(b) Record the double entry in George's books if Harry buys the goods on credit and pays some time later.

Solution

(a) **Cash sale**

The double entry is simply to:

Debit the bank account with £1,000 because £1,000 has been paid in.

Credit the sales account with £1,000 because income has increased by £1,000.

Bank

	£		£
Sales	1,000		

Sales

	£		£
		Bank	1,000

(b) **Credit sale**

The double entry will be made at two separate times.

(i) *At the time the sale is made*

At the time the sale is made we credit £1,000 to the sales account because a sale has been made, but we cannot make any entry in the bank account at the time of the sale because no cash is received. However, the dual effect principle means that there must be another effect to this transaction, and in this case it is that the business has acquired a receivable.

The double entry is:

Debit receivables account with £1,000 (this is an asset of the business).

Credit the sales account with £1,000 because income has increased by £1,000.

Receivables

	£		£
Sales	1,000		

Sales

	£		£
		Receivables	1,000

(ii) *When Harry pays the £1,000*

The double entry now will be:

Debit the bank account with £1,000 because £1,000 has been paid in.

Credit the receivables account because Harry has paid and the receivable has been reduced by £1,000.

Receivables

	£		£
Sales	1,000	Bank	1,000

Sales

	£		£
		Receivables	1,000

Bank

	£		£
Receivables	1,000		

5.1 Summary

The net effect of the above credit sale is that the receivable has a nil balance because Harry has paid and we are left with a credit in the sales account and a debit in the cash book. This is exactly as for a cash sale – we just had to go through the intermediate step of the receivable account to get there.

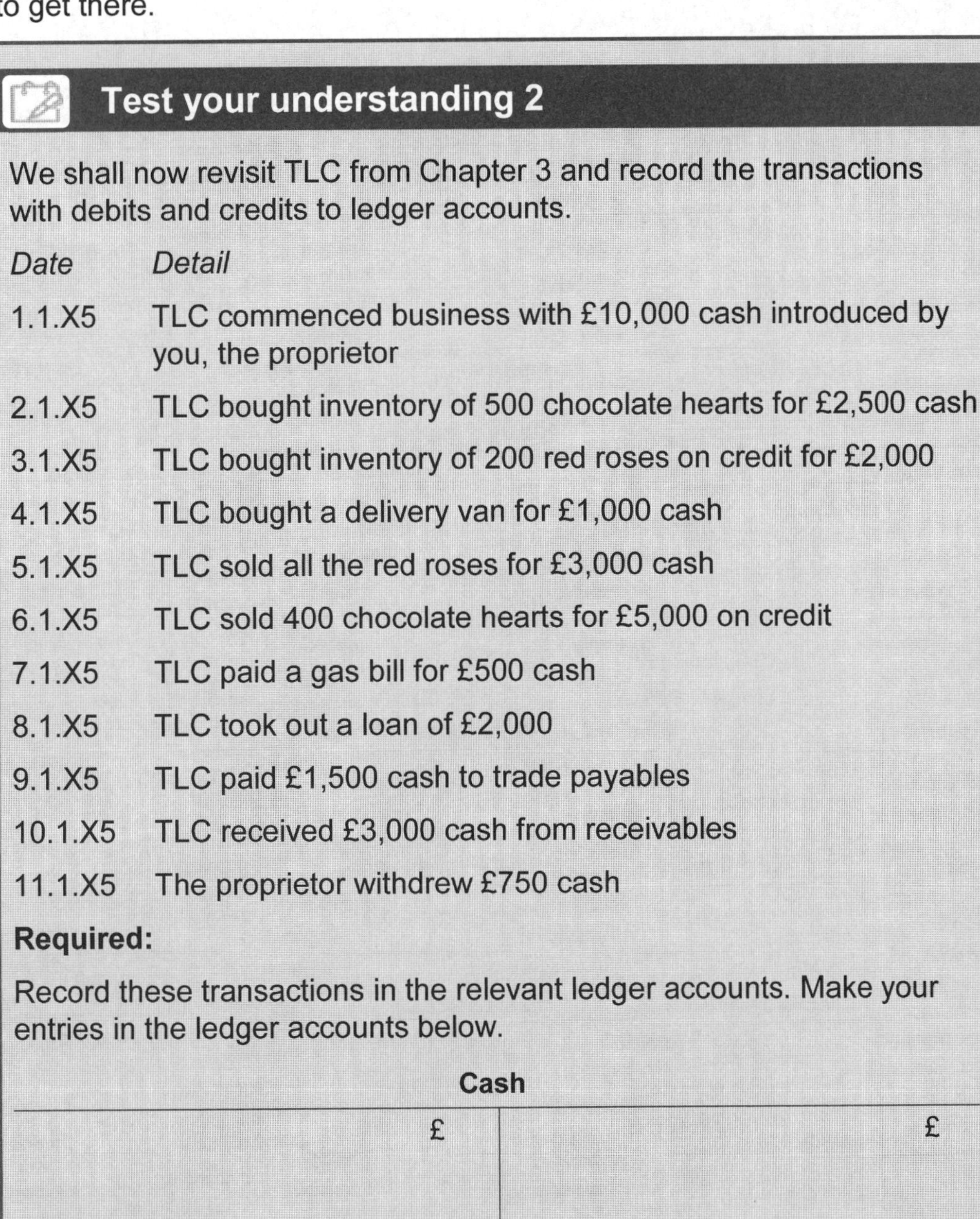

Test your understanding 2

We shall now revisit TLC from Chapter 3 and record the transactions with debits and credits to ledger accounts.

Date	*Detail*
1.1.X5	TLC commenced business with £10,000 cash introduced by you, the proprietor
2.1.X5	TLC bought inventory of 500 chocolate hearts for £2,500 cash
3.1.X5	TLC bought inventory of 200 red roses on credit for £2,000
4.1.X5	TLC bought a delivery van for £1,000 cash
5.1.X5	TLC sold all the red roses for £3,000 cash
6.1.X5	TLC sold 400 chocolate hearts for £5,000 on credit
7.1.X5	TLC paid a gas bill for £500 cash
8.1.X5	TLC took out a loan of £2,000
9.1.X5	TLC paid £1,500 cash to trade payables
10.1.X5	TLC received £3,000 cash from receivables
11.1.X5	The proprietor withdrew £750 cash

Required:

Record these transactions in the relevant ledger accounts. Make your entries in the ledger accounts below.

Cash

	£		£

	Capital	
	£	£

	Purchases	
	£	£

	Payables	
	£	£

	Delivery van	
	£	£

	Sales	
	£	£

Receivables

£	£

Gas

£	£

Loan

£	£

Drawings

£	£

Test your understanding 3

Z, the owner of a consultancy firm, has the following transactions:

(a) Pays £4,000 into the bank as capital.

(b) Buys a computer for £1,000.

(c) Pays rent of £400.

(d) Earns £800 for consultancy services.

Write up the ledger accounts for the above.

Test your understanding 4

B makes the following cash transactions:

(a) Pays £4,000 into the bank as capital.

(b) Buys goods for £700.

(c) Buys champagne to entertain the staff for £300.

(d) Purchases three computers for £3,000.

(e) Sells goods for £1,500 cash.

(f) Draws £500 cash.

(g) Purchases goods for £1,200 cash.

(h) Pays telephone bill of £600.

(i) Receives telephone bill rebate of £200.

(j) Buys stationery for £157.

Write up the ledger accounts for the above.

Test your understanding 5

A sells books to B for £1,000 on credit.

A also sells books to C for £90 credit.

B pays £500 and C pays £90.

Write up these transactions in the sales ledger accounts of A, using individual receivable accounts for each customer.

6 Balancing a ledger account

6.1 Procedure for balancing a ledger account

Step 1 Total both the debit and the credit side of the ledger account and make a note of each total.

Step 2 Insert the higher of the two totals as the total on both sides of the ledger account leaving a line beneath the final entry on each side of the account.

Step 3 On the side with the smaller total insert the figure needed to make this column add up to the total. Call this figure the balance carried down (or 'Bal c/d' as an abbreviation).

Step 4 On the opposite side of the ledger account, below the total insert this same figure and call it the balance brought down (or 'Bal b/d' as an abbreviation).

6.2 Step by step example

Example 11

The bank account of a business has the following entries:

Bank

	£		£
Capital	1,000	Purchases	200
Sales	300	Drawings	100
Sales	400	Rent	400
Capital	500	Stationery	300
Sales	800	Purchases	400

Calculate the balance on the account and bring the balance down as a single amount.

Solution

Step 1 Total both sides of the account and make a note of the totals. (Note that these totals that are asterisked below would not normally be written into the ledger account itself. They are only shown here to explain the process more clearly.)

Bank

	£		£
Capital	1,000	Purchases	200
Sales	300	Drawings	100
Sales	400	Rent	400
Capital	500	Stationery	300
Sales	800	Purchases	400
*Sub-total debits**	*3,000*	*Sub-total credits**	*1,400*

Step 2 Insert the higher total as the total of both sides.

Bank

	£		£
Capital	1,000	Purchases	200
Sales	300	Drawings	100
Sales	400	Rent	400
Capital	500	Stationery	300
Sales	800	Purchases	400
*Sub-total debits**	*3,000*	*Sub-total credits**	*1,400*
Total	3,000	Total	3,000

Step 3 Insert a balancing figure on the side of the account with the lower sub-total. This is referred to as the 'balance carried down' or 'bal c/d' for short.

Bank

	£		£
Capital	1,000	Purchases	200
Sales	300	Drawings	100
Sales	400	Rent	400
Capital	500	Stationery	300
Sales	800	Purchases	400
*Sub-total debits**	*3,000*	*Sub-total credits**	*1,400*
		Bal c/d	1,600
Total	3,000	Total	3,000

Step 4 Insert the balance carried down figure beneath the total on the other side of the account. This is referred to as 'bal b/d' for short.

Bank

	£		£
Capital	1,000	Purchases	200
Sales	300	Drawings	100
Sales	400	Rent	400
Capital	500	Stationery	300
Sales	800	Purchases	400
*Sub-total debits**	*3,000*	*Sub-total credits**	*1,400*
		Bal c/d	1,600
Total	3,000	Total	3,000
Bal b/d	1,600		

The closing balance carried down at the end of the period is also the opening balance brought down at the start of the next period. This opening balance remains in the account as the starting position and any further transactions are then added into the account. In this case the balance brought down is a debit balance as there is money in the bank account making it an asset.

Example 12

Consider again the ledger accounts from the earlier example Percy in this chapter which are reproduced below and balance them.

Bank

Date			£	*Date*			£
1 Jan	Capital	(1)	20,000	1 Jan	Van	(2)	500
5 Jan	Sales	(6)	2,000		Purchases	(3)	1,000
					Drawings	(4)	50
				5 Jan	Purchases	(5)	500
				15 Jan	Rent	(7)	200

Capital

Date			£	*Date*			£
				1 Jan	Bank	(1)	20,000

Van

Date			£	*Date*			£
1 Jan	Bank	(2)	500				

Purchases

Date			£	*Date*			£
1 Jan	Bank	(3)	1,000				
5 Jan	Bank	(5)	500				

Drawings

Date			£	*Date*			£
1 Jan	Bank	(4)	50				

Sales

Date			£	*Date*			£
				5 Jan	Bank	(6)	2,000

Rent

Date			£	*Date*			£
15 Jan	Bank	(7)	200				

Solution

(a) **The bank account**

Bank

Date		£	*Date*		£
1 Jan	Capital	20,000	1 Jan	Van	500
5 Jan	Sales	2,000		Purchases	1,000
				Drawings	50
			5 Jan	Purchases	500
			15 Jan	Rent	200

Step 1 Total both the debit and the credit side of the ledger account and make a note of each total – debit side £22,000, credit side £2,250.

Step 2 Insert the higher of the two totals, £22,000, as the total on both sides of the ledger account leaving a line beneath the final entry on each side of the account.

Bank

Date		£	*Date*		£
1 Jan	Capital	20,000	1 Jan	Van	500
5 Jan	Sales	2,000		Purchases	1,000
				Drawings	50
			5 Jan	Purchases	500
			15 Jan	Rent	200
		22,000			22,000

Step 3 On the side with the smaller total insert the figure needed to make this column add up to the total. Call this figure the balance carried down (or Bal c/d as an abbreviation).

Step 4 On the opposite side of the ledger account, below the total insert this same figure and call it the balance brought down (or Bal b/d as an abbreviation).

Bank

Date		£	*Date*		£
1 Jan	Capital	20,000	1 Jan	Van	500
5 Jan	Sales	2,000		Purchases	1,000
				Drawings	50
			5 Jan	Purchases	500
			15 Jan	Rent	200
			31 Jan	Balance c/d	19,750
		22,000			22,000
1 Feb	Balance b/d	19,750			

This shows that the business has £19,750 left in the bank account at the end of January and therefore also on the first day of February. As the balance that is brought down to start the next period is on the debit side of the account this is known as a debit balance and indicates that this is an asset – money in the bank account.

(b) **Capital**

Capital

Date		£	*Date*		£
			1 Jan	Bank	20,000

As there is only one entry in this account there is no need to balance the account. The entry is on the credit side and is known as a credit balance. A credit balance is a liability of the business and this account shows that the business owes the owner £20,000 of capital.

(c) **Van**

Van

Date		£	*Date*		£
1 Jan	Bank	500			

Again, there is no need to balance this account as there is only one entry. This is a debit balance as it is an asset – the non-current asset, the van, which cost £500.

(d) **Purchases**

Purchases

Date		£	*Date*		£
1 Jan	Bank	1,000			
5 Jan	Bank	500	31 Jan	Balance c/d	1,500
		1,500			1,500
1 Feb	Balance b/d	1,500			

This now shows that during the month £1,500 of purchases was made. This is a debit balance as purchases are an expense of the business.

(e) **Drawings**

Drawings

Date		£	*Date*		£
1 Jan	Bank	50			

This is a debit balance as drawings are a reduction of the capital owed to the owner which is a credit balance.

(f) **Sales**

Sales

Date		£	*Date*		£
			5 Jan	Bank	2,000

There is no need to balance the account as there is only one entry – a £2,000 credit balance representing income.

(g) **Rent**

Rent

Date		£	*Date*		£
15 Jan	Bank	200			

As there is only one entry there is no need to balance the account. This is a debit balance indicating that there has been an expense of £200 of rent incurred during the month.

Test your understanding 6

Given below is a bank account ledger account for the month of March. You are required to 'balance off' the ledger account.

Bank

Date		£	*Date*		£
1 Mar	Capital	12,000	3 Mar	Purchases	3,000
7 Mar	Sales	5,000	15 Mar	Non-current asset	2,400
19 Mar	Sales	2,000	20 Mar	Purchases	5,300
22 Mar	Sales	3,000	24 Mar	Rent	1,000
			28 Mar	Drawings	2,000

Test your understanding 7

The following bank account has been written up for the month of May 20X9. There was no opening balance.

Bank

	£		£
Capital	10,000	Computer	1,000
Sales	2,000	Telephone	567
Sales	3,000	Rent	1,500
Sales	2,000	Rates	125
		Stationery	247
		Petrol	49
		Purchases	2,500
		Drawings	500
		Petrol	42

Bring down the balance on the account.

 Test your understanding 8

The following bank account has been written up during May 20X9. There was no brought forward balance.

Bank

	£		£
Capital	5,000	Purchases	850
Sales	1,000	Fixtures	560
Sales	876	Van	1,500
Rent rebate	560	Rent	1,300
Sales	1,370	Rates	360
		Telephone	220
		Stationery	120
		Petrol	48
		Car repairs	167

Bring down the balance on the account.

Test your understanding 9

The following bank account has been written up during June 20X9.

Bank

	£		£
Balance b/f	23,700	Drawings	4,000
Sales	2,300	Rent	570
Sales	1,700	Purchases	6,000
Receivables	4,700	Rates	500
		Salaries	3,600
		Car expenses	460
		Petrol	49
		Petrol	38
		Electricity	210
		Stationery	89

Bring down the balance on the account.

7 The trial balance

7.1 Introduction

Definition – Trial balance

The trial balance is a list showing the balance brought down on each ledger account. It is a check point to ensure that every debit has an equal and opposite credit entry and therefore the totals of the trial balance columns should balance. However, it does not confirm that the account you have debited or credited is correct.

7.2 Format of the trial balance

An example of a simple trial balance is given below:

	Debit	*Credit*
	£	£
Sales		5,000
Opening inventory	100	
Purchases	3,000	
Rent	200	
Car	3,000	
Receivables	100	
Payables		1,400
	6,400	6,400

The trial balance is produced immediately after the double entry has been completed and balances extracted on the accounts.

The first column will detail the name of the ledger account and the balance will be noted in either the debit or credit column depending on the side it has been brought down on.

If the double entry has been completed correctly, the total of the debits will equal the total of the credits. Drafting a trial balance is a way of ensuring that double entries have been correctly completed.

Example 13

The following are the balances on the accounts of Ernest at 31 December 20X8.

	£
Sales	47,140
Purchases	26,500
Receivables	7,640
Payables	4,320
General expenses	9,430
Loan	5,000
Plant and machinery at cost	7,300
Motor van at cost	2,650
Drawings	7,500
Rent and rates	6,450
Insurance	1,560
Bank overdraft	2,570
Capital	10,000

Required:

Prepare Ernest's trial balance as at 31 December 20X8.

Solution

Step 1 Set up a blank trial balance

Step 2 Work down the list of balances one by one using what you have learned so far about debits and credits. Assets and expenses are debit balances and liabilities and income are credit balances.

The mnemonic DEAD CLIC may help.

Debit:	**Credit:**
Expenses	Liabilities
Assets	Income
Drawings	Capital

Trial balance at 31 December 20X8

	Dr	*Cr*
	£	£
Sales		47,140
Purchases	26,500	
Receivables	7,640	
Payables		4,320
General expenses	9,430	
Loan		5,000
Plant and machinery at cost	7,300	
Motor van at cost	2,650	
Drawings	7,500	
Rent and rates	6,450	
Insurance	1,560	
Bank overdraft		2,570
Capital		10,000
	69,030	69,030

Take care with drawings. These are a reduction of the capital owed back to the owner therefore as a reduction of a liability they must be a debit balance.

The bank overdraft is an amount owed to the bank therefore it must be a credit balance.

 **Test your understanding 10**

Continuing with the example of Percy, complete the trial balance.

Test your understanding 11

The following are the balances on the accounts of XYZ at 31 August 20X9:

	£
Sales	41,770
Purchases	34,680
Receivables	6,790
Payables	5,650
General expenses	12,760
Loan	10,000
Plant and machinery at cost	5,000
Motor van at cost	6,000
Drawings	2,000
Rent and rates	6,700
Insurance	4,000
Bank overdraft	510
Capital	20,000

Prepare XYZ's trial balance as at 31 August 20X9.

Test your understanding 12

Tony makes the following transactions during the month of July 20X9:

(a) Purchases good on credit for £1,000.

(b) Pays cash for rent of £500.

(c) Makes sales on credit for £1,500.

(d) Buys a computer for £900 cash.

(e) Pays cash for wages of £1,000.

(f) Receives cash from a credit customer of £400.

(g) Pays £300 cash to a credit supplier.

(h) Pays £200 cash for a telephone bill.

(i) Receives £50 cash refund for overcharge on telephone bill.

(j) Makes cash purchases of £400.

(k) Makes cash sales of £2,000.

Write up the ledger accounts for these transactions, balance the accounts off and extract Tony's Trial Balance at 31 July 20X9.

8 Summary

In this chapter we have studied cash and credit transactions. It is important to always start with the bank account and remember that cash received is a debit in the bank account and cash paid out is a credit in the bank account. If you get that right then the rest really does fall into place.

You should also be aware of the definitions of assets, expenses and income and the normal entries that you would make in the accounts for these.

Balancing an account is a very important technique which you must be able to master. You must understand how to bring the balance down onto the correct side and what that balance represents.

Test your understanding answers

Test your understanding 1

The figures in brackets are used here to indicate the transaction number in the test your understanding. They can be used to match the debit entry for the transaction with the corresponding credit entry.

Capital

	£		£
		Cash at bank (1)	150,000

Property

	£		£
Cash at bank (2)	140,000		

Purchases

	£		£
Cash at bank (3)	5,000		
Cash at bank (5)	8,000		

Sales

	£		£
		Cash at bank (4)	7,000
		Cash at bank (7)	15,000

Sundry expenses

	£		£
Cash at bank (6)	100		

Wages expense

	£		£
Cash at bank (8)	2,000		

Postage

	£		£
Cash at bank (9)	100		

Cash at bank

	£		£
Capital (1)	150,000	Property (2)	140,000
Sales (4)	7,000	Purchases (3)	5,000
Sales (7)	15,000	Purchases (5)	8,000
		Sundry expenses (6)	100
		Wages payable (8)	2,000
		Postage (9)	100

Test your understanding 2

Cash

Date	*Narrative*	£	*Date*	*Narrative*	£
1.1.X5	Capital	10,000	2.1.X5	Purchases	2,500
5.1.X5	Sales	3,000	4.1.X5	Delivery van	1,000
8.1.X5	Loan	2,000	7.1.X5	Gas	500
10.1.X5	Receivables	3,000	9.1.X5	Payables	1,500
			11.1.X5	Drawings	750

Capital

Date	*Narrative*	£	*Date*	*Narrative*	£
			1.1.X5	Cash	10,000

Purchases

Date	*Narrative*	£	*Date*	*Narrative*	£
2.1.X5	Cash	2,500			
3.1.X5	Payables	2,000			

Payables

Date	*Narrative*	£	*Date*	*Narrative*	£
9.1.X5	Cash	1,500	3.1.X5	Purchases	2,000

Delivery van

Date	*Narrative*	£	*Date*	*Narrative*	£
4.1.X5	Cash	1,000			

Sales

Date	*Narrative*	£	*Date*	*Narrative*	£
			5.1.X5	Cash	3,000
			6.1.X5	Receivables	5,000

Receivables

Date	*Narrative*	£	*Date*	*Narrative*	£
6.1.X5	Sales	5,000	10.1.X5	Cash	3,000

Gas

Date	*Narrative*	£	*Date*	*Narrative*	£
7.1.X5	Cash	500			

Loan

Date	Narrative	£	Date	Narrative	£
			8.1.X5	Cash	2,000

Drawings

Date	Narrative	£	Date	Narrative	£
11.1.X5	Cash	750			

Test your understanding 3

Bank

		£			£
(a)	Capital	4,000	(b)	Computer	1,000
(d)	Sales	800	(c)	Rent	400

Capital

		£			£
			(a)	Bank	4,000

Rent

		£			£
(c)	Bank	400			

Sales

		£			£
			(d)	Bank	800

Computers

		£			£
(b)	Bank	1,000			

Test your understanding 4

Capital

	£		£
		(a) Bank	4,000

Purchases

	£		£
(b) Bank	700		
(g) Bank	1,200		

Entertainment

	£		£
(c) Bank	300		

Computers

	£		£
(d) Bank	3,000		

Sales

	£		£
		(e) Bank	1,500

Drawings

	£		£
(f) Bank	500		

Telephone

	£		£
(h) Bank	600	(i) Bank	200

Stationery

		£			£
(j)	Bank	157			

Bank

		£			£
(a)	Capital	4,000	(b)	Purchases	700
(e)	Sales	1,500	(c)	Entertainment	300
(i)	Telephone	200	(d)	Computers	3,000
			(f)	Drawings	500
			(g)	Purchases	1,200
			(h)	Telephone	600
			(j)	Stationery	157

Test your understanding 5

Sales

	£		£
		B	1,000
		C	90

Receivable B

	£		£
Sales	1,000	Bank	500

Receivable C

	£		£
Sales	90	Bank	90

Bank

	£		£
Receivable B	500		
Receivable C	90		

Test your understanding 6

Bank

Date		£	*Date*		£
1 Mar	Capital	12,000	3 Mar	Purchases	3,000
7 Mar	Sales	5,000	15 Mar	Non-current asset	2,400
19 Mar	Sales	2,000	20 Mar	Purchases	5,300
22 Mar	Sales	3,000	24 Mar	Rent	1,000
			28 Mar	Drawings	2,000
			31 Mar	Balance c/d	8,300
		22,000			22,000
1 Apr	Balance b/d	8,300			

Test your understanding 7

Bank

	£		£
Capital	10,000	Computer	1,000
Sales	2,000	Telephone	567
Sales	3,000	Rent	1,500
Sales	2,000	Rates	125
		Stationery	247
		Petrol	49
		Purchases	2,500
		Drawings	500
		Petrol	42
Sub-total	17,000	Sub-total	6,530
		Balance c/d	10,470
	17,000		17,000
Balance b/d	10,470		

Test your understanding 8

Bank

	£		£
Capital	5,000	Purchases	850
Sales	1,000	Fixtures	560
Sales	876	Van	1,500
Rent rebate	560	Rent	1,300
Sales	1,370	Rates	360
		Telephone	220
		Stationery	120
		Petrol	48
		Car repairs	167
Sub-total	8,806	Sub-total	5,125
		Balance c/d	3,681
	8,806		8,806
Balance b/d	3,681		

Test your understanding 9

Bank

	£		£
Balance b/d	23,700	Drawings	4,000
Sales	2,300	Rent	570
Sales	1,700	Purchases	6,000
Receivables	4,700	Rates	500
		Salaries	3,600
		Car expenses	460
		Petrol	49
		Petrol	38
		Electricity	210
		Stationery	89
Sub-total	32,400	Sub-total	15,516
		Balance c/d	16,884
	32,400		32,400
Balance b/d	16,884		

Test your understanding 10

Trial balance

	Dr	Cr
	£	£
Bank	19,750	
Capital		20,000
Van	500	
Purchases	1,500	
Drawings	50	
Sales		2,000
Rent	200	
	22,000	22,000

Test your understanding 11

Trial balance at 31 August 20X9

	Dr	Cr
	£	£
Sales		41,770
Purchases	34,680	
Receivables	6,790	
Payables		5,650
General expenses	12,760	
Loan		10,000
Plant and machinery at cost	5,000	
Motor van at cost	6,000	
Drawings	2,000	
Rent and rates	6,700	
Insurance	4,000	
Bank overdraft		510
Capital		20,000
	77,930	77,930

Test your understanding 12

Purchases

	£		£
(a) Payables	1,000		
(j) Bank	400	Balance c/d	1,400
	1,400		1,400
Balance b/d	1,400		

Payables

	£		£
(g) Bank	300	(a) Purchases	1,000
Balance c/d	700		
	1,000		1,000
		Balance b/d	700

Rent

	£		£
(b) Bank	500	Balance c/d	500
	500		500
Balance b/d	500		

Sales

	£		£
		(c) Receivables	1,500
Balance c/d	3,500	(k) Bank	2,000
	3,500		3,500
		Balance b/d	3,500

Receivables

	£		£
(c) Sales	1,500	(f) Bank	400
		Balance c/d	1,100
	1,500		1,500
Balance b/d	1,100		

Computers

	£		£
(d) Bank	900	Balance c/d	900
	900		900
Balance b/d	900		

Wages

	£		£
(e) Bank	1,000	Balance c/d	1,000
	1,000		1,000
Balance b/d	1,000		

Telephone

	£		£
(h) Bank	200	(i) Bank	50
		Balance c/d	150
	200		200
Balance b/d	150		

Bank

		£			£
(f)	Receivables	400	(b)	Rent	500
(i)	Telephone	50	(d)	Computer	900
(k)	Sales	2,000	(e)	Wages	1,000
			(g)	Payables	300
			(h)	Telephone	200
			(j)	Purchases	400
Balance c/d		850			
		3,300			3,300
			Balance b/d		850

Trial balance as at 31 July 20X9:

	Dr	*Cr*
	£	£
Purchases	1,400	
Payables		700
Rent	500	
Sales		3,500
Receivables	1,100	
Computers	900	
Wages	1,000	
Telephone	150	
Bank overdraft		850
	5,050	5,050

Accounting for credit sales, VAT and discounts

5

Introduction

In this chapter we will consider, in more detail, the accounting for credit sales considering the effects of discounts and VAT as well as reviewing the accounting for receipts from receivables.

ASSESSMENT CRITERIA

Distinguish between prompt payment, trade and bulk discounts (1.2)

Demonstrate an understanding of the process of recording financial transactions (1.4)

Enter sales invoices and credit notes into books of prime entry (2.2)

Check the accuracy of receipts from customers (2.3)

Transfer data from the books of prime entry to the ledgers (5.1)

CONTENTS

1 Recording credit sales

1.1 The sales day book

In chapter 2 we were introduced to the sales day book (SDB) which is where a credit sale is primarily recorded. The sales day book details the names and references in relation to the customer we have sold goods to or provided a service to on credit. It also contains a breakdown of the transaction value – the net, VAT and gross (total) amounts (as detailed on the invoice).

The SDB is not part of the double entry; it is not part of the ledger accounts. The totals from the sales day book are used to perform the double entry to enter into the general ledger on a timely basis.

1.2 Accounting for credit sales and VAT

When recording a credit sale, the financial effects of the transaction include; the recognition of a receivable, the income generated from the sale and the amount of VAT that has been charged and is liable to be paid to HM Revenue & Customs.

The sales day book has been reproduced below along with summaries of the accounting entries required.

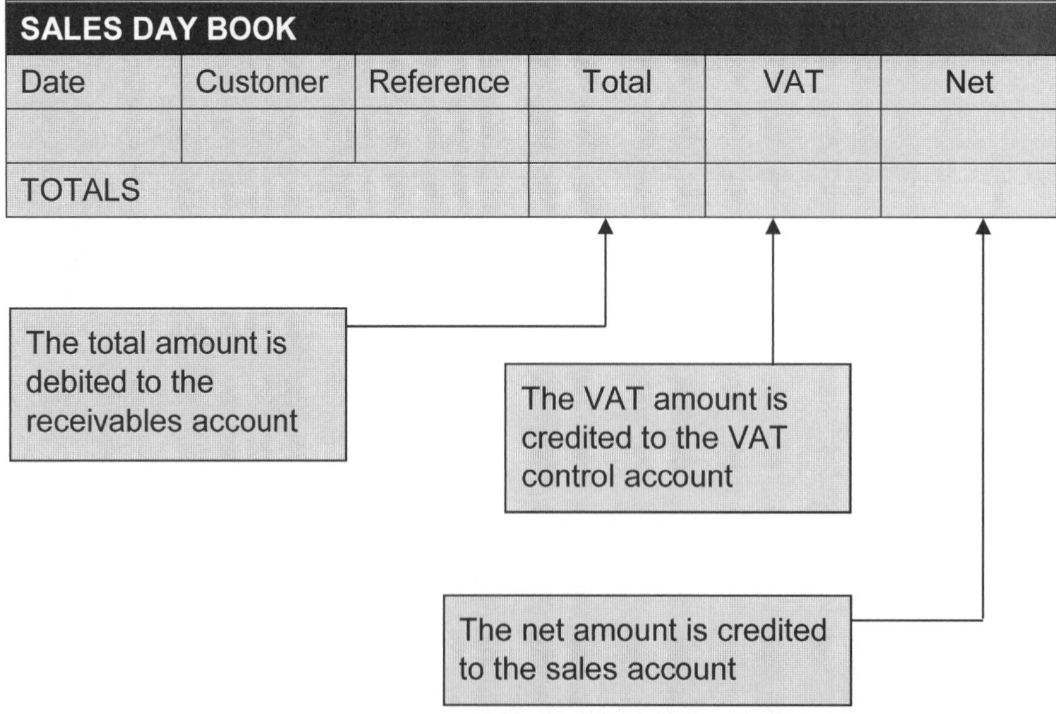

SALES DAY BOOK					
Date	Customer	Reference	Total	VAT	Net
TOTALS					

1.3 Summary of entries

In summary, the accounting entries for a credit sale with VAT are:

Debit	Receivables account with the gross amount
Credit	Sales account with the net amount
Credit	VAT control account with the VAT amount

The total amount is debited to the receivables account. This is recognising the asset of a credit customer owing us (the business) the gross amount of the transaction, including VAT.

The net amount is credited to the sales account. This is recognising an increase to income. It is only the net amount that is credited to the sales account as the VAT charged on the transaction is merely collected by the business on behalf of HM Revenue & Customs.

The VAT amount is credited to the VAT control account in recognition that this amount is owed to HMRC – this is a liability.

2 Discounts

2.1 Introduction

We have already been introduced to different types of discounts in an earlier chapter but we shall revise them here. There are three main types of discount that a business might offer to its credit customers; a bulk discount, a trade discount and a prompt payment discount.

2.2 Bulk discounts

A bulk discount is a percentage of the list price of the goods being sold that is deducted when purchasing large quantities.

A bulk discount is a definite amount deducted from the list price total of the invoice. The amounts recorded in the sales day book will be after a bulk discount has been deducted.

2.3 Trade discounts

A trade discount is a percentage of the list price of the goods being sold that is deducted for certain customers. This discount may be offered for frequent and valued customers, encouraging loyalty.

A trade discount is a definite amount deducted from the list price total of the invoice. The amounts recorded in the sales day book will be after the trade discount has been deducted.

2.4 Prompt payment discounts

A prompt payment discount (which may also be referred to as a cash or settlement discount) is offered to customers if they settle the invoice within a certain time period. It is up to the customer to decide whether or not to pay within the required timescale and therefore take advantage of the prompt payment discount.

The discount is expressed as a percentage of the invoice total but is not deducted from the invoice total as it is not certain when the invoice is sent out whether or not it will be taken advantage of. Instead the details of the prompt payment discount being offered will be noted at the bottom of the invoice.

A prompt payment discount can be offered but it is up to the customer whether or not to take advantage of it. The amounts recorded in the sales day book will be before any deductions of prompt payment discounts, as at that point we do not know if the discount will be taken advantage of or not.

3 VAT and discounts

3.1 Calculating VAT

A business makes no profit out of any VAT charged on its sales. Instead this amount is paid over to HM Revenue and Customs.

Test your understanding 1

Calculate the VAT on the following sales:

(a) A sale for £140.00 net of VAT

(b) A sale for £560.00 net of VAT

(c) A sale for £720.00 inclusive of VAT

(d) A sale for £960.00 inclusive of VAT

3.2 Bulk and trade discounts

At the time of generating and recording an invoice it is known if a bulk or trade discount has been given. There are no later conditions to be met.

VAT is calculated on the net amount of the transaction after the deduction of these discounts.

Example 1

L sells £1,000 of goods net of VAT (at 20%) to M on credit. There is an agreed 10% trade discount with M. Enter these transactions in the ledger accounts.

Solution

Step 1 Calculate the discount and VAT on the sale.

	£
Original list price of goods	1,000.00
Less: 10% trade discount	(100.00)
Net invoice value	900.00
VAT (20% x £900)	180.00
Total (gross) invoice value	1,080.00

Step 2 Enter the invoice amounts into the ledger accounts.

Receivables

	£		£
Sales and VAT	1,080.00		

Sales

	£		£
		Receivables	900.00

VAT

	£		£
		Receivables	180.00

3.3 Prompt payment discounts

Prompt payment VAT legislation was amended (Revenue and Customs Brief 49 (2014)) and the changes took effect from 1 April 2015. The AAT made these changes examinable for Bookkeeping Transactions from September 2016.

Although a customer may be offered a prompt payment discount no reflection of this discount is shown within the accounting records until the customer does take advantage of this, if they choose to do so. When initially raising an invoice, VAT should be charged on the full price of the goods or services (although this would be after deducting trade or bulk discounts).

If the customer takes advantage of the prompt payment discount the VAT would be adjusted to reflect the discount taken. This adjustment could be by way of a credit note – the chosen method for the Bookkeeping Transactions assessment criteria. The credit note to reflect this prompt payment discount is entered into the discounts allowed day book. This is considered in more detail in section 4.

Example 2

Leo, a trader, sells goods for £500 (exclusive of VAT at 20%). He offers a 10% discount if payment is made within 7 days.

The amounts shown as due on the invoice will be:

Sales price	£500
VAT	£100
Amount due	£600

The invoice will state that a prompt payment discount of £60 can be deducted from the amount due, if payment is made within 7 days. If the trader takes the discount the supplier must then issue a credit note for £60 i.e. £50 + VAT of £10. This credit note will be recorded in the discounts allowed day book.

Test your understanding 2

Calculate the VAT **paid** on the following sales:

(a) A sale for £280.00 net of VAT where a prompt payment discount of 2% is offered but not taken advantage of.

(b) A sale for £480.00 net of VAT where a prompt payment discount of 3% is offered but not taken advantage of.

(c) A sale for £800.00 net of VAT where a prompt payment discount of 5% is offered and is taken advantage of.

(d) A sale of £650.00 net of VAT where a prompt payment discount of 4% is offered and is taken advantage of.

4 Accounting for receipts from receivables and prompt payment discounts

4.1 Accounting for receipts from receivables

When a receivable makes a payment for an amount owed the double entry is:

Debit	Bank account
Credit	Receivable account

The debit to the bank account is recognising the increase in our funds – we have received money from the receivable.

The credit entry to the receivable account is to reduce the receivable balance now that the receivable has made a payment to reduce what they owed the business.

When initially recording a receipt from a receivable, the amounts will be recorded into the cash receipts book. Recording receipts from receivables into the cash receipts book was reviewed in chapter 2.

4.2 Checking the accuracy of receipts from customers

Prior to making the accounting entries for the receipt from a receivable, it should be established whether the amount being received from the customer is correct.

Discrepancies causing under or over payment may occur. Such discrepancies may be due to the incorrect application and calculation of discounts so errors need to be identified. Checks should be made by agreeing the receipt to supporting documentation, re-performing calculations and agreeing discounts to a discount policy.

There are numerous reasons why a credit customer may make the incorrect payment including it being a genuine mistake or perhaps there being a dispute over the invoices due. In the event of a genuine mistake the seller should contact the customer to explain the issue and request for the issue to be rectified. If there is a dispute the seller should contact the customer attempting to resolve the issue.

4.3 Accounting for prompt payment discounts

If a receivable takes advantage of a prompt payment discount, the receivable will pay less than what has been recorded within the accounting records. The adjustment required impacts the receivable account, the VAT account and a discounts allowed account.

When accounting for a discount allowed to a credit customer, we do not revise the original sales value, instead we recognise an expense for this discount.

When initially recording a discount allowed to a customer, due to the customer taking advantage of a prompt payment discount, the amounts will be recorded into the discounts allowed day book.

The discounts allowed day book has been reproduced along with a summary of the accounting entries required.

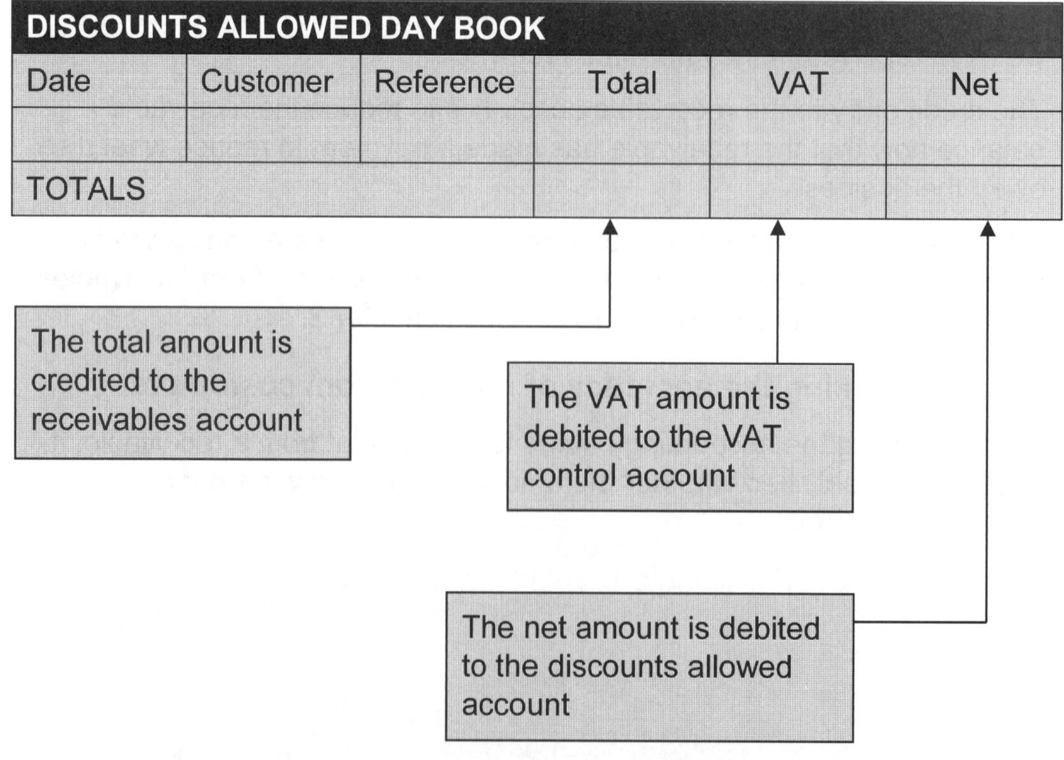

DISCOUNTS ALLOWED DAY BOOK					
Date	Customer	Reference	Total	VAT	Net
TOTALS					

To summarise, the accounting entries for a prompt payment discount are:

Debit	Discounts allowed account with the net amount
Debit	VAT account with the VAT amount
Credit	Receivable account with the gross amount

The gross amount is credited to the receivables account. This is recognising the reduction to the receivable of the discount and associated VAT charge.

The net amount is debited to the discounts allowed account. This is recognising an expense of allowing a discount. Note that this is for the VAT exclusive amount.

The VAT amount based on the discount allowed is debited to the VAT account in recognition that this amount is no longer owed to HMRC as there has been a reduction to the original price due to the customer taking advantage of a prompt payment discount.

The example that follows shows the procedures of calculating invoice amounts and amounts due from receivables as well as how to account for these transactions.

Example 3

Enzo sells goods for £200 net of VAT (at 20%) to Emilia on credit. Enzo offers Emilia a 2% prompt payment discount if Emilia pays within 10 days. Emilia does pay within the required time and takes the prompt payment discount.

Required:

(a) Calculate the invoice value.

(b) Record the required entries for the credit sale to Emilia in the sales day book and the relevant accounts in the general ledger of Enzo.

(c) Calculate the amount paid by Emilia (taking the prompt payment discount).

(d) Record the receipt by Enzo of Emilia's payment in the cash receipts book, the prompt payment discount in the discounts allowed day book and make the required entries into the ledger accounts in the general ledger of Enzo.

Solution

(a) Calculate the invoice value.

	£
Sales value net of VAT	200.00
VAT = 200 × 20%	40.00
Invoice value	240.00

(b) Record the required entries for the credit sale to Emilia in the sales day book and the relevant accounts in the general ledger of Enzo.

SALES DAY BOOK			
Customer	**Total £**	**VAT £**	**Net £**
Emilia	240.00	40.00	200.00

Receivables

	£		£
Sales and VAT	240.00		

Sales

	£		£
		Receivables	200.00

VAT

	£		£
		Receivables	40.00

(c) Calculate the amount paid by Emilia (taking the prompt payment discount).

	£
Sales value net of VAT	200.00
Less: prompt payment discount = 2% × 200	(4.00)
VAT (196 × 20%)	39.20
Amount paid by Emilia	235.20

(d) Record the receipt by Enzo of Emilia's payment in the cash receipts book, the prompt payment discount allowed in the discounts allowed day book and make the required entries into the ledger accounts in the general ledger of Enzo.

CASH RECEIPTS BOOK				
Narrative	**Total £**	**VAT £**	**Receivables £**	**Cash sales £**
Emilia	235.20		235.20	

DISCOUNTS ALLOWED DAY BOOK			
Narrative	**Total**	**VAT**	**Net**
Emilia	4.80	0.80	4.00

Because Emilia takes the prompt payment discount, she pays Enzo £4.80 less than the invoice value – this is made up by the £4 reduction to the net price of the goods (2% of £200) and a £0.80 reduction to the VAT charge (the VAT should be 20% based on the discounted amount of £196).

In order to clear the receivables account we have to credit that account with the £4.80, debit a discount allowed account with £4 and debit the VAT account with £0.80.

The discount allowed of £4 is an expense of the business as we have allowed our customer to pay less than the invoice value in order for us to have the benefit of receiving the money earlier.

The £0.80 debit to VAT is reducing down the original VAT calculated on the sale as the price of the goods has now decreased because of the discount given to the customer.

Receivables

	£		£
Sales and VAT	240.00	Bank	235.20
		Discount allowed	4.80

Sales

	£		£
		Receivables	200.00

VAT

	£		£
Receivables	0.80	Receivables	40.00

Discount allowed

	£		£
Receivables	4.00		

Bank

	£		£
Receivables	235.20		

Now that we have reviewed accounting for receipts from receivables and prompt payment discounts, work through the following examples to practise the double entries involved.

Example 4

C sells £2,000 of goods net of VAT (at 20%) to Z on credit. He offers Z a 5% prompt payment discount if Z pays within 5 days. Z does not pay his account within 5 days and so does not take the prompt payment discount. Z pays after 10 days. Enter these transactions in the accounts.

Solution

Step 1 Calculate the VAT on the sale.

	£
Sales value net of VAT	2,000.00
VAT = 2,000 × 20%	400.00
Invoice value	2,400.00

At the point of raising the invoice it is not known whether the prompt payment discount will be taken or not. The discount offer would be stated at the bottom of the invoice but the sales value would not be adjusted on the invoice.

Step 2 Enter the invoice in the accounts.

Receivables

	£		£
Sales and VAT	2,400.00		

Sales

	£		£
		Receivables	2,000.00

VAT

	£		£
		Receivables	400.00

Step 3 Enter the payment by Z in the accounts.

Receivables

	£		£
Sales and VAT	2,400.00	Bank	2,400.00

Sales

	£		£
		Receivables	2,000.00

VAT

	£		£
		Receivables	400.00

Bank

	£		£
Receivables	2,400.00		

As Z does not take advantage of the prompt payment discount, there is no entry for the prompt payment discount at all in the accounts.

Example 5

Two months later C sells another £2,000 of goods net of VAT (at 20%) to Z on credit. He offers Z a 5% prompt payment discount if Z pays within 5 days. This time Z does pay his account within 5 days and takes the prompt payment discount. Enter these transactions in the accounts.

Solution

Step 1 Calculate the VAT on the sale.

Note: This is exactly the same as the previous example.

	£
Sales value net of VAT	2,000.00
VAT = 2,000 × 20%	400.00
Invoice value	2,400.00

Step 2 Enter the invoice in the accounts.

Note: This is exactly the same as the previous example because the value of the invoice is exactly the same.

Receivables

	£		£
Sales and VAT	2,400.00		

Sales

	£		£
		Receivables	2,000.00

VAT

	£		£
		Receivables	400.00

Step 3 Calculate the amount paid by Z.

Note: The amount paid by Z will be different from the previous example because Z does take the 5% prompt payment discount offered.

	£
Sales value net of VAT	2,000.00
Less: prompt payment discount = 5% × 2,000	(100.00)
VAT (1,900 × 20%)	380.00
Amount paid by Z	2,280.00

Step 4 Enter this amount in the accounts.

Receivables

	£		£
Sales and VAT	2,400.00	Bank	2,280.00

Bank

	£		£
Receivables	2,280.00		

Because Z takes the prompt payment discount, he pays C £120 less than the invoice value – this is made up by the £100 reduction to the net price of the goods (5% of £2,000) and a £20 reduction to the VAT charge (the VAT should be 20% based on the discounted amount of £1,900).

In order to clear the receivables account we have to credit that account with the £120, debit a discount allowed account with £100 and debit the VAT account with £20.

The discount allowed of £100 is an expense of the business as we have allowed our customer to pay less than the invoice value in order for us to have the benefit of receiving the money earlier.

The £20 debit to VAT is reducing down the original VAT calculated on the sale as the price of the goods has now decreased because of the discount given to the customer.

Sales

	£		£
		Receivables	2,000.00

VAT

	£		£
Receivables	20.00	Receivables	400.00

Receivables

	£		£
Sales and VAT	2,400.00	Bank	2,280.00
		Discount allowed	100.00
		VAT	20.00

Discount allowed

	£		£
Receivables	100.00		

Bank

	£		£
Receivables	2,280.00		

Test your understanding 3

A sells £600 of goods to B – VAT is still to be added. A offers B a prompt payment discount of 3%.

(a) What will the accounting entries be to record the initial sale if:

- (i) B does not take the prompt payment discount.
- (ii) B does take the prompt payment discount.

(b) Calculate the amount that B will pay A if:

- (i) B does not take the prompt payment discount.
- (ii) B does take the prompt payment discount.

(c) What are the accounting entries for recording the payment received from B if the prompt payment discount has been taken?

5 Summary

We have covered some fairly tricky areas in this chapter and it is very important that you really do understand them.

The calculations of VAT (sales tax) are fairly straightforward but do make sure you can calculate the VAT element of a sale when you are given the sales value gross of VAT.

Quite tricky is the adjustment needed when a customer takes advantage of a prompt payment discount. You have to ensure the discounted price of the goods is accounted for as well as the reduction to the VAT amount.

It is necessary for you to be able to check the accuracy of receipts from customers, identifying any discrepancies that may have occurred.

Test your understanding answers

Test your understanding 1

(a) VAT = £140.00 × 20% = £28.00

(b) VAT = £560.00 × 20% = £112.00

(c) VAT = £720.00 × $\frac{20}{120}$ = £120.00

(d) VAT = £960.00 × $\frac{20}{120}$ = £160.00

Test your understanding 2

(a) VAT = £280 × 20% = £56.00

(b) VAT = £480 × 20% = £96.00

(c) VAT = £(800 – (5% × 800)) × 20% = £152.00

(d) VAT = £(650 – (4% × 650)) × 20% = £124.80

Although a prompt payment discount was offered in (a) and (b) the discount was not taken advantage of so the VAT paid is not discounted.

In (c) and (d) the prompt payment discounts offered were taken advantage of and so the VAT paid would be calculated based on the discounted sales price.

Test your understanding 3

(a) What will the accounting entries be to record the initial sale if:

(i) B does not take the prompt payment discount.

(ii) B does take the prompt payment discount.

The invoice value and the accounting entries required will be the same regardless of whether B takes the prompt payment discount or not.

Invoice value:

	£
Net price	600.00
VAT £600 × 20%	120.00
Invoice value	720.00

Accounting entries:

Debit receivables	£720.00
Credit sales	£600.00
Credit VAT	£120.00

(b) Calculate the amount that B will pay A if:

(i) **B does not take the prompt payment discount:**

Amount paid by B: £720.00

(ii) **B does take the prompt payment discount:**

If B does take the prompt payment discount the original invoice value will be the same as seen in part (a). However the payment if the discount is taken is calculated as follows:

	£
Net price	600.00
Less: prompt payment discount (£600 × 3%)	(18.00)
Revised sales price	582.00
VAT (£582 × 20%)	116.40
Amount paid by B:	698.40

The net amount of the discount is £18.00, with a reduction to VAT of £3.60 and therefore a total deduction to the amount owed by the receivable of £21.60.

(c) What are the accounting entries for recording the payment received from B if the prompt payment discount has been taken?

Accounting entries:

For the bank receipt:

Debit bank	£698.40
Credit receivables	£698.40

For the discount allowed:

Debit discounts allowed	£18.00
Debit VAT	£3.60
Credit receivables	£21.60

Accounting for credit purchases, VAT and discounts

Introduction

In this chapter we move on from considering the accounting entries for sales and look here at the equivalent accounting entries for purchases.

ASSESSMENT CRITERIA

Distinguish between prompt payment, trade and bulk discounts (1.2)

Demonstrate an understanding of the process of recording financial transactions (1.4)

Check the accuracy of supplier invoices and credit notes (3.1)

Enter supplier invoices and credit notes into books of prime entry (3.2)

Prepare payments to suppliers (3.3)

Transfer data from the books of prime entry to the ledgers (5.1)

CONTENTS

1 Recording credit purchases

1.1 The purchases day book

In an early chapter we were introduced to the purchases day book which is where a credit purchase is primarily recorded. The purchases day book (PDB) details the names and references in relation to the supplier we have bought goods from or received a service from on credit. It also contains a breakdown of the transaction value – the net, VAT and gross (total) amounts (as detailed on the invoice).

The PDB is not part of the double entry; it is not part of the ledger accounts. The totals from the purchases day book are used to perform the double entry to enter into the general ledger on a timely basis.

1.2 Accounting for credit purchases and VAT

When recording a credit purchase, the financial effects of the transaction include; the recognition of a payable, expense from a purchase and an amount of VAT that has been paid but which we can use to offset against a VAT liability to HM Revenue & Customs.

The purchases day book has been reproduced below along with summaries of the accounting entries required.

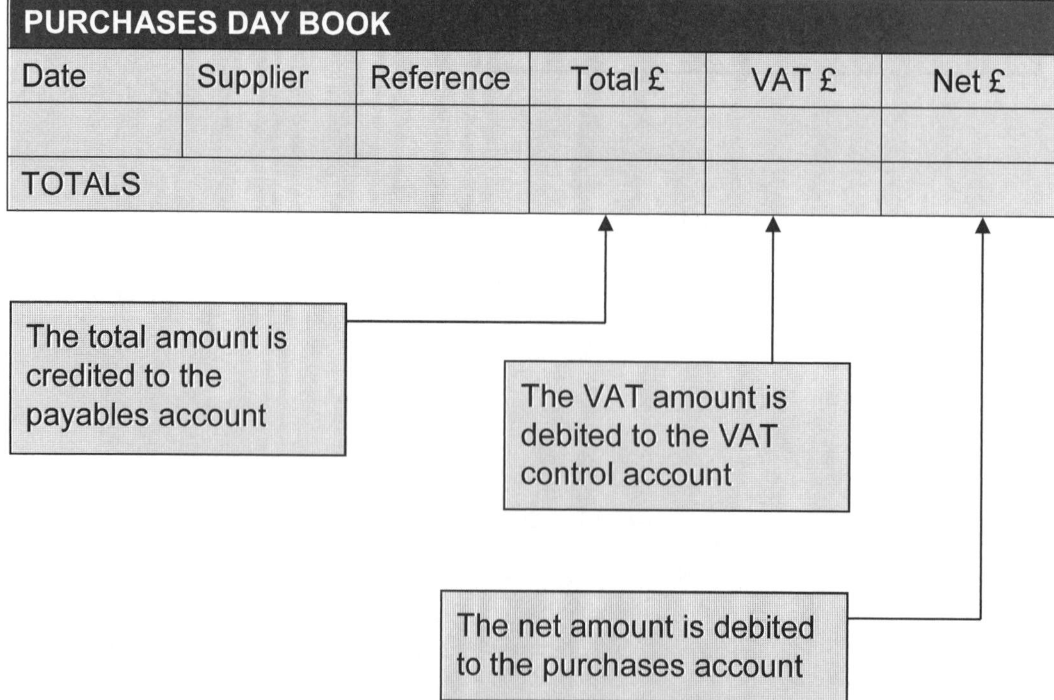

PURCHASES DAY BOOK

Date	Supplier	Reference	Total £	VAT £	Net £
TOTALS					

1.3 Summary of entries

In summary the accounting entries for a credit purchase with VAT are:

Debit	Purchases account with the net amount
Debit	VAT account with the VAT
Credit	Payables account with the gross amount

Purchases have been debited with the net amount as the VAT is not a cost to the business. Instead the VAT is an amount that can be offset against the amount of VAT due to HMRC and therefore the VAT is a debit entry in the VAT account.

The payables account is credited with the gross amount as this is the amount that must be paid to the supplier.

Work through the following example to practise the double entry for credit purchases.

Example 1

B sells goods on credit to Y for £500 plus VAT at 20%. Y pays B the full amount due. Record these transactions in the accounts of Y.

Solution

Step 1 Calculate the VAT on the purchase and enter the transaction in the payables, purchases and VAT accounts.

Calculation of VAT

	£
Net value of sale	500.00
VAT at 20%	100.00
Gross value of purchase	600.00

Payables

	£		£
		Purchases and VAT	600.00

Purchases

	£		£
Payables	500.00		

VAT

	£		£
Payables	100.00		

Step 2 Enter £600.00 paid by Y in the payables & the bank account.

Payables

	£		£
Bank	600.00	Purchases and VAT	600.00

Purchases

	£		£
Payables	500.00		

VAT

	£		£
Payables	100.00		

Bank

	£		£
		Payables	600.00

2 VAT and discounts

2.1 Introduction

We studied discounts and VAT (sales tax) when studying sales in chapter 5. The calculation of VAT and discounts are **exactly** the same when considering purchases. Remember that it is the seller who offers the discounts and it is the seller who charges the VAT, the fact that we are now studying purchases does not change the calculations.

The purchaser will receive a 'sales invoice' from the seller. This will have details of discounts and VAT exactly as we saw before when studying sales. The purchaser will call this a 'purchase invoice' and enter it in the books accordingly as we shall see.

We shall not therefore go through all the details of VAT and discounts but will simply revise this with a short example.

Example 2

Carl buys £1,000 of goods from Susan on credit. Susan sends a sales invoice with the goods offering a 5% prompt payment discount if Carl pays within 7 days. Carl does pay within 7 days.

Calculate:

(a) the VAT

(b) the total value of the invoice, and

(c) the amount that Carl will pay.

Solution

(a) VAT = £1,000 × 20% = £200

Note: although the discount is offered at the point of the invoice being generated it does not impact the calculation of VAT or the net goods value until the prompt payment discount is taken advantage of.

(b) **Total value of invoice**

	£
Goods	1,000.00
VAT	200.00
Invoice value	1,200.00

(c) **Amount Carl will pay**

	£
Goods	1,000.00
Less prompt payment discount (5% × 1,000)	(50.00)
Revised goods amount	950.00
VAT (950 × 20%)	190.00
Amount Carl will pay	1,140.00

Test your understanding 1

Calculate the VAT for the following:

(a) X purchases £400 goods from Y net of VAT at 20%.

(b) X purchases £650 goods from Y net of VAT at 20%.

(c) X purchases £528 goods from Y including VAT at 20%.

(d) X purchases £120 goods from Y including VAT at 20%.

Test your understanding 2

Calculate the VAT **paid** on the following:

(a) X purchases £850 goods from Y and takes the 3% prompt payment discount offered.

(b) X purchases £600 goods from Y and takes the 5% prompt payment discount offered.

(c) X purchases £325 goods from Y and does not take the 2% prompt payment discount offered.

(d) X purchases £57 goods from Y and does not take the 4% prompt payment discount offered.

3 Accounting for payments to suppliers and prompt payment discounts

3.1 Accounting for payments to payables

When we make a payment for an amount owed to a payable the double entry is:

Debit	Payable account
Credit	Bank account

The credit to the bank account is recognising the decrease in bank funds – we have paid money to the payable.

The debit entry to the payable account is to reduce the payable balance now that we have made the payment, the liability is reduced.

When initially recording a payment to a payable, the amounts will be recorded into the cash payments book. Recording payments to payables into the cash payments book was reviewed in chapter 2.

3.2 Preparing payments to suppliers

Prior to making the accounting entries for a payment to a payable, checks should be performed on the invoice received to identify any discrepancies. The details of quantities and amounts should be agreed to the purchase order, the delivery note and the goods received note to ensure correct billing.

3.3 Accounting for prompt payment discounts

If a business takes advantage of a prompt payment discount, the business will pay a lower amount to the payable than the amount that is recorded as the payable balance in the accounting records. The adjustment required for this discount received impacts the payable account; the VAT account and a discounts received account.

When accounting for a discount received from a credit supplier, we do not revise the original purchase value; instead we recognise this discount as a form of income.

When initially recording a prompt payment discount received from a supplier, the amounts will be recorded into a discounts received day book.

The discounts received day book has been reproduced along with the summaries of the accounting entries required.

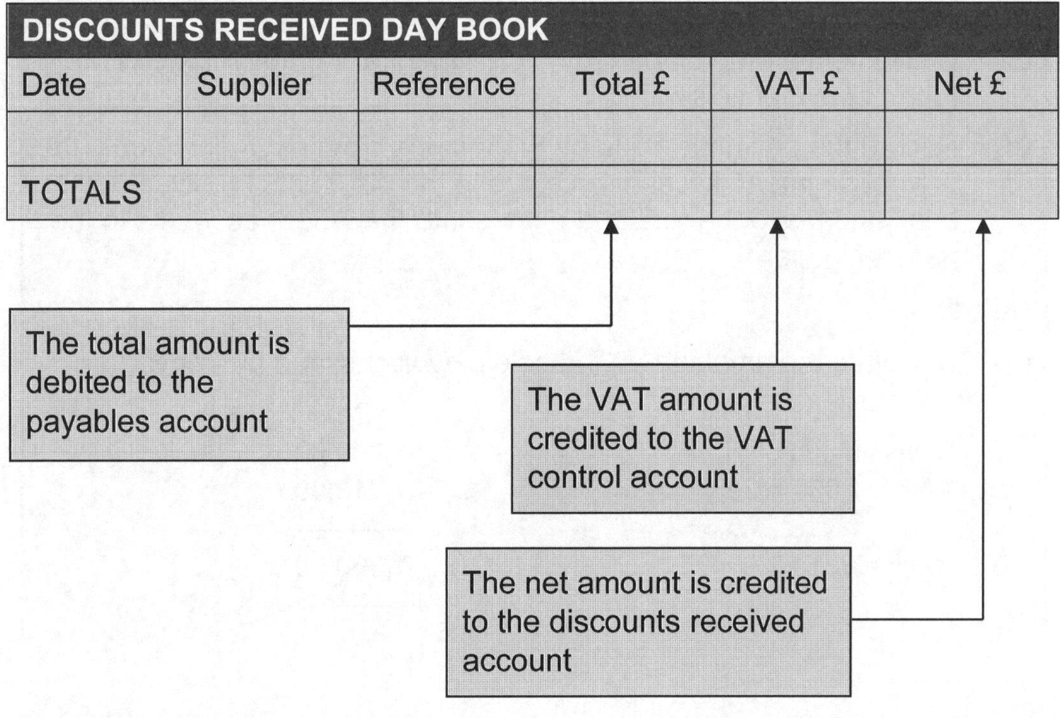

DISCOUNTS RECEIVED DAY BOOK					
Date	Supplier	Reference	Total £	VAT £	Net £
TOTALS					

To summarise, the accounting entries for a prompt payment discount received are:

Debit	Payables with the gross amount
Credit	VAT account with the VAT amount
Credit	Discounts received account with the net amount

The gross amount is debited to the payables account. This is recognising the reduction to the payable of the discount and associated VAT charge.

The net amount is credited to the discounts received account. This is recognising a form of income from receiving a discount. Note this is for the VAT exclusive amount.

The VAT amount based on the discount received is credited to the VAT account in recognition that the VAT on the purchase that was originally debited has now decreased.

Example 3

Tanya sells goods for £1,050 net of VAT at 20% to Flora on credit. Flora is offered a 5% prompt payment discount if payment is made within 5 working days. Flora does pay within the required time and takes advantage of the prompt payment discount that was offered by Tanya.

Required:

(a) Calculate the amounts on the sales invoice issued by Tanya.

(b) Record the required entries for the credit purchase in Flora's accounting records – the purchases day book and the relevant ledger accounts in the general ledger.

(c) Calculate the amount paid by Flora when taking advantage of the prompt payment discount.

(d) Record the payment made by Flora in the cash payments book, the prompt payment discount received in the discounts received day book and make the required entries into the ledger accounts in the general ledger.

Solution

(a) Calculate the amounts on the sales invoice issued by Tanya.

	£
Sales value net of VAT	1,050.00
VAT = 1,050 × 20%	210.00
Invoice value	1,260.00

(b) Record the required entries for the credit purchase in Flora's accounting records – the purchases day book and the relevant accounts in the general ledger.

PURCHASES DAY BOOK			
Supplier	**Total £**	**VAT £**	**Net £**
Tanya	1,260.00	210.00	1,050.00

Purchases

	£		£
Payables	1,050.00		

VAT

	£		£
Payables	210.00		

Payables

	£		£
		Purchases & VAT	1,260.00

(c) Calculate the amount paid by Flora when taking advantage of the prompt payment discount.

	£
Purchases value net of VAT	1,050.00
Less: prompt payment discount	
= 5% × 1,050	(52.50)
VAT (997.50 × 20%)	199.50
Amount paid by Flora	1,197.00

(d) Record the payment made by Flora in the cash payments book, the prompt payment discount received in the discounts received day book and make the required entries into the ledger accounts in the general ledger.

CASH PAYMENTS BOOK				
Narrative	**Total** £	**VAT** £	**Payables** £	**Other** £
Tanya	1,197.00		1,197.00	

DISCOUNTS RECEIVED DAY BOOK			
Narrative	**Total** £	**VAT** £	**Net** £
Tanya	63.00	10.50	52.50

As Flora takes the prompt payment discount, she pays Tanya £63 less than the invoice value – this is made up by the £52.50 reduction to the net price of the goods (5% of £1,050) and a £10.50 reduction to the VAT charge (the VAT should be 20% based on the discounted amount of £997.50).

In order to clear the balance on the payables account we have to debit that account with £63, credit a discounts received account with £52.50 and credit the VAT account with £10.50.

The discount received of £52.50 is treated as an income of the business. The £10.50 credit to VAT is reducing down the original VAT calculated on the purchase price, which has now reduced due to taking advantage of the prompt payment discount.

Purchases

	£		£
Payables	1,050.00		

VAT

	£		£
Payables	210.00	Payables	10.50

Payables

	£		£
Bank	1,197.00	Purchases and VAT	1,260.00
Discounts received and VAT	63.00		

Discounts received

	£		£
		Payables	52.50

Bank

	£		£
		Payables	1,197.00

Example 4

B sells £1,000 of goods to Y net of VAT on credit. He gives Y a deduction of 20% trade discount from the £1,000 net value. Y pays his account in full. Enter these amounts in the accounts of Y.

Solution

Step 1 Calculate the value of the sale net of discount and the VAT at 20% thereon.

	£
Sales value	1,000
Less: 20% discount	(200)
Net value	800
VAT at 20%	160
Total invoice value	960

Step 2 Enter the invoice in the payables, purchases and VAT accounts.

Payables

	£		£
		Purchases and VAT	960

Purchases

	£		£
Payables	800		

VAT

	£		£
Payables	160		

Note: Note that the trade discount does not feature at all in the accounts. The invoice value is expressed after deduction of the trade discount and it is this invoiced amount that is entered in the purchases day book and relevant ledger accounts.

Step 3 Enter the cash paid by Y.

Payables

	£		£
Bank	960	Purchases and VAT	960

Purchases

	£		£
Payables	800		

VAT

	£		£
Payables	160		

Bank

	£		£
		Payables	960

Example 5

C sells £2,000 of goods net of VAT to Z on credit. He offers Z a 5% prompt payment discount if Z pays within 7 days. Z pays his account within 7 days and takes the prompt payment discount. Enter these transactions in the accounts of Z.

Solution

Step 1 Calculate the VAT on the purchase.

	£
Invoice value net of VAT	2,000.00
VAT = 20% × 2,000	400.00
Invoice value	2,400.00

Step 2 Enter the invoice in the accounts of Z.

Payables

	£		£
		Purchases and VAT	2,400.00

Purchases

	£		£
Payables	2,000.00		

VAT

	£		£
Payables	400.00		

Step 3 Calculate the amount paid by Z.

	£
Invoice value net of VAT	2,000.00
Less: prompt payment discount = 5% × 2,000	(100.00)
VAT (1,900 × 20%)	380.00
Amount paid by Z	2,280.00

Step 4 Enter this amount in the accounts.

Payables

	£		£
Bank	2,280.00	Purchases and VAT	2,400.00

As Z takes the prompt payment discount, he pays C £120 less than the invoice value – this is made up by the £100 reduction to the net price of the goods (5% of £2,000) and a £20 reduction to the VAT charge (the VAT should be 20% based on the discounted amount of £1,900).

In order to clear the balance on the payables account we have to debit that account with £120, credit a discounts received account with £100 and credit the VAT account with £20.

The discount received of £100 is treated as an income of the business. The £20 credit to VAT is reducing down the original VAT calculated on the purchase price, which has now reduced due to taking advantage of the prompt payment discount.

Payables

	£		£
Bank	2,280.00	Purchases and VAT	2,400.00
Discounts received and VAT	120.00		

Purchases

	£		£
Payables	2,000.00		

VAT

	£		£
Payables	400.00	Payables	20.00

Bank

	£		£
		Payables	2,280.00

Discount received

	£		£
		Payables	100.00

Test your understanding 3

Z buys £600 of goods net of VAT at 20% from A and takes the 3% prompt payment discount offered.

Post these transactions in the ledger accounts of Z.

Purchases

	£		£

Payables

	£		£

Bank

	£		£

VAT

£	£

Discounts received

£	£

3.4 Checking the accuracy of supplier invoices

We have considered the calculations that are required when dealing with invoices reviewing the impact of VAT and discounts. We should apply this knowledge when checking the accuracy of supplier invoices. This is studied in more detail in chapter 8.

4 Summary

The topics covered in this chapter will have been familiar to you as you have already studied the similar topics for sales.

Make sure you understand the accounting entries required when a business takes advantage of a prompt payment discount offered by a credit supplier.

Test your understanding answers

Test your understanding 1

(a) VAT = £400 × 20% = £80.00

(b) VAT = £650 × 20% = £130.00

(c) VAT = £528 × $\frac{20}{120}$ = £88.00

(d) VAT = £120 × $\frac{20}{120}$ = £20.00

Test your understanding 2

(a) VAT =£(850 – (3% × 850)) × 20% = £164.90

(b) VAT =£(600 – (5% × 600)) × 20% = £114.00

(c) VAT =£325 × 20% = £65.00

(d) VAT =£57× 20% = £11.40

Test your understanding 3

Calculate the invoice value and amount paid by Z.

	£
Net price	600.00
VAT £600 × 20%	120.00
Invoice value	720.00
Less: Discount 3% × 720	(21.60)
Amount paid	698.40

The discount can be broken down as follows:

	£
Discount on net amount £600 × 3%	18.00
Discount on VAT amount £120 × 3%	3.60
Total discount received	21.60

Purchases

	£		£
Payables	600.00		

Payables

	£		£
Bank	698.40	Purchases and VAT	720.00
Discounts received and VAT	21.60		
	720.00		720.00

Bank

	£		£
		Payables	698.40

VAT

	£		£
Payables	120.00	Payables	3.60

Discounts received

	£		£
		Payables	18.00

Control accounts and subsidiary ledgers

7

Introduction

We have already seen how different transactions including credit sales and credit purchases are recorded into the books of prime entry. In this chapter we introduce the control accounts which form part of the general ledger and the individual memorandum accounts which are maintained for receivables and payables in the subsidiary sales and purchases ledgers.

ASSESSMENT CRITERIA

Demonstrate an understanding of the process of recording financial transactions (1.4)

Transfer data from the books of prime entry to the ledgers (5.1)

CONTENTS

1 The accounting system

1.1 Introduction

In order to simplify the process of recording transactions and exercise greater control, we divide the recording of the transactions into three parts.

(1) The first part is the **books of prime entry**.

(2) The second part is transferring the amounts from the books of prime entry into the **ledger accounts** within the **general ledger** where the double entry takes place.

(3) The third part is the **subsidiary (memorandum) ledgers** – individual receivable and payable accounts known as the '**sales ledger'** and the '**purchases ledger'**.

Invoices, credit notes, receipts and payments will form the basis of accounting entries in all parts.

2 The general and subsidiary ledgers

2.1 The general ledger

Definition – General ledger

A general ledger contains all the ledger accounts for recording transactions occurring within an entity.

Note: The AAT's preferred term is 'general ledger' but the general ledger may also be referred to as the 'main' or 'nominal' ledger.

The general ledger is the place where the double entry takes place in the appropriate ledger accounts. The general ledger contains all the accounts you have become familiar with so far, for example:

Capital

Drawings

Van

Rent

Electricity

Purchases

Sales

Bank

etc.

Two of these typical accounts are the receivables and payables accounts.

When credit sales are posted to the receivables account and credit purchases are posted to the payables account we can balance it off and see how much in total is owed to us by our customers and owed by us to our suppliers. However, we cannot see how much each individual customer owes us and how much we owe each individual supplier.

We need another set of ledger accounts, a subsidiary ledger, which records the individual amounts owed by the receivables and to the payables, as well as having the main receivables and payables account with the totals in it, in the general ledger.

The receivables account in the general ledger will now be referred to as the **sales ledger control account**.

Definition – Sales ledger control account

The sales ledger control account contains the total value of all the invoices and credit notes issued to and cash receipts from credit customers for a given period.

The payables account in the general ledger will now be referred to as the **purchases ledger control account**.

Definition – Purchases ledger control account

The purchases ledger control account contains the total value of all the invoices and credit notes received from and cash payments made to credit suppliers for a given period.

2.2 The subsidiary ledgers

Definition – Subsidiary ledger

A subsidiary ledger provides details behind the entries in the general ledger. Subsidiary ledgers are maintained for individual receivables and payables.

Subsidiary ledgers (which can also be known as memorandum ledgers) do not form part of the double entry system i.e. no corresponding debit and credit entries are required.

Definition – Subsidiary sales ledger

A subsidiary sales ledger is more commonly referred to as the 'sales ledger'. It is a set of accounts for individual receivables.

Definition – Subsidiary purchases ledger

A subsidiary purchases ledger is more commonly referred to as the 'purchases ledger'. It is a set of accounts for individual payables.

As well as information about our receivables in total we have to keep track of each individual receivable. How much has been invoiced? What payments have been received? How much is owed to us?

We do this in the sales ledger. The sales ledger contains a separate ledger account for each individual receivable.

As we require information about individual receivables, the same applies to individual payables. How much have we been invoiced? What have we paid? How much do we owe?

We do this in the purchases ledger. The purchases ledger contains a separate ledger account for each individual payable.

3 Credit sales

We have now looked at the three elements of a typical accounting system. We must now see how it all fits together.

We will first consider three credit sales invoices.

Customer	*Amount*
A	£1,500
B	£2,000
C	£2,500

Step 1

Each invoice is recorded in the sales day book and in the personal account of each receivable in the sales ledger. The entry required for each invoice is a debit in each individual receivable account to indicate that this is the amount that each one owes us.

Step 2

At the end of the period the sales day book is totalled and the total is entered into the sales ledger control account (SLCA) in the general ledger.

The full double entry is as we saw in a previous chapter (ignoring VAT at the moment):

Debit	Sales ledger control account (receivables)
Credit	Sales

Step 3

Now consider the following cheques being received in payment of these debts.

Customer	*Amount*
A	£1,000
B	£2,000

Each receipt is recorded in the cash book and in the personal account of each receivable in the sales ledger. The entry for cash received in the individual accounts is a credit entry to indicate that they no longer owe us these amounts – reducing the asset we originally recognised.

Step 4

At the end of the period the cash book is totalled and the total is entered into the sales ledger control account (total receivables account) in the general ledger.

The full double entry is:

Debit	Cash account (money in)
Credit	Sales ledger control account (receivables)

This is illustrated on the next page.

Summary

1 The invoices are entered into the SDB and the cheques are entered into the cash book.

2 The totals from the SDB and the cash book are posted to the SLCA.

3 The individual invoices and cash receipts from receivables are posted to the subsidiary sales ledger.

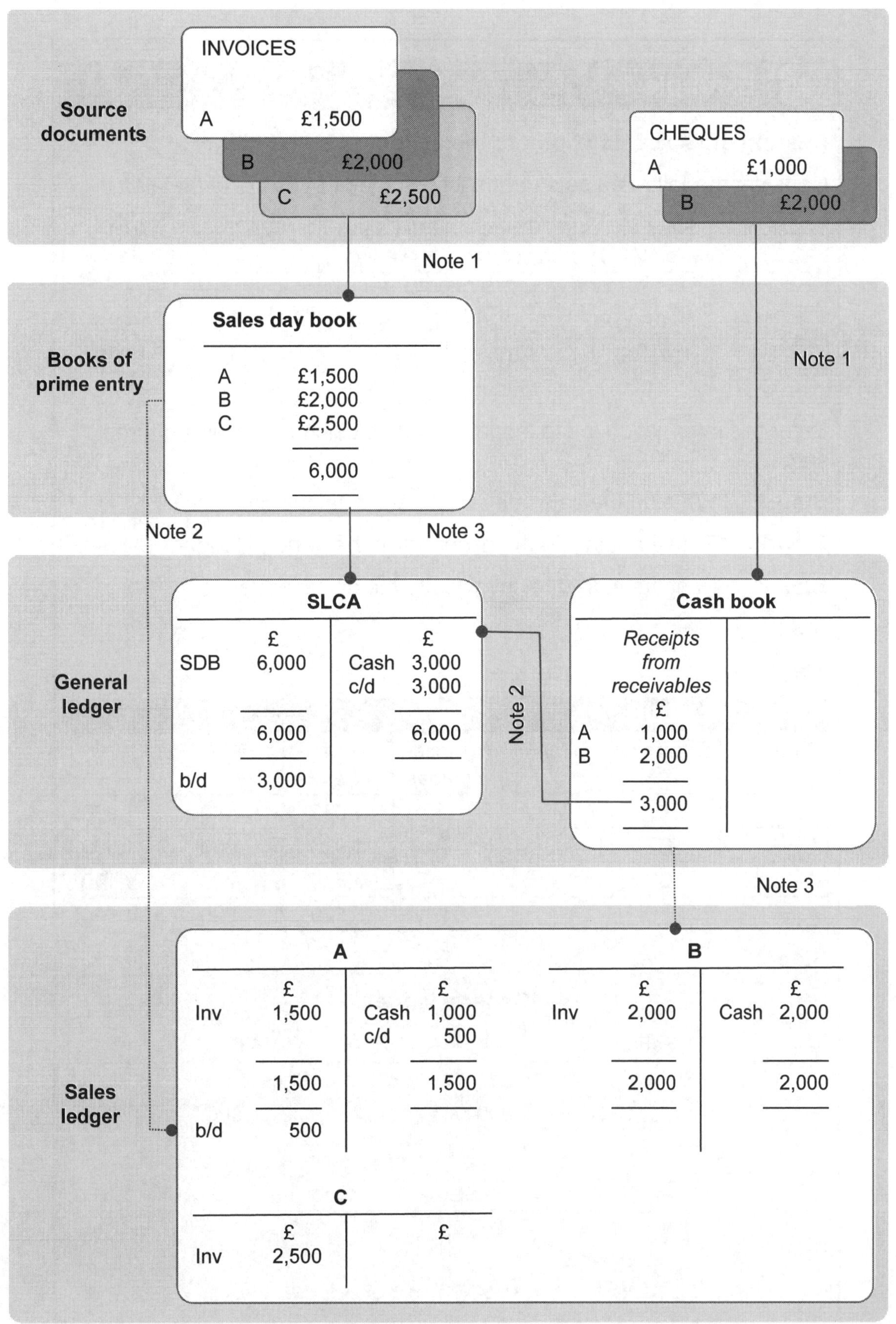
Source documents
INVOICES
A £1,500
B £2,000
C £2,500
CHEQUES
A £1,000
B £2,000
Note 1
Books of prime entry
Sales day book
A £1,500
B £2,000
C £2,500
6,000
Note 1
Note 2
Note 3
General ledger
SLCA
£ £
SDB 6,000 Cash 3,000
c/d 3,000
6,000 6,000
b/d 3,000
Note 2
Cash book
Receipts from receivables
£
A 1,000
B 2,000
3,000
Note 3
Sales ledger
A
£ £
Inv 1,500 Cash 1,000
c/d 500
1,500 1,500
b/d 500
B
£ £
Inv 2,000 Cash 2,000
2,000 2,000
C
£ £
Inv 2,500

Example 1

Posting the sales day book to the accounts in the ledgers

Consider the following sales transactions made by Roberts Metals.

Customer	*Sales value (ex VAT)*	*Trade discount*	*Net sales value*	*VAT*	*Total*
	£	£	£	£	£
A	1,000	10%	900	180	1,080
B	2,000	20%	1,600	320	1,920
C	3,000	30%	2,100	420	2,520

Enter this information in the ledger accounts using the following three steps.

Step 1 Write up the sales day book, and total the columns.

Step 2 Post the totals to the accounts in the general ledger.

Step 3 Post the individual invoices to the sales ledger.

Solution

Step 1

SALES DAY BOOK						
Date	*Customer*	*Ref.*	*Invoice number*	*Total* £	*VAT* £	*Sales* £
	A			1,080	180	900
	B			1,920	320	1,600
	C			2,520	420	2,100
			TOTALS	5,520	920	4,600

Step 2

General ledger

Sales

	£		£
		SLCA	4,600

VAT

	£		£
		SLCA	920

SLCA

	£		£
Sales & VAT	5,520		

Step 3

Sales ledger

A

	£		£
SDB	1,080		

B

	£		£
SDB	1,920		

C

	£		£
SDB	2,520		

Note to solution

(a) The totals of the SDB are entered in the general ledger.

(b) The individual invoices (total value including VAT) are entered in the individual receivables accounts in the sales ledger. This is the amount that the receivable will pay.

(c) Note that there are no entries for trade discounts either in the SDB or in the ledger accounts.

Test your understanding 1

An analysed sales day book has the following totals for a week.

Date	*Invoice no*	*Customer name*	*Code*	*Total*	*VAT*	*Europe*	*Asia*	*America*
				£	£	£	£	£
23/04/X0		Total		65,340	10,890	21,250	15,400	17,800

How would the totals be posted to the general ledger accounts?

Test your understanding 2

You work in the accounts department of Keyboard Supplies, a supplier of a wide range of electronic keyboards to a variety of music shops on credit. Given below are three sales invoices that you have just sent out to customers and these are to be written up into the sales day book given below.

Sales of four different types of keyboard are made and the sales are analysed into each of these four types and coded as follows:

Atol keyboards	01
Bento keyboards	02
Garland keyboards	03
Zanni keyboards	04

Required:

(a) Write up the analysed sales day book and total each of the columns.

INVOICE

Keyboard Supplies
Trench Park Estate
Fieldham
Sussex TN21 4AF
Tel: 01829 654545
Fax: 01829 654646

Invoice to:
BZS Music
42 Westhill
Nutford TN11 3PQ

Deliver to:
As above

Invoice no: 06116
Tax point: 18 April 20X1
VAT reg no: 466 1128 30
Purchase order no: 77121

Code	*Description*	*Quantity*	*VAT rate %*	*Unit price £*	*Amount excl of VAT £*
B4012	Bento Keyboard	3	20	180.00	540.00
Z2060	Zanni Keyboard	6	20	164.00	984.00
					1,524.00
Trade discount 20%					304.80
					1,219.20
VAT					243.84
Total amount payable					1,463.04

Prompt payment discount of 3% if paid within 10 days, net 30 days

INVOICE

Keyboard Supplies
Trench Park Estate
Fieldham
Sussex TN21 4AF
Tel: 01829 654545
Fax: 01829 654646

Invoice to:
M T Retail
Fraser House
Perley TN7 8QT

Deliver to:
As above

Invoice no: 06117
Tax point: 18 April 20X1
VAT reg : 466 1128 30
Purchase order no: PO4648

Code	*Description*	*Quantity*	*VAT rate %*	*Unit price £*	*Amount excl of VAT £*
A6060	Atol Keyboard	1	20	210.00	210.00
Z4080	Zanni Keyboard	1	20	325.00	325.00
					535.00
VAT					107.00
Total amount payable					642.00

Net 30 days

INVOICE

Keyboard Supplies
Trench Park Estate
Fieldham
Sussex TN21 4AF
Tel: 01829 654545
Fax: 01829 654646

Invoice to:
Hammer & Co
1 Acre Street
Nutford TN11 6HA

Deliver to:
As above

Invoice no: 06118
Tax point: 18 April 20X1
VAT reg : 466 1128 30
Purchase order no: 7486

Code	*Description*	*Quantity*	*VAT rate %*	*Unit price £*	*Amount excl of VAT £*
G4326	Garland Keyboard	3	20	98.00	294.00
B2040	Bento Keyboard	5	20	115.00	575.00
					869.00
VAT					173.80
Total amount payable					1,042.80

Prompt payment discount of 3% if paid within 10 days, net 30 days

Sales day book									
Date	*Invoice no*	*Customer name*	*Code*	*Total* £	*VAT* £	*01* £	*02* £	*03* £	*04* £

(b) Complete the required accounting entries from the SDB in part (a) to the accounts within the general ledger.

Account	Amount £	Debit/credit
SLCA		
VAT		
Sales – 01		
Sales – 02		
Sales – 03		
Sales – 04		

Test your understanding 3

Graham Haddow runs a buildings maintenance and decorating business and sends out invoices for the work that he has done. He analyses his sales between the maintenance work and decorating work. You are given three sales invoices that he sent out last week.

Required:

(a) Enter the sales invoice details into the analysed sales day book given and total all of the columns.

INVOICE

Graham Haddow
59 East Street
Medford
MF6 7TL
Tel: 0122 280496

Invoice to:
Portman & Co
Portman House
Tonbridge TN1 4LL

Invoice no: 07891
Tax point: 1 May 20X1
VAT reg : 431 7992 06
Your reference: P2

	Amount excl of VAT £
Repair of window	66.00
Clearing of guttering	73.00
	139.00
VAT	27.80
Total amount payable	166.80

Prompt payment discount of 2% if paid within 14 days, net 30 days

INVOICE

Invoice to:
Stanton Associates
323 Main Road
Tonbridge TN1 6EL

Graham Haddow
59 East Street
Medford
MF6 7TL
Tel: 0122 280496

Invoice no:	07892
Tax point:	3 May 20X1
VAT reg :	431 7992 06
Your reference:	S3

	Amount excl of VAT £
Decoration of meeting room	1,100.00
VAT	220.00
Total amount payable	1,320.00

Prompt payment discount of 2% if paid within 14 days, net 30 days

INVOICE

Invoice to:
Boreham Bros
40/54 Hill Drive
Medford MF2 8AT

Graham Haddow
59 East Street
Medford
MF6 7TL
Tel: 0122 280496

Invoice no:	07893
Tax point:	5 May 20X1
VAT reg :	431 7992 06
Your reference:	B7

	Amount excl of VAT £
Repair of door frames	106.00
Re-decorating of door frames	130.00
	236.00
VAT	47.20
Total amount payable	283.20

Sales day book							
Date	*Invoice no*	*Customer name*	*Code*	*Total* £	*VAT* £	*Maintenance* £	*Decorating* £

(b) Complete the required accounting entries from the SDB in part (a) to the accounts within the general ledger.

Account	Amount £	Debit/credit
SLCA		
VAT		
Sales – Maintenance		
Sales – Decorating		

4 Sales returns

4.1 Introduction

When customers return goods, the accounting system has to record the fact that goods have been returned. If the goods were returned following a cash sale then cash would be repaid to the customer. If goods were returned following a credit sale then the SLCA in the general ledger and the customer's individual account in the sales ledger will need to be credited with the value of the goods returned.

Example 2

Returns following a cash sale

X sells £500 of goods to A for cash plus £100 VAT

X subsequently agrees that A can return £200 worth of goods (excluding the VAT)

Record these transactions in the ledger accounts.

Solution

Step 1

First of all we need to set up a new account called the 'sales returns account' in the general ledger. This will be used in addition to the sales account and cash book with which you are familiar.

Step 2

Enter the cash sale in the accounts.

Debit bank account for cash received	£600
Credit sales with net amount	£500
Credit VAT account with VAT	£100

Bank account

	£		£
Sales & VAT	600		

Sales

	£		£
		Bank	500

Sales returns

	£		£

VAT

	£		£
		Bank	100

Step 3

X will repay A £200 plus VAT of (£200 × 20%) = £40. We therefore need to enter the sales return, the cash and the VAT in the accounts.

Debit sales returns account	£200
Debit VAT account £200 × 20%	£40
Credit bank account with cash paid out	£240

Bank

	£		£
Sales & VAT	600	Sales returns & VAT	240

Sales

	£		£
		Bank	500

Sales returns

	£		£
Bank	200		

VAT

	£		£
Bank	40	Bank	100

4.2 Sales returns for credit sales – no VAT

When a credit customer returns goods, he does not receive cash for the return. Instead the seller will issue a credit note to record the fact that goods have been returned. This credit note is sent to the customer and is entered in the seller's books.

Example 3

X sells goods on credit to A for £500. A returns goods worth £200. X sends a credit note for £200 to A. Enter these transactions in the general ledger of X's books. There is no VAT.

Solution

Step 1

Record the invoice issued for the credit sale for £500:

Debit the SLCA in the general ledger with £500.

Credit the sales account in the general ledger with £500.

SLCA

	£		£
Sales	500		

Sales

	£		£
		SLCA	500

Step 2

Record the credit note for £200. The return is debited to a 'sales returns account' to reflect the reduction in sales. The SLCA is credited to show that the receivable has been reduced.

SLCA

	£		£
Sales	500	Sales returns	200

Sales

	£		£
		SLCA	500

Sales returns

	£		£
SLCA	200		

4.3 Sales returns with VAT

When a return is made and we include VAT, the VAT has to be accounted for both on the invoice when the sale is made, and on the credit note when the goods are returned. This VAT has to be entered in the books.

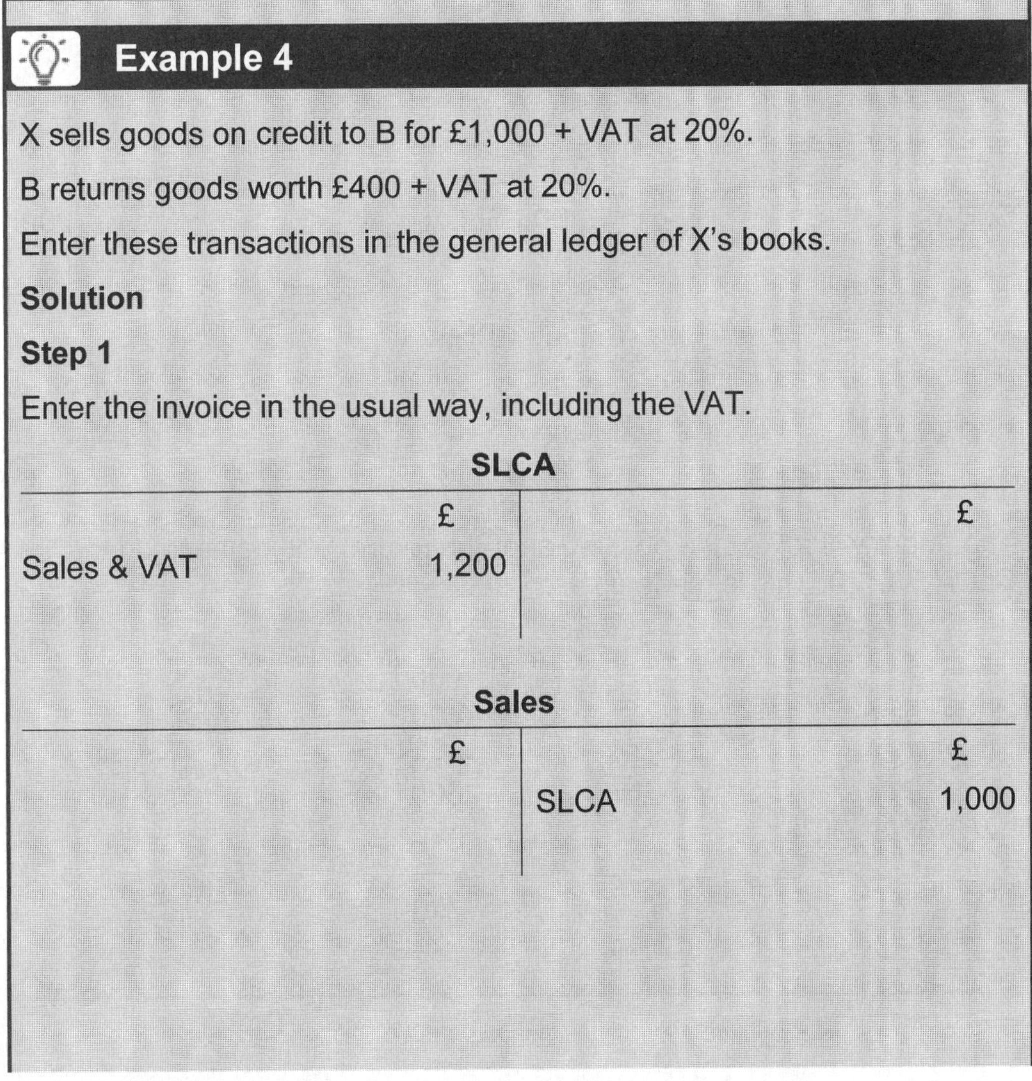

Example 4

X sells goods on credit to B for £1,000 + VAT at 20%.

B returns goods worth £400 + VAT at 20%.

Enter these transactions in the general ledger of X's books.

Solution

Step 1

Enter the invoice in the usual way, including the VAT.

SLCA

	£		£
Sales & VAT	1,200		

Sales

	£		£
		SLCA	1,000

VAT

	£		£
		SLCA	200

Step 2

Enter the credit note. The VAT on the return will be £400 × 20% = £80.

SLCA

	£		£
Sales & VAT	1,200	Sales returns & VAT	480

Sales

	£		£
		SLCA	1,000

VAT

	£		£
SLCA	80	SLCA	200

Sales returns

	£		£
SLCA	400		

The books will reflect the position after the return. The balance on the SLCA is £720. This is made up as:

	£
Sale	1,000
Sale return	(400)
	600
VAT 600 × 20%	120
	720

Example 5

A and B are credit customers of Ellis Electricals. The balances on their accounts in the sales ledger are £1,200 and £2,400 (VAT inclusive amounts) because both A and B made earlier purchases which have not yet been paid.

A returns goods which cost £600 excluding VAT. B returns goods which cost £400 excluding VAT. VAT is at 20%.

Enter the above returns in the sales returns day book and in the general and sales ledgers of Ellis Electricals.

Solution

Step 1

Enter the original sales invoices in the general ledger.

SLCA

	£		£
Sales & VAT	3,600		

Sales

	£		£
		SLCA	3,000

VAT

	£		£
		SLCA	600

Step 2

Write up the sales returns day book.

SALES RETURNS DAY BOOK

Date	*Customer*	*Ref.*	*Credit note number*	*Total £*	*VAT £*	*Sales returns £*
	A			720	120	600
	B			480	80	400
				1,200	200	1,000

Step 3

Enter the SRDB totals in the general ledger accounts.

SLCA

	£		£
Sales & VAT	3,600	Sales returns & VAT	1,200

Sales

	£		£
		SLCA	3,000

VAT

	£		£
SLCA	200	SLCA	600

Sales returns

	£		£
SLCA	1,000		

Step 4

Enter the individual amounts in the sales ledger.

A

	£		£
SDB	1,200	SRDB	720

B

	£		£
SDB	2,400	SRDB	480

Test your understanding 4

Given below are the totals of an analysed sales returns day book for a week.

Date	Customer name	Credit note no	Code	Total	VAT	Europe	Asia	America
				£	£	£	£	£
23/04/X0				3,360	560	1,458	650	692

Post these totals to the general ledger accounts.

5 Credit purchases

5.1 Introduction

When we studied accounting for sales earlier, we dealt with the three parts of the accounting records as they affected sales.

In the case of purchases, the parts are exactly the same except that instead of a 'sales day book' we have the 'purchases day book', and instead of the sales ledger we have the purchases ledger. The third part, namely the general ledger contains the account for the total payables, the purchases ledger control account (PLCA). Remember that, as for sales, the double entry goes through the general ledger, and the purchases ledger is just a memorandum ledger that holds the details of the individual payable's accounts (it is sometimes called the subsidiary (purchases) ledger).

Below we will illustrate how these parts fit together with a diagram.

5.2 Fitting it all together

Consider these three credit purchases invoices.

Supplier	*Amount*
X	£4,000
Y	£5,000
Z	£6,000

Step 1

Each invoice is recorded in the purchases day book by the purchaser.

Step 2

At the end of the period the purchases day book is totalled and the total is entered into the purchases ledger control account in the general ledger.

The full double entry is as we saw in a previous chapter (ignoring VAT at the moment):

Debit	Purchases
Credit	Purchases ledger control account (payables)

The individual entries are recorded in the individual payable accounts in the purchases ledger.

Now consider these cheques being paid to the payables.

Supplier	*Amount*
X	£2,000
Y	£3,000

Step 3

Each payment is recorded in the cash book.

Step 4

At the end of the period the cash book is totalled and the total is entered into the purchases ledger control account in the general ledger. The individual entries are recorded in the individual payable accounts in the purchases ledger.

This is illustrated on the next page.

Summary

1 The invoices are entered into the PDB and the cheques are entered into the cash book.

2 The totals from the cash book and PDB are posted to the PLCA.

3 The individual invoices and cash paid are posted to the purchases ledger.

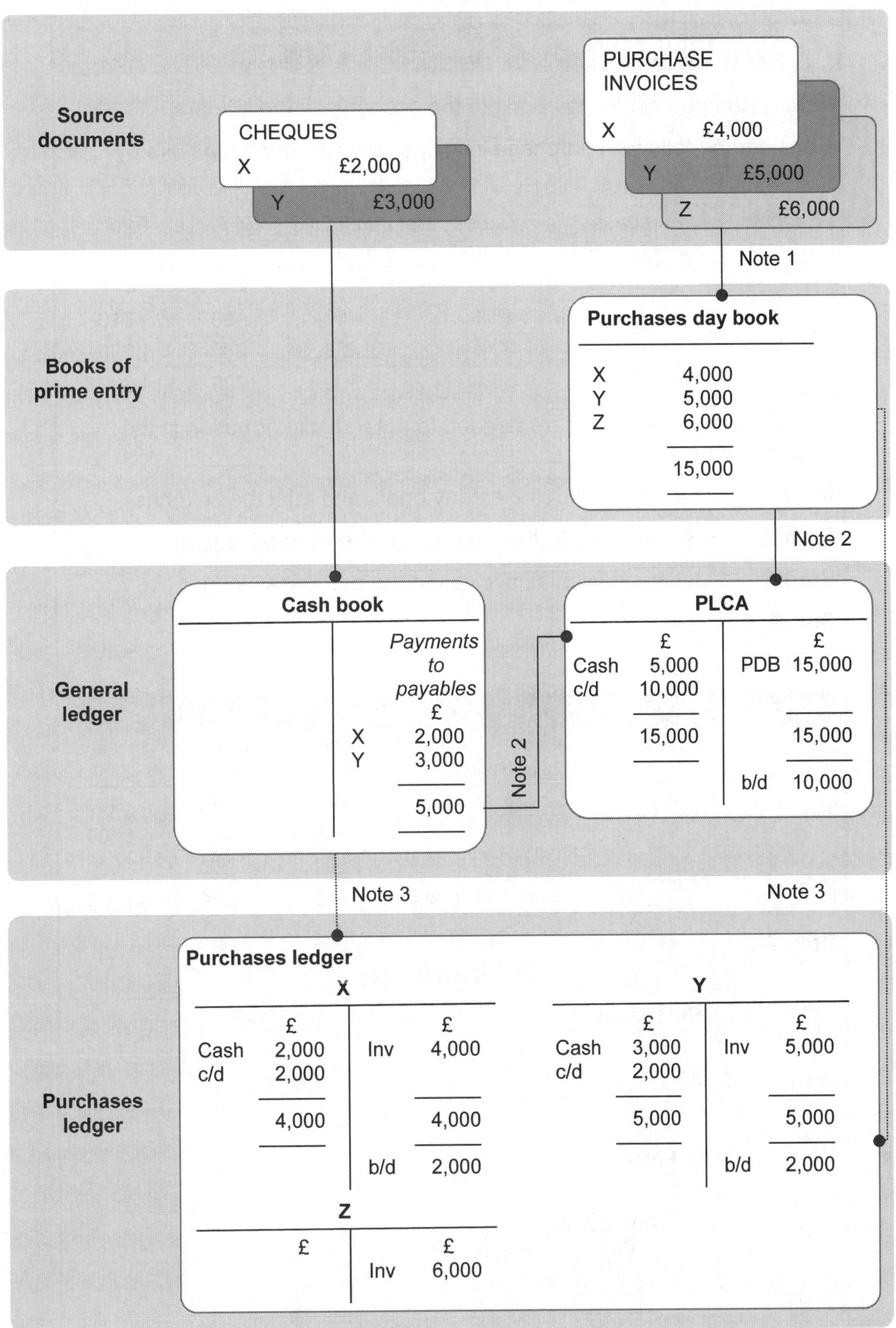
Source documents
CHEQUES
X £2,000
Y £3,000
PURCHASE INVOICES
X £4,000
Y £5,000
Z £6,000
Note 1
Books of prime entry
Purchases day book
X 4,000
Y 5,000
Z 6,000
15,000
Note 2
General ledger
Cash book
Payments to payables
£
X 2,000
Y 3,000
5,000
Note 2
PLCA
£
Cash 5,000
c/d 10,000
15,000
£
PDB 15,000
15,000
b/d 10,000
Note 3
Note 3
Purchases ledger
Purchases ledger
X
£
Cash 2,000
c/d 2,000
4,000
£
Inv 4,000
4,000
b/d 2,000
Y
£
Cash 3,000
c/d 2,000
5,000
£
Inv 5,000
5,000
b/d 2,000
Z
£
£
Inv 6,000

Example 6

Posting the purchases day book to the accounts in the ledgers.

Consider the following purchase invoices received from suppliers by Roberts Metals.

Supplier	*Purchases value (ex VAT)*	*Trade discount*	*Net purchases value*	*VAT*	*Total*
	£	£	£	£	£
X	500	10%	450	90	540
Y	1,750	20%	1,400	280	1,680
Z	5,000	30%	3,500	700	4,200

The following three steps are needed to enter this information in the ledger accounts.

Step 1 Write up the purchases day book, and total the columns.

Step 2 Post the totals to the accounts in the general ledger.

Step 3 Post the individual invoices to the purchases ledger.

Solution

Step 1

PURCHASES DAY BOOK

Date	*Supplier*	*Reference*	*Invoice number*	*Total* £	*VAT* £	*Purchases* £
	X			540	90	450
	Y			1,680	280	1,400
	Z			4,200	700	3,500
			TOTALS	6,420	1,070	5,350

Step 2

General ledger

Purchases

	£		£
PLCA	5,350		

VAT

	£		£
PLCA	1,070		

PLCA

	£		£
		Purchases & VAT	6,420

Step 3

Purchases ledger

X

	£		£
		PDB	540

Y

	£		£
		PDB	1,680

Z

	£		£
		PDB	4,200

Note to solution

(a) The totals of the PDB are entered in the general ledger.

(b) The individual invoices (total value including VAT) are entered in the individual payable accounts in the purchases ledger. This is the amount that will be paid to the payable.

(c) Note that there are no entries for trade discounts either in the PDB or in the ledger accounts.

Test your understanding 5

Date	*Invoice no*	*Supplier*	*Code*	*Total*	*VAT*	*Dept 1*	*Dept 2*	*Dept 3*
				£	£	£	£	£
		Total		90,000	15,000	20,000	15,000	40,000

How would the totals be posted to the general ledger accounts?

Test your understanding 6

Curtain Decor is a business that makes curtains and blinds to order. Its purchases are analysed between fabric purchases, header tape purchases and others. A separate purchases returns day book is not kept so any credit notes received are recorded as negative amounts in the purchases day book. The business only has five credit suppliers and they are as follows:

Mainstream Fabrics	PL01
C R Thorne	PL02
Fabric Supplies Ltd	PL03
Lillian Fisher	PL04
Headstream & Co	PL05

(a) Today's date is 12 April 20X1 and given below are three invoices and a credit note. These are to be entered into the analysed purchases day book and each column is to be totalled.

INVOICE

Invoice to:
Curtain Décor
Field House
Warren Lane
Hawkhurst TN23 1AT

Fabric Supplies Ltd
12/14 Tike Road
Wadfield
TN11 4ZP
Tel: 01882 467111
Fax: 01882 467112

Deliver to:

As above

Invoice no: 06783
Tax point: 7 April 20X1
VAT reg: 532 6741 09

Code	*Description*	*Quantity*	*VAT rate %*	*Unit price* £	*Amount excl of VAT* £
B116-14	Header Tape 14cm	30 m	20	4.62	138.60
P480-G	Fabric – Green	56 m	20	14.25	798.00
					936.60
VAT					187.32
Total amount payable					1,123.92

Prompt payment discount of 2% if paid within 10 days

INVOICE

Lillian Fisher
61 Park Crescent
Hawkhurst
TN23 8GF
Tel: 01868 463501
Fax: 01868 463502

Invoice to:
Curtain Décor
Field House
Warren Lane
Hawkhurst TN23 1AT

Deliver to:

As above

Invoice no: 0328
Tax point: 7 April 20X1
VAT reg: 469 7153 20

Code	*Description*	*Quantity*	*VAT rate %*	*Unit price £*	*Amount excl of VAT £*
TB06	Tie Back Cord – Yellow	10 m	20	6.55	65.50
TB09	Tie Back Cord – Green	4 m	20	6.55	26.20
					91.70
VAT					18.34
Total amount payable					110.04

CREDIT NOTE

Headstream & Co
140 Myrtle Place
Fenham
TN16 4SJ
Tel: 01842 303136
Fax: 01842 303137

Credit note to:
Curtain Décor
Field House
Warren Lane
Hawkhurst TN23 1AT

Credit note no: CN0477
Tax point: 7 April 20X1
VAT reg: 663 4892 77

Code	*Description*	*Quantity*	*VAT rate %*	*Unit price £*	*Amount excl of VAT £*
HT479	Header Tape 22 cm	2 m	20	8.30	16.60
CCF614Y	CC Fabric – Yellow	4 m	20	12.85	51.40
					68.00
VAT					13.60
Total credit					81.60

INVOICE

Invoice to:
Curtain Décor
Field House
Warren Lane
Hawkhurst TN23 1AT

Mainstream Fabrics
Tree Tops House
Farm Road
Tonbridge
TN2 4XT
Tel: 01883 214121
Fax: 01883 214122

Deliver to:

As above

Invoice no: 07359
Tax point: 8 April 20X1
VAT reg: 379 4612 04

Code	*Description*	*Quantity*	*VAT rate %*	*Unit price £*	*Amount excl of VAT £*
DG4167F	Design Guild Fabric – Fuchsia	23 m	20	13.60	312.80
					312.80
Trade discount 10%					31.28
					281.52
VAT					56.30
Total amount payable					337.82

Prompt payment discount of 1½% if paid within 14 days

Purchases day book

Date	*Invoice no*	*Code*	*Supplier*	*Total*	*VAT*	*Fabric*	*Header tape*	*Other*

(b) Complete the required accounting entries from the PDB in part (a) to the accounts within the general ledger.

Account	Amount £	Debit/credit
PLCA		
VAT		
Purchases – fabric		
Purchases – Header tape		
Purchases – Other		

Test your understanding 7

Kingdon Builders analyse their purchases into wood, bricks and cement, and small consumables such as nails and screws. You are given three purchase invoices, recently received, to enter into the purchases day book given.

An extract from the purchase ledger coding manual is given:

Supplier	*Purchase ledger code*
JR Ryan & Co	PL08
HT Todd plc	PL13
Magnum Supplies	PL16

Today's date is 3 May 20X1.

(a) Enter the invoices into the analysed purchases day book and total each of the columns.

INVOICE

Invoice to:
Kingdon Builders
Brecon House
Stamford Road
Manchester
M16 4PL

Magnum Supplies
140/150 Park Estate
Manchester
M20 6EG
Tel: 0161 561 3202
Fax: 0161 561 3200

Deliver to:

As above

Invoice no: 077401
Tax point: 1 May 20X1
VAT reg: 611 4337 90

Code	*Description*	*Quantity*	*VAT rate %*	*Unit price £*	*Amount excl of VAT £*
BH47732	House Bricks – Red	400	20	1.24	496.00
					496.00
Trade discount 15%					74.40
					421.60
VAT					84.32
Total amount payable					505.92

Prompt payment discount of 2% if paid within 10 days

INVOICE

Invoice to:
Kingdon Builders
Brecon House
Stamford Road
Manchester
M16 4PL

J.R. Ryan & Co
59 Parkway
Manchester
M2 6EG
Tel: 0161 560 3392
Fax: 0161 560 5322

Deliver to:

As above

Invoice no: 046193
Tax point: 1 May 20X1
VAT reg: 661 2359 07

Code	*Description*	*Quantity*	*VAT rate %*	*Unit price* £	*Amount excl of VAT* £
DGT 472	SDGS Softwood 47 × 225 mm	11.2 m	20	8.44	94.53
NBD021	Oval Wire Nails	7 boxes	20	2.50	17.50
					112.03
Trade discount 10%					11.20
					100.83
VAT					20.16
Total amount payable					120.99

INVOICE

Invoice to:
Kingdon Builders
Brecon House
Stamford Road
Manchester
M16 4PL

HT Todd plc
30 Longfield Park
Kingsway
M45 2TP
Tel: 0161 511 4666
Fax: 0161 511 4777

Deliver to:

As above

Invoice no: 47823
Tax point: 1 May 20X1
VAT reg: 641 3229 45
Purchase order no: 7211

Code	*Description*	*Quantity*	*VAT rate %*	*Unit price £*	*Amount excl of VAT £*
PLY8FU	Plywood Hardboard	16 sheets	20	17.80	284.80
BU611	Ventilator Block	10	20	8.60	86.00
					370.80
VAT					74.16
Total amount payable					444.96

Prompt payment discount of 3% if paid within 14 days

Purchases day book

Date	*Invoice no*	*Code*	*Supplier*	*Total*	*VAT*	*Wood*	*Bricks/ Cement*	*Consum-ables*

(b) Complete the required accounting entries from the PDB in part (a) to the accounts within the general ledger.

Account	Amount £	Debit/credit
PLCA		
VAT		
Purchases – Wood		
Purchases – Bricks/cement		
Purchases – Consumables		

6 Purchases returns

6.1 Introduction

When a business buys and then returns goods to a supplier, the accounting system has to record the fact that goods have been returned. If the goods were returned following a cash purchase then cash would be repaid by the supplier to the customer who had bought the goods. If goods were returned following a credit purchase then the PLCA in the general ledger will need to be debited and the individual supplier's account in the purchases ledger will need to be debited with the value of the goods returned (we shall see the other entries required below).

Example 7

Returns following a cash purchase

Y buys £1,000 plus £200 VAT of goods from B for cash.

B subsequently agrees that Y can return £500 worth of goods (excluding VAT at 20%).

Record these transactions in the ledger accounts of Y.

Solution

Step 1

First of all we need to set up a new account called the 'purchases returns account' in the general ledger.

Step 2

Enter the cash purchases in the accounts of Y.

Credit cash book for cash paid	£1,200.00
Debit purchases with expense	£1,000.00
Debit VAT account with VAT	£200.00

Bank

	£		£
		Purchases and VAT	1,200

Purchases

	£		£
Bank	1,000		

Purchases returns

	£		£

VAT

	£		£
Bank	200		

Step 3

B will repay Y £500 plus VAT of £100. We therefore need to enter the purchases returns, the cash and the VAT in the accounts.

Bank

	£		£
Purchases returns and VAT	600	Purchases and VAT	1,200

Purchases

	£		£
Bank	1,000		

Purchases returns

	£		£
		Bank	500

VAT

	£		£
Bank	200	Bank	100

6.2 Purchases returns for credit purchases with VAT

When a credit customer returns goods, he does not receive cash for the return; the seller will issue a credit note to record the fact that goods have been returned. This credit note is sent to the customer and is entered in the customer's books.

When a return is made for goods that incur VAT, we include VAT; the VAT was accounted for on the invoice when the purchase was made, and now has to be accounted for on the credit note when the goods are returned. This VAT has to be entered in the books.

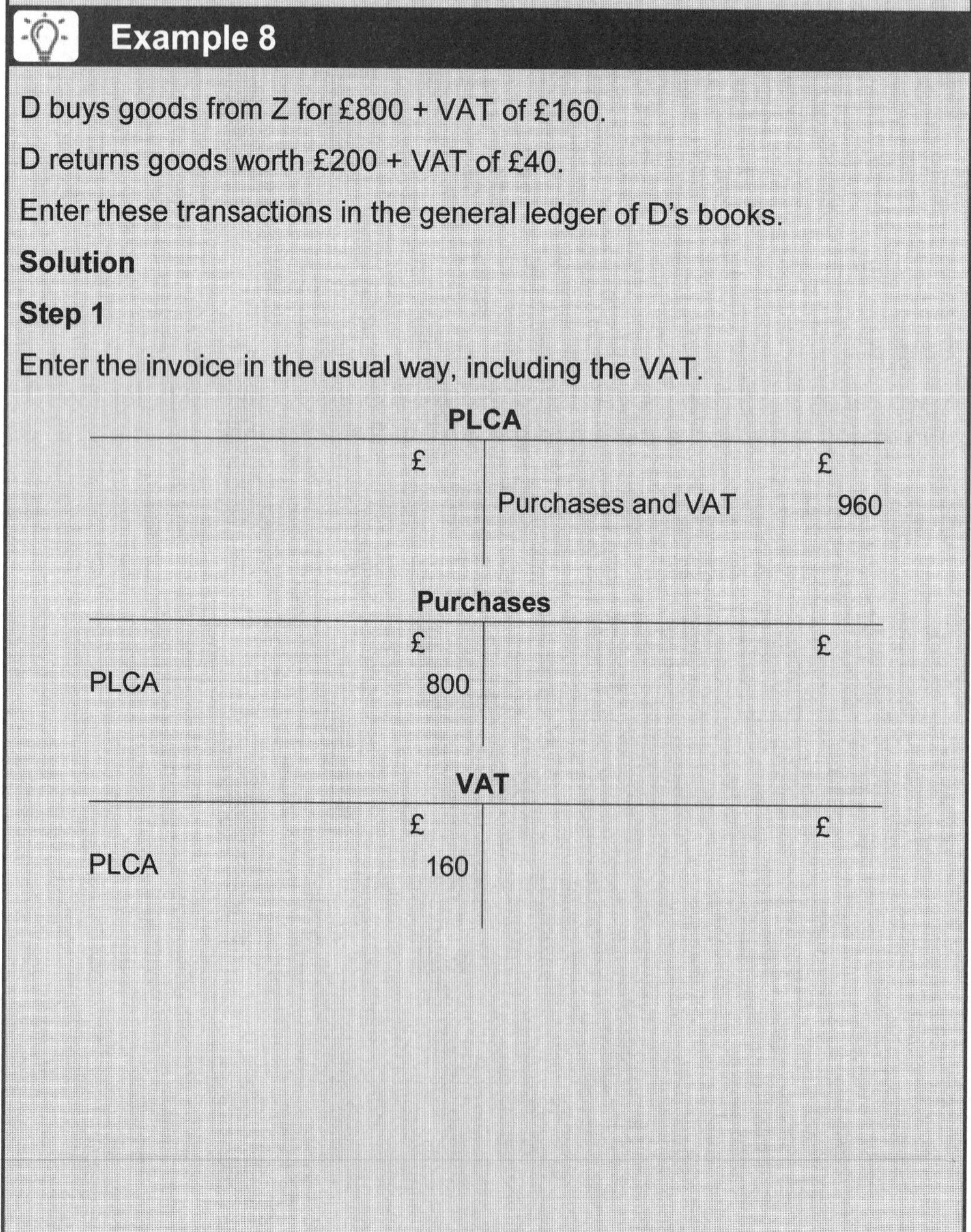

Example 8

D buys goods from Z for £800 + VAT of £160.

D returns goods worth £200 + VAT of £40.

Enter these transactions in the general ledger of D's books.

Solution

Step 1

Enter the invoice in the usual way, including the VAT.

PLCA

	£		£
		Purchases and VAT	960

Purchases

	£		£
PLCA	800		

VAT

	£		£
PLCA	160		

Step 2

Enter the credit note. The VAT on the return is £40. This gives a total credit note of £240.

PLCA

	£		£
Purchases returns and VAT	240	Purchases and VAT	960

Purchases

	£		£
PLCA	800		

VAT

	£		£
PLCA	160	PLCA	40

Purchases returns

	£		£
		PLCA	200

The books will reflect the position after the return. The balance on the PLCA is £720. This is made up as:

	£
Purchase	800
Purchase return	(200)
	600
VAT 600 × 20%	120
	720

Example 9

John bought goods for £750 + VAT from X and £1,000 + VAT from Y.

John returns goods which cost £200 excluding VAT to X, and goods which cost £400 excluding VAT to Y. VAT is at 20%.

Enter the purchases and returns in the general and purchases ledger of John, using a purchases returns day book.

Solution

Step 1

Enter the original purchases invoices in the general ledger.

PLCA

	£		£
		Purchases and VAT	2,100

Purchases

	£		£
PLCA	1,750		

VAT

	£		£
PLCA	350		

Step 2

Write up the purchases returns day book.

PURCHASES RETURNS DAY BOOK

Date	*Supplier*	*Reference*	*Credit note number*	*Total* £	*VAT* £	*Purchases returns* £
	X			240	40	200
	Y			480	80	400
				720	120	600

Step 3

Enter the PRDB totals in the general ledger accounts.

PLCA

	£		£
Purchases returns and VAT	720	Purchases and VAT	2,100

Purchases

	£		£
PLCA	1,750		

VAT

	£		£
PLCA	350	PLCA	120

Purchases returns

	£		£
		PLCA	600

Step 4

Enter the individual amounts in the purchases ledger. The amounts will be debited to the individual payable accounts as the return is reducing the amount that is owed to the payable.

X

	£		£
PRDB	240	PDB	900

Y

	£		£
PRDB	480	PDB	1,200

Test your understanding 8

Given below are the totals of an analysed purchases returns day book for a week.

Date	*Supplier*	*Credit note no*	*Code*	*Total*	*VAT*	*Dept 1*	*Dept 2*	*Dept 3*
				£	£	£	£	£
23/04/X0				9,600	1,600	1,000	2,000	5,000

Post these totals to the general ledger accounts.

7 Summary

In this chapter we have reviewed how transactions are recorded.

Initially a transaction is recorded in the relevant book of prime entry (day book).

The double entry takes place in the general ledger, with the total of the gross sales being recorded in a sales ledger control account (SLCA) which we have previously called receivables. The total of the gross purchases is recorded in a purchases ledger control account (PLCA) which we have previously called payables.

Subsidiary sales ledgers contain individual entries for individual receivables whereas the subsidiary purchases ledgers contain individual entries for individual payables.

It is in the Foundation Certificate level's Bookkeeping Controls unit that control accounts are studied in more detail. The reconciliation of the sales and purchases ledger control accounts to the individual ledgers will be reviewed including identifying and explaining discrepancies upon performing a reconciliation.

Test your understanding answers

Test your understanding 1

The required double entry is as follows:

Debit	Sales ledger control account	£65,340
Credit	VAT	£10,890
	Europe sales	£21,250
	Asia sales	£15,400
	America sales	£17,800

Note carefully that it is the net amount that is credited to each sales account and the gross amount (including VAT) that is debited to the sales ledger control account. The VAT total is credited to the VAT account.

The ledger entries would appear as follows:

Sales ledger control account

	£		£
SDB	65,340		

VAT

	£		£
		SDB	10,890

Europe sales

	£		£
		SDB	21,250

Asia sales

	£		£
		SDB	15,400

America sales

	£		£
		SDB	17,800

Test your understanding 2

(a)

Sales day book									
Date	*Invoice no*	*Customer name*	*Code*	*Total £*	*VAT £*	*01 £*	*02 £*	*03 £*	*04 £*
18/4/X1	06116	B Z S Music		1,463.04	243.84		432.00		787.20
18/4/X1	06117	M T Retail		642.00	107.00	210.00			325.00
18/4/X1	06118	Harmer & Co		1,042.80	173.80		575.00	294.00	
				3,147.84	524.64	210.00	1,007.00	294.00	1,112.20

Note that when a trade discount has been deducted on the invoice in total it must be deducted from each type of sale when entering the figures in the analysed sales day book.

(b)

Account	Amount £	Debit/credit
SLCA	3,147.84	Debit
VAT	524.64	Credit
Sales – 01	210.00	Credit
Sales – 02	1,007.00	Credit
Sales – 03	294.00	Credit
Sales – 04	1,112.20	Credit

Test your understanding 3

(a)

Sales day book							
Date	*Invoice no*	*Customer name*	*Code*	*Total* £	*VAT* £	*Maintenance* £	*Decorating* £
01/5/X1	07891	Portman & Co	P2	166.80	27.80	139.00	
03/5/X1	07892	Stanton Assocs	S3	1,320.00	220.00		1,100.00
05/5/X1	07893	Boreham Bros	B7	283.20	47.20	106.00	130.00
				1,770.00	295.00	245.00	1,230.00

(b)

Account	Amount £	Debit/credit
SLCA	1,770.00	Debit
VAT	295.00	Credit
Sales – Maintenance	245.00	Credit
Sales – Decorating	1,230.00	Credit

Test your understanding 4

Sales returns – Europe account

	£		£
SLCA	1,458		

Sales returns – Asia account

	£		£
SLCA	650		

Sales returns – America account

	£		£
SLCA	692		

VAT account

	£		£
SLCA	560		

Sales ledger control account

	£		£
		Sales returns & VAT	3,360

Note carefully that it is the net amount that is debited to each returns account and the gross amount to the sales ledger control account. The difference, the VAT, is debited to the VAT account.

Test your understanding 5

The required double entry is as follows:

Debit	VAT	£15,000
	Department 1 purchases	£20,000
	Department 2 purchases	£15,000
	Department 3 purchases	£40,000
Credit	Purchases ledger control account	£90,000

Note carefully that it is the net amount that is debited to each purchases account and the gross amount (including VAT) that is credited to the purchases ledger control account. The VAT total is debited to the VAT account.

The ledger entries would appear as follows:

Purchases ledger control account

	£		£
		Purchases & VAT	90,000

VAT

	£		£
PLCA	15,000		

Department 1 purchases

	£		£
PLCA	20,000		

Department 2 purchases

	£		£
PLCA	15,000		

Department 3 purchases

	£		£
PLCA	40,000		

Test your understanding 6

(a)

Purchases day book

Date	*Invoice no*	*Code*	*Supplier*	*Total*	*VAT*	*Fabric*	*Header tape*	*Other*
07/4/X1	06783	PL03	Fabric Supplies Ltd	1,123.92	187.32	798.00	138.60	
07/4/X1	0328	PL04	Lillian Fisher	110.04	18.34			91.70
07/4/X1	CN0477	PL05	Headstream & Co	(81.60)	(13.60)	(51.40)	(16.60)	
08/4/X1	07359	PL01	Mainstream Fabrics	337.82	56.30	281.52		
				1,490.18	248.36	1,028.12	122.00	91.70

(b)

Account	Amount £	Debit/credit
PLCA	1,490.18	Credit
VAT	248.36	Debit
Purchases – fabric	1,028.12	Debit
Purchases – Header tape	122.00	Debit
Purchases – Other	91.70	Debit

Test your understanding 7

(a)

Purchases day book								
Date	*Invoice no*	*Code*	*Supplier*	*Total*	*VAT*	*Wood*	*Bricks/ Cement*	*Consum -ables*
1/5/X1	077401	PL16	Magnum Supplies	505.92	84.32		421.60	
1/5/X1	046193	PL08	JR Ryan & Co	120.99	20.16	85.08		15.75
1/5/X1	47823	PL13	HT Todd plc	444.96	74.16	284.80	86.00	
				1,071.87	178.64	369.88	507.60	15.75

(b)

Account	Amount £	Debit/credit
PLCA	1,071.87	Credit
VAT	178.64	Debit
Purchases – Wood	369.88	Debit
Purchases – Bricks/cement	507.60	Debit
Purchases – Consumables	15.75	Debit

Test your understanding 8

Purchases returns – Department 1 account

	£		£
		PLCA	1,000

Purchases returns – Department 2 account

	£		£
		PLCA	2,000

Purchases returns – Department 3 account

	£		£
		PLCA	5,000

VAT account

	£		£
		PLCA	1,600

Purchases ledger control account

	£		£
Purchases returns & VAT	9,600		

Note carefully that it is the net amount that is credited to each returns account and the gross amount to the purchases ledger control account. The difference, the VAT, is credited to the VAT account.

Payments and receipts

Introduction

We will now consider the procedures and requirements of making and recording payments and receipts which includes maintaining the cash book and petty cash records.

ASSESSMENT CRITERIA

Indicate the purpose of business documents (1.1)

Distinguish between prompt payment, trade and bulk discounts (1.2)

Demonstrate an understanding of the process of recording financial transactions (1.4)

Check the accuracy of receipts from customers (2.3)

Check the accuracy of supplier invoices and credit notes (3.1)

Prepare payments to suppliers (3.3)

Enter receipts and payments into a two column analysed cash book (4.1)

Enter receipts and payments into an analysed petty cash book (4.2)

Total and balance the cash book and petty cash book (4.3)

Transfer data from the books of prime entry to the ledgers (5.1)

CONTENTS

1 Statements of accounts

1.1 Introduction

When sales to a customer are on a credit basis, it is important that there are procedures in place to ensure the monies outstanding are received promptly.

In practice most customers do not settle their debt after receiving every invoice, as customers can purchase from their suppliers numerous times within a month. Therefore, payment will tend to be made when a statement has been sent by the supplier. The statement will detail all the invoices, credit notes and any payments that have occurred within the month. The information contained on the statement will come from the individual receivable's account within the subsidiary sales ledger.

When these statements are sent out and then received by the customer, the customer should compare them to the account they hold for the supplier in their subsidiary purchases ledger.

Once the statement has been reconciled against the customer's own accounting records, the customer will then pay the amount due.

Definition – Receivable (customer) statement

A statement that shows all the invoices and credit notes that have been sent to a particular credit customer for that month, together with any amounts outstanding from previous months. The statement also details any payments received from credit customers.

Definition – Payable (supplier) statement

A statement that shows all the invoices and credit notes that have been received from a particular credit supplier for that month, together with any amounts outstanding from previous months. The statement also details any payments sent to the credit supplier.

1.2 Preparing a receivables' statement

A receivables' statement will normally be prepared from the information in the receivables' individual account in the sales ledger. Different businesses will use different formats but the basics that must be shown are all invoices, credit notes, payments received and discounts for the period together with a running total of the balance. An example is shown in section 1.3.

1.3 Procedure for preparing a statement of account

When preparing a statement for a credit customer, it is important that all details are correct therefore a logical and accurate approach is required.

Step 1

- Find the customer's account in the filing system of the sales ledger.

Step 2

- Work through the account by date order listing each transaction in turn on the statement – invoices as debits and credit notes, payments and discounts as credits.

Step 3

- Return to the start of the statement and calculate the balance at each transaction date to appear in the balance column.

Example 1

Given below are the sales ledger accounts for two of Nick Brookes' customers. We will start by balancing each account to show the total amount due by each customer. Note: the accounts provide details of the invoice and credit note numbers as well as bank receipts and discounts allowed.

Mayer Ltd **SL01**

		£			£
03/04	INV001	189.60	10/04	CN001	50.40
14/04	INV005	211.20	18/04	Bank	136.30
21/04	INV007	259.20			
26/04	INV009	196.80	Balance c/d		670.10
		856.80			856.80
Balance b/d		670.10			

Penken Bros **SL04**

		£			£
10/04	INV004	162.00	17/04	CN002	40.80
24/04	INV008	171.60	21/04	Bank	115.11
28/04	INV011	141.60	21/04	Discount allowed	3.03
				Balance c/d	316.26
		475.20			475.20
Balance b/d		316.26			

We can now use this information to prepare statements for these two customers as at the end of April 20X2.

Solution

To: Mayer Ltd	NICK BROOKES 225 School Lane Weymouth Dorset WE36 5NR Tel: 0149 29381 Fax: 0149 29382 Date: 30/04/X2

STATEMENT

Date	*Transaction*	*Debit* £	*Credit* £	*Balance* £
03/04	INV001	189.60		189.60
10/04	CN001		50.40	139.20
14/04	INV005	211.20		350.40
18/04	Payment		136.30	214.10
21/04	INV007	259.20		473.30
26/04	INV009	196.80		670.10

May we remind you that our credit terms are 30 days
With prompt payment discount of 3% for payment within 14 days

To: Penken Bros	NICK BROOKES 225 School Lane Weymouth Dorset WE36 5NR Tel: 0149 29381 Fax: 0149 29382 Date: 30/04/X2

STATEMENT

Date	*Transaction*	*Debit* £	*Credit* £	*Balance* £
10/04	INV004	162.00		162.00
17/04	CN002		40.80	121.20
21/04	Payment		115.11	
21/04	Discount		3.03	3.06
24/04	INV008	171.60		174.66
28/04	INV011	141.60		316.26

May we remind you that our credit terms are 30 days
With prompt payment discount of 3% for payment within 14 days

These are documents that are being sent to customers; therefore it is extremely important they are completely accurate. Always check the figures and additions.

Test your understanding 1

You are to prepare a statement to be sent out to one customer, Jack Johnson, for the month of May 20X6. At the start of May this customer did not owe your business, Thames Traders, any money. The sales ledger account for Jack for the month of May is given below.

Jack Johnson

Date		£	Date		£
03 May	Invoice 1848	38.79	08 May	Credit note 446	12.40
07 May	Invoice 1863	50.70	15 May	Cash receipt	77.09
10 May	Invoice 1870	80.52	24 May	Credit note 458	16.50
18 May	Invoice 1881	42.40			
23 May	Invoice 1892	61.20			
30 May	Invoice 1904	27.65			

You are required to prepare a statement for Jack on the blank statement given below.

Thames Traders

To: Date:

STATEMENT

Date	*Transaction*	*Debit* £	*Credit* £	*Balance* £

May we remind you that our credit terms are 30 days

1.4 Checking suppliers' statements

We will now consider the perspective of the business receiving a supplier statement. Before any payments are made it is important to check the supplier's statement is correct. Each invoice and credit note should be checked either to the original documentation or to the supplier's account in the purchases ledger.

Differences between the balances on the supplier statement and the individual supplier's account may occur due to omissions, incorrect amounts being recorded, duplicated transactions or timing differences such as a payment being sent to a supplier but not being received at the time the statement was prepared.

When the accuracy of the statement has been ascertained then it must be determined exactly which invoices from the statement are to be paid.

Example 2

Given below is a statement from a supplier together with that supplier's account from the purchases ledger.

To: Scott Brothers
34 Festival Way
Oldham
OL2 3BD

Nemo Limited
Date: 31 August 20X3

STATEMENT

Date	*Transaction*	*Total* £	*Current* £	*30+* £	*60+* £
12 May 20X3	Invoice 2569	92.35			92.35
13 June 20X3	CN 2659	(23.60)			(23.60)
09 July 20X3	Invoice 2701	102.69		102.69	
18 July 20X3	Invoice 2753	133.81		133.81	
02 Aug 20X3	Invoice 2889	56.50	56.50		
10 Aug 20X3	Invoice 2901	230.20	230.20		
28 Aug 20X3	Invoice 3114	243.24	243.24		
	TOTALS	835.19	529.94	236.50	68.75

May we remind you our credit terms are 30 days

Nemo Ltd

		£			£
13 June	CN 2659	23.60	12 May	Invoice 2569	92.35
			09 July	Invoice 2701	102.69
			18 July	Invoice 2753	133.81
			02 Aug	Invoice 2889	56.50
			10 Aug	Invoice 2901	203.20
			28 Aug	Invoice 3114	243.24

To check that the supplier's statement is correct prior to paying any amounts, the statement should be carefully checked to the supplier's account in the purchases ledger.

Solution

Invoice number 2901 is in the purchases ledger at a total of £203.20 whereas it appears on the supplier's statement as £230.20.

The purchase invoice itself should be accessed from the filing system to determine whether the amount is £203.20 or £230.20. If the supplier's statement is incorrect then a polite telephone call should be made or an email or letter sent to the supplier, Nemo Ltd, explaining the problem.

1.5 Which invoices to pay

Once the supplier's statement has been checked for accuracy then it has to be decided which invoices shall be paid. Most organisations will have a policy regarding the payment of supplier's invoices or, alternatively, a fairly senior figure in the business will decide each month which invoices are to be paid.

Example 3

Using the supplier's statement shown above suppose that payment has been authorised for all amounts that have been outstanding for 30 days or more. What amount should the cheque be made out for?

Solution

	£
60+ days total	68.75
30+ days total	236.50
Cheque amount	305.25

2 Receiving and making payments

2.1 Introduction

Different types of business will receive money from their customers and pay money to their suppliers in different forms.

Definitions

Cash

Money in coins or notes.

Credit card

A plastic card that is issued by a bank allowing the holder to purchase goods or services on credit.

Debit card

A plastic card that is issued by a bank allowing the holder to transfer money electronically from their bank account when making a purchase of goods or services.

Cheque

An order to a bank written on a specially printed form that states a sum to be paid from the drawer's (account holder's) account.

BACS

BACS (Bankers' Automated Clearing Services) is an electronic system to make payments directly from one bank account to another. They're mainly used for direct debits and direct credits. Transfers usually take three working days.

Faster Payment

Faster Payments Service (FPS) is an electronic system which makes payments directly from one bank account to another. Transfers typically take a few seconds.

Standing order

An instruction to a bank by an account holder to make regular fixed payments to a particular person or organisation.

Direct debit

An instruction to a bank by an account holder authorising the organisation the account holder wants to pay, to collect varying amounts from the account. Advanced notice of the amounts and dates of collection must be given.

3 Remittances

3.1 Introduction

When a customer makes a payment for a credit sale, they will also send a remittance advice to detail the invoices that are being paid.

Definition – Remittance advice

A remittance advice is a blank document that the customer completes when making a payment to the supplier. It shows the total payment being made and which invoices (less credit notes) the payment is paying off.

3.2 Remittance lists

All cash received should be listed on a remittance list by the supplier. The list should give details of:

- the customer
- the invoice numbers to which the payment relates (if known)
- the amount paid, and
- any discount allowed (see later in this chapter).

The list should be totalled and signed.

3.3 Using remittance advices

When a business issues an invoice to a customer, the invoice will often have a detachable slip. This slip, which is to be returned by the customer when making a payment, is the remittance advice identifying what the payment is for.

A remittance advice is used to either advise of a payment being made directly to the seller's bank account or to accompany a cheque. This makes it much easier for the business receiving the payment to know which outstanding invoices (less credit notes) are actually being paid. An example of a remittance advice follows on the next page.

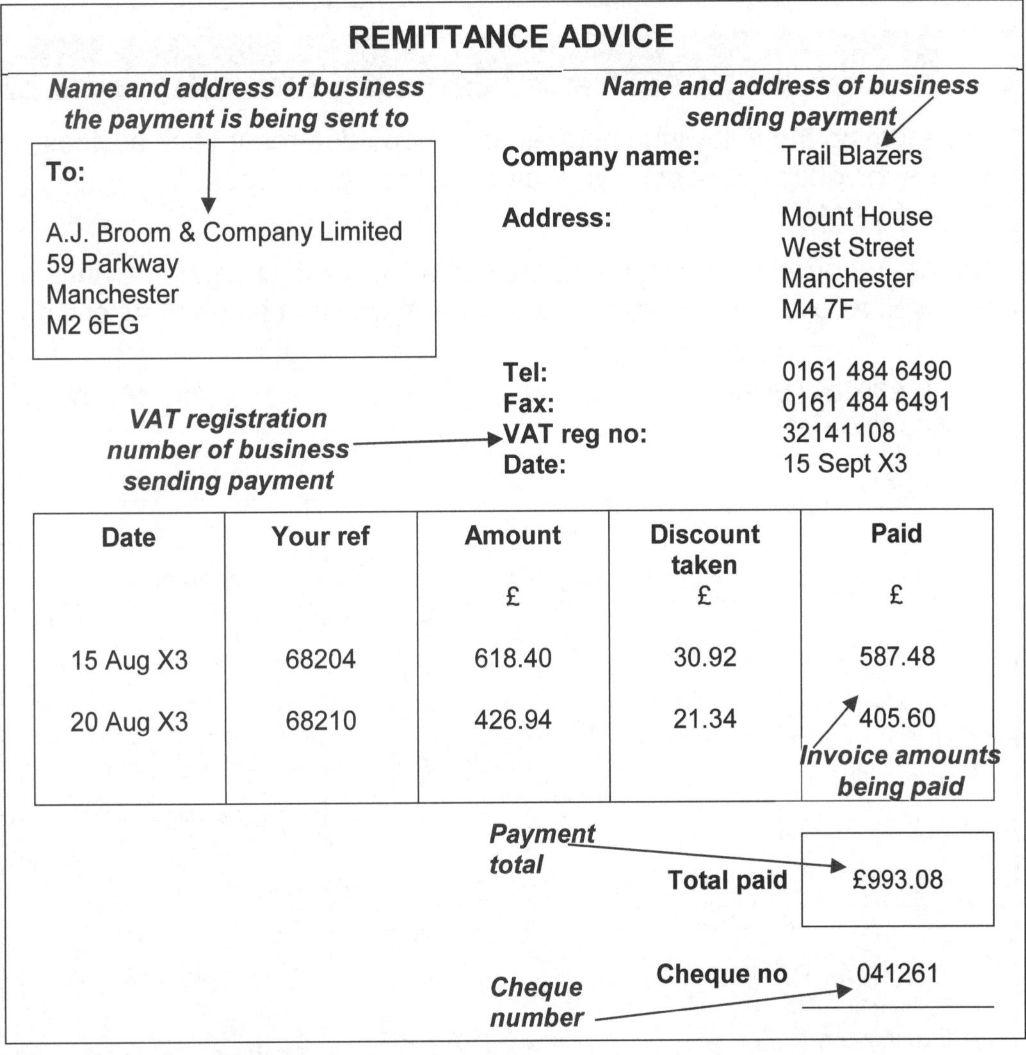

REMITTANCE ADVICE

To:

A.J. Broom & Company Limited
59 Parkway
Manchester
M2 6EG

Company name: Trail Blazers

Address: Mount House, West Street, Manchester, M4 7F

Tel: 0161 484 6490
Fax: 0161 484 6491
VAT reg no: 32141108
Date: 15 Sept X3

Date	Your ref	Amount £	Discount taken £	Paid £
15 Aug X3	68204	618.40	30.92	587.48
20 Aug X3	68210	426.94	21.34	405.60

Total paid £993.08

Cheque no 041261

When receiving payments from customers it is vital to ensure the correct amounts are paid. When agreeing receipts you should check:

- Does the payment amount agree to the invoice and remittance advice?
- If a cheque payment is received, can it be banked i.e. is it valid?
- Does the amount paid agree with what is shown as owed?
- Is the customer eligible (within the required timescale) to take any prompt payment discount offered?
- Has the customer calculated the discount percentage correctly?

Test your understanding 2

A remittance advice is a document sent by a supplier to a customer to advise the customer that goods ordered have been sent off to the customer. True/False

Example 4

This morning the following cheques and supporting remittance advices were received in the post by your organisation, A. J. Broom & Company Ltd.

You are required to check the remittance advice and cheque amounts to the invoices given to ensure that the correct amount has been received.

WESTERN BANK
21 High Street
Bristol
BS1 4TZ

20 – 16 – 80

14 Sept **20** X3

Pay A.J. Broom & Company Ltd — or order

Two Thousand and nine pounds
And 4 pence

Account Payee

£2,009.04

P Smithson
PATRICK CARPENTERS

046178 20–16–80 41643121

CENTRAL BANK
52 Warwick Road
Birmingham
B13 4XT

40 – 18 – 30

15 Sept **20** X3

Pay A.J. Broom & Company Ltd — or order

One thousand three hundred and
Six pounds and 16 pence

Account Payee

£1,306.16

J P Roberts
ROBERTS CONSTRUCTION

020106 40–18–30 31164992

REMITTANCE ADVICE

To:	Company name:	Patrick Carpenters
	Address:	Simba Industrial Est.
A.J. Broom & Company Limited		Leeds
59 Parkway		
Manchester	Tel:	0714 304 2990
M2 6EG	Fax:	0714 304 2963
	VAT reg:	318 4861 27
	Date:	14 Sept 20X3

Date	Your ref	Amount	Discount taken	Paid
		£	£	£
23 Aug	68229	1,649.04	–	1,649.04
23 Aug	3217	(360.00)	–	(360.00)
4 Sept	68237	720.00	–	720.00
			Total paid	£ 2,009.04
			Cheque no	046178

REMITTANCE ADVICE

To:	Company name:	Roberts Construction
	Address:	Chillian Park
A.J. Broom & Company Limited		Oldham
59 Parkway		
Manchester	Tel:	0201 632 497
M2 6EG	Fax:	0201 632 498
	VAT reg:	331 4986 91
	Date:	15 Sept 20X3

Date	Your ref	Amount	Discount taken	Paid
		£	£	£
23 Aug	68230	1,306.16	–	1,306.16
			Total paid	£ 1,306.16
			Cheque no	020106

Invoice 68229

Patrick Carpenters
Samba Industrial Estate
Leeds

A.J. Broom & Company Limited

59 Parkway
Manchester
M2 6EG
Tel: 0161 560 3392
Fax: 0161 560 5322

Tax Point:	23 August 20X3
VAT reg:	452 4585 48

Code	*Supply*	*Description*	*Quantity*	*VAT rate*	*Unit price*	*Amount excl of VAT*
				%	£	£
336 BTB	Sale	Roof tiles – black	10	20	123.00	1,230.00
667 LL5	Sale	Softwood plank – 20 cm	14	20	10.30	144.20
						1,374.20
VAT						274.84
Total amount payable						**1,649.04**

Invoice 68237

Patrick Carpenters
Samba Industrial Estate
Leeds

A.J. Broom & Company Limited

59 Parkway
Manchester
M2 6EG
Tel: 0161 560 3392
Fax: 0161 560 5322

Tax Point:	4 September 20X3
VAT reg :	452 4585 48

Code	*Supply*	*Description*	*Quantity*	*VAT rate*	*Unit price*	*Amount excl of VAT*
				%	£	£
630 CC4	Sale	Oak veneer in Panels	3	20	200.00	600.00
VAT						120.00
Total amount payable						**720.00**

Credit note 3217

A.J. Broom & Company Limited

59 Parkway
Manchester
M2 6EG
Tel: 0161 560 3392
Fax: 0161 560 5322

Tax Point:	23 August 20X3
VAT reg:	452 4585 48

Patrick Carpenters
Samba Industrial Estate
Leeds

Code	*Supply*	*Description*	*Quantity*	*VAT rate %*	*Unit price £*	*Amount excl of VAT £*
950 BB3	Return	Cotswold bricks	1	20	300.00	300.00
VAT						60.00
Total amount credited						**360.00**

Invoice 68230

A.J. Broom & Company Limited

59 Parkway
Manchester
M2 6EG
Tel: 0161 560 3392
Fax: 0161 560 5322

Tax Point:	23 August 20X3
VAT reg no:	452 4585 48

Roberts Construction
Chillian Park
Oldham

Code	*Supply*	*Description*	*Quantity*	*VAT rate %*	*Unit price £*	*Amount excl of VAT £*
160 TT7	Sale	Insulation	5	20	95.50	477.50
632 BS4	Sale	Brick tiles	20	20	33.25	665.00
						1,142.50
Trade discount 4%						45.70
						1,096.80
VAT						219.36
Total amount payable						**1,316.16**

Solution

From Patrick Carpenters

	£
Invoice number 68229	1,649.04
Invoice number 68237	720.00
Credit note 3217	(360.00)
	2,009.04

This agrees with the cheque.

From Roberts Construction

Invoice number 68230 £1,316.16

This does not agree with the cheque as the cheque is made out for £1,306.16 This discrepancy should be brought to the attention of the manager responsible for credit control at Roberts Construction and a polite letter should be written to the customer explaining an error has been made. Request can be made for payment but if this is a regular customer then the additional amount may simply be added to the next cheque that Roberts Construction sends.

3.4 Payments received with no accompanying remittance advice

If a payment from a customer is received with no remittance advice or other confirmation of which invoices are being paid then it will be necessary to examine the details of this customer's transactions in the sales ledger.

The individual account for this receivable must be extracted from the subsidiary ledger in an attempt to match the payment received to invoices and credit notes.

Example 5

A payment has been received into the business bank account from A J Holland, a credit customer, for £878.00 but no remittance advice has been sent to advise which transactions the payment relates to.

In the absence of this supporting document the individual receivable account for A J Holland has been found in the sales ledger, to investigate which transactions are being paid and to ensure that the correct payment amount has been received.

A J Holland

	£		£
13/05/X2 Invoice 2256	336.67	20/05/X2 Credit 249	54.09
18/05/X2 Invoice 2271	846.23		
20/05/X2 Invoice 2280	447.69		
25/05/X2 Invoice 2288	147.73		

Solution

By a process of trial and error it can be discovered that the invoices that are being paid off are number 2256, 2280 and 2288 less the credit note. It would appear therefore that the payment is for the correct amount although there might be some concern as to why invoice 2271 has not been paid; maybe there is some dispute over the amount of this invoice which should be investigated.

Always check figures carefully as such errors are often easy to miss.

3.5 Checking cheques

When cheques are received in the post it is important that they are checked for their validity, particularly in respect of:

- the date: a cheque can become out of date as it is only valid for 6 months from the date of issue
- the payee's name: should be the same as the one shown on the account the cheque is being paid into
- the words and figures agree; if they disagree the cheque should be returned by the bank for amendment or a new cheque issued
- the cheque is signed.

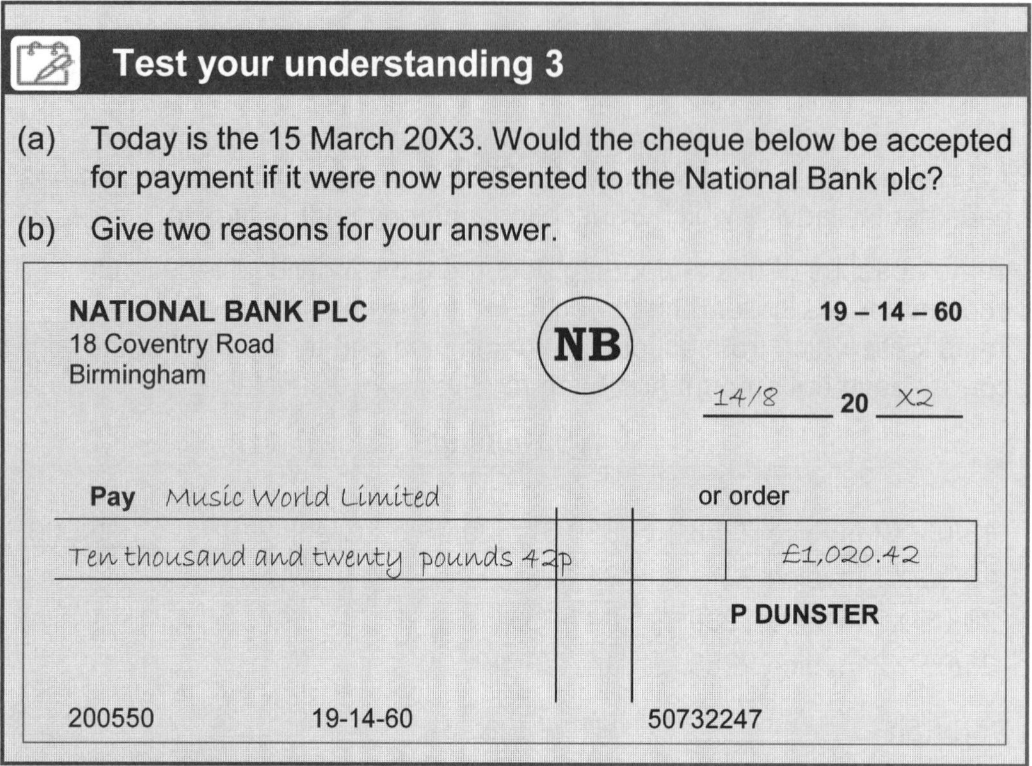

Test your understanding 3

(a) Today is the 15 March 20X3. Would the cheque below be accepted for payment if it were now presented to the National Bank plc?

(b) Give two reasons for your answer.

NATIONAL BANK PLC
18 Coventry Road
Birmingham

NB

19 – 14 – 60

14/8 **20** X2

Pay Music World Limited or order

Ten thousand and twenty pounds 42p | £1,020.42

P DUNSTER

200550 19-14-60 50732247

4 Recording cash receipts and cash payments

4.1 The cash book

The cash book was introduced in chapter 2. It is the book of prime entry for recording receipts and payments.

Definition – The cash book

A cash book is a record of cash receipts and payments that conforms to the double entry system.

An analysed cash book is a cash book with additional columns for analysing principal sources and payments for cash.

There are many different forms of the cash book that you may encounter. As already discussed in chapter 2, Bookkeeping Transactions requires knowledge of a two-column cash book which maintains separate columns for 'bank' and 'cash' transactions for both receipts and payments. You may also hear of a three-column cash book which in addition to a bank and a cash column for receipts and payments would also have a discount column for both receipts and payments.

A three-column cash book is not examinable for Bookkeeping Transactions as instead of incorporating discount columns within the cash book, the AAT has set out separate discount day books which we introduced in chapter 2 and also reviewed in chapters 5 and 6.

There are two ways a cash book can be used within the accounting system. As set out in the assessment criteria of Bookkeeping Transactions, you need to be aware that the cash book can be a book of prime entry on its own or it can be a book of prime entry that also forms part of the double entry bookkeeping system.

It will always be made clear if the cash book forms part of the double entry bookkeeping system as well as being a book of prime entry. If this is the case, the impact on the cash or bank account is already dealt with and no separate posting is required to the bank or cash ledger account – as effectively the cash book is forming the ledger account in the general ledger. The cash book as part of the general ledger is reviewed in section 5 of this chapter. The examples we see before then will be where the cash book is a book of prime entry alone.

4.2 Recording cash receipts

We will now review an example for recording cash receipts, which shows how transactions are posted into the cash book and transferred to the appropriate accounts within the general and subsidiary ledgers.

Example 6

The following is an example of the general and sales ledgers, including entries from the sales and sales returns day books. For the purposes of this example, the narratives in the ledger accounts are references to the appropriate day books.

General ledger

Sales

	£		£
		SDB	4,600.00

VAT

	£		£
SRDB	140.00	SDB	805.00

SLCA

	£		£
SDB	5,405.00	SRDB	940.00

Sales returns

	£		£
SRDB	800.00		

Sales ledger

A

	£		£
SDB	1,057.50		

B

	£		£
SDB	1,880.00		

C

	£		£
SDB	2,467.50	SRDB	940.00

The following transactions took place:

Receivable A pays £1,057.50

Receivable B pays £1,000.00

Enter this information in the cash receipts book and in the appropriate ledger accounts in the general and subsidiary ledgers.

Solution

The following steps are needed.

Step 1 Enter these transactions in the cash book.

Step 2 Total the cash book and post the totals to the general ledger.

Step 3 Post the individual amounts of cash paid by receivables to the individual accounts in the sales ledger.

Step 1

CASH RECEIPTS BOOK

Date	*Narrative*	*Ref*	*Cash* £	*Bank* £	*VAT* £	*Receivables* £	*Cash sales* £
	A			1,057.50	See note 2 – step 2	1,057.50	
	B			1,000.00		1,000.00	
Totals				2,057.50		2,057.50	

Step 2

We have brought forward the balances from the general ledger in the earlier example and now post the cash received book (CRB) totals to the general ledger.

General ledger

Sales

	£		£
		SLCA	4,600.00

VAT

	£		£
SLCA	140.00	SLCA	805.00

SLCA

	£		£
Sales & VAT	5,405.00	Sales returns & VAT	940.00
		Bank	2057.50

Sales returns

	£		£
SLCA	800.00		

Bank

	£		£
SLCA	2,057.50		

Note 1: We have posted the total of the SLCA column of the CRB to the sales ledger control account. This is the same as the total column in this example, but in more complex examples it may not be. The entry to the sales ledger control account is a credit entry as this is reducing the amount owed by our receivables.

Note 2: A common confusion is for people to wonder about the VAT – surely some of the money paid by A and B is actually paying the VAT part of the invoice. Yes it is, but we have already accounted for this VAT element when we entered the invoices themselves into the ledger accounts via the sales day book.

The total of the invoices in the SDB were debited to the SLCA and the VAT and sales were the corresponding credits. We therefore now post the total cash including VAT to the sales ledger control account but nothing is posted to the VAT account as this has already been done when dealing with the invoices.

Note 3: This is now the full double entry for the cash received completed.

Debit Bank account (cash receipts book)

Credit Sales ledger control account (receivables)

We have credited the sales ledger control account and the debit entry is posted to the bank account as the cash receipts book does not form part of the double entry system.

Note: if the cash receipts book was not only a day book but also formed part of the double entry bookkeeping system, the entry in the cash receipts book itself is the related debit entry. In this case there would be no need for any further debit entry to a separate cash/bank ledger account.

Step 3

We have brought forward the balance from the sales ledger in the earlier example and now post the cash received to the individual sales ledger accounts. Again, as with the sales ledger control account, this is a credit entry in each case as the cash received is reducing the amount owed by each receivable.

A

	£		£
b/d	1,057.50	CRB	1,057.50

B

	£		£
b/d	1,880.00	CRB	1,000.00

C

	£		£
b/d	2,467.50	SRDB	940.00

4.3 Prompt payment discounts allowed to customers

Prompt payment discounts have already been considered in chapter 5. However we shall now look at this in more detail using an example to show how the transactions are entered into the day books and ledger accounts.

Example 7

The sales day book with prompt payment discounts.

Consider the following sales transactions made by Roberts Metals.

Customer	*Sales value (ex VAT)*	*Trade discount*	*Net sales value*	*VAT*	*Total*
	£	£	£	£	£
A	1,000	10%	900	180	1,080
B	2,000	20%	1,600	320	1,920
C	3,000	30%	2,100	420	2,520

In addition to the trade discount, customer A has been offered an additional 5% discount if he pays his invoice within 5 days.

Enter this information in the sales day book and ledger accounts.

Solution

Recording the invoice

The following steps are needed.

Step 1 Write up the sales day book.

Step 2 Post the totals to the accounts in the general ledger.

Step 3 Post the individual invoices to the sales ledger.

At the point of issuing the invoice it is not known if the prompt payment discount will be taken or not. It simply does not impact the invoice amounts at the point of making the sale.

Step 1

SALES DAY BOOK

Date	*Customer*	*Reference*	*Invoice number*	*Total* £	*VAT* £	*Sales* £
	A			1,080	180	900
	B			1,920	320	1,600
	C			2,520	420	2,100
			TOTALS	5,520	920	4,600

Step 2

Sales

	£		£
		SLCA	4,600

VAT

	£		£
		SLCA	920

SLCA

	£		£
Sales & VAT	5,520		

Step 3

A

	£		£
SDB	1,080		

B

	£		£
SDB	1,920		

C

	£		£
SDB	2,520		

Recording the cash received

Customer A pays within the required time for the discount allowed. Details of the payments from customers A and B are below:

Customer A: Payment £1,026 (see working 1)

Customer B: Payment £1,000

Working 1:

Discounted sales price £900 × 95% = £855

VAT on discounted price £855 × 20% = £171

Total payment £1,026

The adjustment to the balance of customer A due to the prompt payment discount being taken will be made by issuing a credit note – recorded in the discounts allowed day book. The cash receipts for customers A and B will be recorded in the cash receipts book.

CASH RECEIPTS BOOK							
Date	*Narrative*	*Ref*	*Cash* £	*Bank* £	*VAT* £	*Receivables* £	*Cash sales* £
	A			1,026	See note 2 – step 2	1,026	
	B			1,000		1,000	
Totals				2,026		2,026	

The deduction to the value of the original net amount and the VAT amount, by issuing a credit note, will now be entered into the discounts allowed day book.

The discount offered to A was 5%. This equates to a deduction from the original net price of £45.00 and a reduction to the VAT amount of £9.00 – in total the discount reducing A's receivable balance will be £54.00. The credit note for receivable A has been entered into the discounts allowed book below:

DISCOUNTS ALLOWED DAY BOOK					
Date	*Narrative*	*Reference*	*Total* £	*VAT* £	*Net* £
	A		54	9	45
Totals			54	9	45

Step 3 – Posting the cash book and discount allowed book totals

The totals are posted as follows to the general ledger.

Sales

	£		£
		SLCA	4,600

VAT

	£		£
SLCA	9	SLCA	920

SLCA

	£		£
Sales & VAT	5,520	Bank	2,026
		Disc. allowed & VAT	54

Discount allowed

	£		£
SLCA	45		

The discount allowed figure in the discount allowed book is entered into the ledger accounts as follows:

The gross amount (inclusive of VAT) is credited to the SLCA, to acknowledge a reduction to the receivable balance.

The net amount (exclusive of VAT) is debited to the discount allowed ledger account, to recognise the expense to the business of allowing the customer the discount.

The VAT amount is debited to the VAT ledger account recognising that due to the net price of the goods being reduced, the amount of VAT recoverable on that sale is now less.

If the cash book only acts as a book of prime entry rather than also being part of the double entry bookkeeping system, a debit entry to the bank or cash ledger account would also be seen here.

Step 4 – Posting to the sales ledger

A

	£		£
SDB	1,080	CRB	1,026
		Disc. all.	54
	1,080		1,080

B

	£		£
SDB	1,920	CRB	1,000
		c/d	920
	1,920		1,920
b/d	920		

C

	£		£
SDB	2,520		

Test your understanding 4

Your organisation receives a number of cheques from receivables through the post each day. The amounts received in payment have been recorded in the cash receipts book. Some of the receivables (G Hunt and J Dent) were in receipt of discounts after taking advantage of prompt payment discounts that had been offered. These discounts have been recorded in the discounts allowed day book.

The organisation also makes some sales to non-credit customers each day which include VAT at the standard rate of 20% and are paid for by cheque.

Today's date is 28 April 20X1 and the cash receipts book and the discounts allowed book are as follows:

CASH RECEIPTS BOOK							
Date	*Narrative*	*Ref*	*Cash* £	*Bank* £	*VAT* £	*Receivables* £	*Cash sales* £
28/4/X1	G Hunt	SL04		114		114	
	L Tessa	SL15		110		110	
	J Dent	SL17		342		342	
	F Trainer	SL21		97		97	
	A Winter	SL09		105		105	
	Non-credit sales			120	20		100
Totals				888	20	768	100

DISCOUNTS ALLOWED DAY BOOK					
Date	*Narrative*	*Reference*	*Total* £	*VAT* £	*Net* £
28/4/X1	G Hunt – SL04	CN658	6	1	5
	J Dent – SL17	CN659	18	3	15
Totals			24	4	20

Required:

Show what the entries in the sales ledger will be:

Account name	Amount £	Dr ✓	Cr ✓

Show what the entries will be in the general ledger for the cash receipts book totals:

Account name	Amount £	Dr ✓	Cr ✓

Show what the entries will be in the general ledger for the discount allowed book totals:

Account name	Amount £	Dr ✓	Cr ✓

4.4 Recording cash payments

We will now review an example for recording cash payments which shows how transactions are posted into the cash book and transferred to the appropriate accounts within the general and subsidiary ledgers.

Example 8

Parma Products buys goods for resale from two suppliers on credit. The business buys £1,000 + VAT at 20% of goods from X and £3,000 + VAT at 20% of goods from Y. Parma receives an invoice and pays £500 + VAT at 20% rent to their landlord via bank transfer. Parma also pays X's invoice in full by cheque. Enter these transactions in the accounts of Parma Products. The rent invoice is not entered in the PDB.

Solution

Step 1 Enter the invoices for goods in the PDB.

PURCHASES DAY BOOK						
Date	*Supplier*	*Reference*	*Invoice number*	*Total* £	*VAT* £	*Purchases* £
	X			1,200	200	1,000
	Y			3,600	600	3,000
			TOTALS	4,800	800	4,000

Step 2 Enter the totals of the PDB in the general ledger.

Purchases

	£		£
PLCA	4,000		

VAT

	£		£
PLCA	800		

PLCA

	£		£
		Purchases & VAT	4,800

Step 3 Enter the cash paid in the analysed cash payments book.

CASH PAYMENTS BOOK								
Date	*Narrative*	*Reference*	*Cash* £	*Bank* £	*VAT* £	*Payables* £	*Rent* £	*Admin* £
	X			1,200		1,200		
	Rent			600	100		500	
Totals				1,800	100	1,200	500	

Note that the VAT on the payment to the credit suppliers has already been accounted for in the general ledger via the entries in the purchases day book. However, the rent invoice was not entered in the PDB so the VAT has to be entered in the VAT column of the cash book from where it will be posted to the VAT account (see Step 4).

Step 4 Post the cash paid totals from the cash book to the general ledger.

Purchases

	£		£
PLCA	4,000		

VAT

	£		£
PLCA	800		
Bank	100		

PLCA

	£		£
Bank	1,200	Purchases & VAT	4,800

Rent

	£		£
Bank	500		

Note 1: All the VAT paid is now debited to the VAT account. You must make sure that you understand how VAT can be posted via the PDB and via the cash book.

Note 2: All of the entries (payables, VAT and rent) made from the cash payments book are debit entries. The credit entry is the total of the cash payments (£1,800) which would be credited to the bank ledger account.

Step 5: Enter the amounts in the purchases ledger.

X

	£		£
CPB	1,200	PDB	1,200

Y

	£		£
		PDB	3,600

The entries to the purchases ledger from the cash payments book are debit entries in the individual payable accounts as the payment means that less is owed to the payable.

4.5 Prompt payment discounts received from suppliers

Prompt payment discounts from suppliers are a tricky complication that we were introduced to in chapter 6. We shall now review an example.

Example 9

Consider a business run by Francis which buys goods costing £2,000 + VAT from Z. Z offers a 5% settlement discount if Francis pays within 10 days. Francis does pay within 10 days.

Enter these new transactions in the books of Francis.

Solution

Step 1 Calculate the value of the invoice.

	£
Cost of goods	2,000
VAT (2,000 × 20%)	400
Total invoice value	2,400

Step 2 Enter the invoice from Z in the purchases day book.

PURCHASES DAY BOOK

Date	*Supplier*	*Reference*	*Invoice number*	*Total* £	*VAT* £	*Purchases* £
	Z			2,400	400	2,000
			TOTALS	2,400	400	2,000

Step 3 Enter the totals of the purchases day book in the general ledger.

Purchases

	£		£
PLCA	2,000		

VAT

	£		£
PLCA	400		

PLCA

	£		£
		Purchases & VAT	2,400

Step 4 Calculate the cash paid by Francis.

	£
Cost of goods	2,000
5% prompt payment discount	(100)
	1,900
VAT (2,000 – (5% × 2,000)) × 20%	380
Total cash paid	2,280

Step 5 Enter the cash paid in the analysed cash payments book and the discount received in the discounts received day book.

CASH PAYMENTS BOOK

Date	*Narrative*	*Reference*	*Cash*	*Bank*	*VAT*	*Payables*	*Rent*
			£	£	£	£	£
	Z			2,280		2,280	
		TOTALS		2,280		2,280	

DISCOUNTS RECEIVED DAY BOOK

Date	*Narrative*	*Reference*	*Total* £	*VAT* £	*Net* £
	Z		120	20	100
Totals			120	20	100

Step 6 Post the cash payments book and discounts received day book totals to the general ledger.

Purchases

	£		£
PLCA	2,000		

VAT

	£		£
PLCA	400	PLCA	20

PLCA

	£		£
Bank	2,280	Purchases & VAT	2,400
Discount received & VAT	120		

Discount received

	£		£
		PLCA	100

Bank

	£		£
		PLCA	2,280

Test your understanding 5

Given below is the cash payments book and discounts received day book for a business.

CASH PAYMENTS BOOK

Date	*Details*	*Cheque no*	*Code*	*Bank* £	*PLCA* £	*Cash purchases* £	*VAT* £
12/3	Homer Ltd	03648	PL12	176.40	176.40		
	Forker & Co	03649	PL07	285.18	285.18		
	Purchases	03650		342.00		285.00	57.00
	Print Ass.	03651	PL08	190.45	190.45		
	ABG Ltd	03652	PL02	220.67	220.67		
	Purchases	03653		198.00		165.00	33.00
	G Greg	03654	PL19	67.89	67.89		
				1,480.59	940.59	450.00	90.00

DISCOUNTS RECEIVED DAY BOOK					
Date	*Narrative*	*Reference*	*Total* £	*VAT* £	*Net* £
12/3	Homer Ltd	CN897	3.60	0.60	3.00
	Forker & Co	CN898	8.82	1.47	7.35
Totals			12.42	2.07	10.35

Required:

Show what the entries in the purchases ledger will be:

Account name	Amount £	Dr ✓	Cr ✓

Show what the entries will be in the general ledger for the cash payments book totals:

Account name	Amount £	Dr ✓	Cr ✓

Show what the entries will be in the general ledger for the discounts received day book totals:

Account name	Amount £	Dr ✓	Cr ✓

5 The cash book as part of the general ledger

5.1 Introduction

The Bookkeeping Transactions assessment may show the cashbook as a ledger account format. This indicates the cashbook forms part of the general ledger, with the entries being one side of the double entry required within the general ledger. Therefore a typical assessment requirement will be to complete the other side of the entry within the general ledger, and to update the individual accounts in the subsidiary ledger.

Example 10

Date	*Detail*	*Bank* £	*Date*	*Detail*	*Bank* £
30/6/X9	Bal b/d	16,173	30/6/X9	Plant & machinery	25,500
30/6/X9	Receivable A	13,200	30/6/X9	Loan repayment	1,500
			30/6/X9	Motor expenses	1,440
			30/6/X9	Bal c/d	933
		29,373			**29,373**

We need to appreciate that the bank account has already been completed with one side of the entry, and the other side of the entry is all that is required in order to complete the double entry postings.

Postings to general ledger (ignoring VAT)

Account	**Amount**	**Dr or Cr**
SLCA	13,200	Cr
Plant and machinery	25,500	Dr
Loan	1,500	Dr
Motor expenses	1,440	Dr

Postings to the sales ledger

Account	**Amount**	**Dr or Cr**
Receivable A account	13,200	Cr

Test your understanding 6

Date	*Detail*	*Bank* £	*Date*	*Detail*	*VAT* £	*Bank* £
30/6/X9	Bal b/d	24,067	30/6/X9	Motor vehicles		20,000
30/6/X9	Bal c/d	2,913	30/6/X9	Motor expenses	80	480
			30/6/X9	Payable B		6,500
		26,980			**80**	**26,980**
			1/7/X9	Bal b/d		2,913

What are the postings to the general and purchases ledgers?

Example 11

You may be asked to only record transactions for one side of the cash book.

Cash book – debit side

Details	**Bank** £
Balance b/d	2,568
Edwards Ltd	3,864

(a) Record the entry into the sales ledger.

(b) Record the entry within the general ledger.

Solution

The cash book has already been completed with one side (debit side) of the entries. The other side (credit side) is all that is required in order to complete the double entry postings.

(a) **Sales ledger**

Details	**Amount** £	**Debit/Credit**
Edwards Ltd	3,864	Credit

(b) **General ledger**

Details	**Amount** £	**Debit/Credit**
Sales ledger control account	3,864	Credit

Test your understanding 7

Cashbook – credit side

Details	**VAT** £	**Bank** £
Motor expenses	60	360
Wages		4,785

Record the THREE transactions within the general ledger.

Details	**Amount** £	**Debit/Credit**

6 Petty cash

6.1 Introduction

Definition – Petty cash

Petty cash is the small amount of cash that most businesses hold in order to make small cash payments, such as payment for coffee and milk for the staff kitchen.

6.2 Petty cash box

Holding cash on business premises is a security risk and therefore it is important the petty cash is secure. It should be kept in a locked petty cash box and usually this itself will be held in the safe. Only the person responsible for the petty cash should have access to the petty cash box.

6.3 Payment of petty cash

Petty cash is usually reimbursed to employees who have already incurred a small cash expense on behalf of the business. These payments should only be made for valid business expenses. For this reason, the petty cashier should only pay out to the employee on receipt of an authorised petty cash voucher and, where appropriate, VAT receipt.

Definition – Petty cash voucher

A petty cash voucher is an internal document that details the business expenditure an employee has incurred out of his own money.

This voucher must be authorised by an appropriate person before any amounts can be paid to that employee out of the petty cash box.

A typical petty cash voucher is shown below:

PETTY CASH VOUCHER

Authorised by F R Clarke	*Received by* L Kent	*No* 4173	
Date	*Description*	*Amount*	
4 April 20X1	Train Fare	12	50
	Total	12	50

Signature of person authorising voucher

Signature of claimant

Sequential voucher number

Details of expenditure including the date and the nature of the expense

Total paid to employee

6.4 Maintaining petty cash records

Upon the petty cash vouchers being received and the employees being reimbursed, the details are recorded in the petty cash book. In Chapter 2 we were briefly introduced to the petty cash book as a book of prime entry. The Bookkeeping Transactions assessment requires you to be able to make entries into the petty cash book.

6.5 Writing up the petty cash book

When cash is paid into the petty cash book, this will be recorded on the receipts side (debit side) of the petty cash book.

Each petty cash voucher will then in turn be written up in the petty cash book on the payments side.

To ensure no vouchers have been mislaid, petty cash vouchers are pre-numbered sequentially. Each voucher is then entered into the petty cash book in the correct order, with each item of expenditure being recorded in the correct expense analysis column.

Example 12

A business has just started to run a petty cash system with an amount of £100. £100 is withdrawn from the bank account and paid into the petty cash box on 3 April 20X1.

During the first week the following authorised petty cash vouchers were paid. These transactions will now be recorded in the petty cash book.

PETTY CASH VOUCHER			
Authorised by T Smedley	*Received by* P Lannall	*No* 0001	
Date	*Description*	*Amount*	
3 April 20X1	Tea/coffee/milk	4	73
	Total	4	73

PETTY CASH VOUCHER			
Authorised by T Smedley	*Received by* R Sellers	*No* 0002	
Date	*Description*	*Amount*	
3 April 20X1	Train fare	14	90
	Total	14	90

PETTY CASH VOUCHER			
Authorised by T Smedley	*Received by* F Dorne	*No* 0003	
Date	*Description*	*Amount*	
4 April 20X1	Stationery	4	00
	VAT	0	80
	Total	4	80

PETTY CASH VOUCHER			
Authorised by T Smedley	*Received by* P Dent	*No* 0004	
Date	*Description*	*Amount*	
5 April 20X1	Postage costs	16	35
	Total	16	35

PETTY CASH VOUCHER			
Authorised by T Smedley	*Received by* H Polly	*No* 0005	
Date	*Description*	*Amount*	
7 April 20X1	Train fare	15	30
	Total	15	30

PETTY CASH VOUCHER			
Authorised by T Smedley	*Received by* P Lannall	*No* 0006	
Date	*Description*	*Amount*	
8 April 20X1	Milk/biscuits	3	85
	Total	3	85

Solution

Petty cash book												
Receipts			**Payments**									
Date	*Narrative*	*Total*	*Date*	*Narrative*	*Voucher no*	*Total*	*Postage*	*Travel*	*Tea & coffee*	*Sundry*	*VAT*
20X1		£	20X1			£	£	£	£	£	£
03/04	Bank	100.00	03/04	Tea/coffee	0001	4.73			4.73		
			03/04	Train fare	0002	14.90		14.90			
			04/04	Stationery	0003	4.80				4.00	0.80
			05/04	Postage	0004	16.35	16.35				
			07/04	Train fare	0005	15.30		15.30			
			08/04	Milk/biscuits	0006	3.85			3.85		

6.6 The imprest system

Many businesses use the imprest system for petty cash. Using an imprest system makes petty cash easier to control and therefore reduces the possibility of error and fraud.

The business decides on a fixed amount of petty cash (the imprest) which is just large enough to cover normal petty cash requirements for a period (usually a week). This amount of petty cash is withdrawn from the bank.

Claims are paid out of petty cash by a voucher being completed for each amount of petty cash paid out. The vouchers are kept in the petty cash box so that the amount of cash held decreases and is replaced by vouchers.

At any given time, the total contents of the box (i.e. petty cash plus amounts withdrawn represented by vouchers) should equal the amount of the imprest.

At the end of the period, a cheque is drawn for the total of the vouchers which restores the petty cash float to the amount of the imprest. The vouchers are removed from the petty cash box and filed.

Example 13

The imprest amount for a petty cash system is £150, which is the amount paid into the petty cash box on 1 November. At the end of the week the total of the vouchers in the petty cash box is £125.05. How much cash is required in order to replenish the petty cash box to the imprest amount?

Solution

£125.05, the amount paid out on the basis of the petty cash vouchers.

6.7 Non-imprest petty cash system

An imprest petty cash system as in the previous example is the most common method of dealing with and controlling petty cash. However some businesses may use a non-imprest system. This might be where a set amount of cash is withdrawn each week and paid into the petty cash box no matter what the level of expenditure in that week.

For example it may be an organisation's policy to cash a cheque for £50 each Monday morning for use as petty cash for the week. The danger here is either that petty cash requirements are more than £50 in the week in which case the petty cash box will run out of money. Alternatively week after week expenditure is significantly less than £50 each week, leading to a large amount of cash building up in the petty cash box.

6.8 Posting the petty cash book

Once the petty cash book has been written up, we must now post the totals of the petty cash book to the general ledger accounts.

The petty cash book can be a book of prime entry alone, or a book of prime entry that also forms part of the double entry bookkeeping system.

6.9 Posting the petty cash receipt

The receipt into the petty cash box has come from cash being withdrawn from the bank account. This will have been done by writing out a cheque for cash and withdrawing this from the bank. Therefore the cheque should be recorded in the cash payments book as a payment when the cash payments book is written up.

The receipt of the cash into the petty cash box is recorded in the receipts side of the petty cash book, i.e. the debit side.

6.10 Posting the petty cash payments – the petty cash book as part of the double entry bookkeeping system

We will consider an example where the petty cash book is part of the double entry bookkeeping system as well as being a book of prime entry.

Example 14

A petty cash book is give below. This is to be posted to the general ledger accounts.

Petty cash book												
Receipts			**Payments**									
Date	*Narrative*	*Total*	*Date*	*Narrative*	*Voucher no*	*Total*	*Postage*	*Travel*	*Tea & coffee*	*Sundry*	*VAT*
20X1		£	20X1			£	£	£	£	£	£
20/08	Bal b/d	100.00	20/08	Tea/coffee	0001	13.68			13.68		
20/08	Bank	50.00	21/08	Train fare	0002	6.80		6.80			
			21/08	Stationery	0003	19.20				16.00	3.20
			22/08	Postage	0004	16.35	16.35				
			23/08	Train fare	0005	15.30		15.30			
			24/08	Milk/biscuits	0006	3.85			3.85		

Solution

Step 1 Each of the columns in the petty cash payments side must be totalled.

The accuracy of your totalling should be checked by ensuring that all of the analysis column totals add back to the total of the 'total' column in the petty cash book payments side.

Petty cash book											
Receipts			**Payments**								
Date	*Narrative*	*Total*	*Date*	*Narrative*	*Voucher no*	*Total*	*Postage*	*Travel*	*Tea & coffee*	*Sundry*	*VAT*
20X1		£	20X1			£	£	£	£	£	£
20/08	Bal b/d	100.00	20/08	Tea/coffee	0001	13.68			13.68		
20/08	Bank	50.00	21/08	Train fare	0002	6.80		6.80			
			21/08	Stationery	0003	19.20				16.00	3.20
			22/08	Postage	0004	16.35	16.35				
			23/08	Train fare	0005	15.30		15.30			
			24/08	Milk/biscuits	0006	3.85			3.85		
				Bal c/d		74.82					
		150.00				150.00	16.35	22.10	17.53	16.00	3.20

Step 2 Each of the analysis column totals must now be entered into the general ledger accounts as debit entries.

VAT account

	£		£
Petty cash book (PCB)	3.20		

The entry has come from the petty cash book and this is the reference – this is now shortened to PCB.

Postage account

	£		£
PCB	16.35		

Travel account

	£		£
PCB	22.10		

Tea and coffee account

	£		£
PCB	17.53		

Sundry expenses account

	£		£
PCB	16.00		

Bank account

	£		£
		PCB	50.00

There is no need for an entry to the petty cash control account as the petty cash book acts as the general ledger account and the closing balance on the account is taken from it when the trial balance is prepared.

6.11 Posting the petty cash payments – the petty cash book not part of the double entry bookkeeping system

When the petty cash book is not part of the double entry system, the accounting entries must show the impact on the expense accounts, the VAT account and the petty cash control account.

In the event of there being a top up to the petty cash, a separate entry will be required. We would need to show the money being withdrawn from the bank and deposited into petty cash.

We will now consider the earlier illustration to review the general ledger postings required when the petty cash book is not part of the double entry accounting system.

Example 15

A petty cash book is give below. This is to be posted to the general ledger accounts.

Petty cash book											
Receipts			Payments								
Date	*Narrative*	*Total*	*Date*	*Narrative*	*Voucher no*	*Total*	*Postage*	*Travel*	*Tea & coffee*	*Sundry*	*VAT*
20X1		£	20X1			£	£	£	£	£	£
20/08	Bal b/d	100.00	20/08	Tea/coffee	0001	13.68			13.68		
20/08	Bank	50.00	21/08	Train fare	0002	6.80		6.80			
			21/08	Stationery	0003	19.20				16.00	3.20
			22/08	Postage	0004	16.35	16.35				
			23/08	Train fare	0005	15.30		15.30			
			24/08	Milk/biscuits	0006	3.85			3.85		

Solution

Step 1 Each of the columns in the petty cash payments side must be totalled.

The accuracy of your totalling should be checked by ensuring that all of the analysis column totals add back to the total of the 'total' column in the petty cash book payments side.

Petty cash book												
Receipts			**Payments**									
Date	*Narrative*	*Total*	*Date*	*Narrative*	*Voucher no*	*Total*	*Postage*	*Travel*	*Tea & coffee*	*Sundry*	*VAT*
20X1		£	20X1			£	£	£	£	£	£
20/08	Bal b/d	100.00	20/08	Tea/coffee	0001	13.68			13.68		
20/08	Bank	50.00	21/08	Train fare	0002	6.80		6.80			
			21/08	Stationery	0003	19.20				16.00	3.20
			22/08	Postage	0004	16.35	16.35				
			23/08	Train fare	0005	15.30		15.30			
			24/08	Milk/biscuits	0006	3.85			3.85		
		150.00				75.18	16.35	22.10	17.53	16.00	3.20

Check the totals:

	£
Postage	16.35
Travel	22.10
Tea and coffee	17.53
Sundry	16.00
VAT	3.20
	75.18

We have been told that the petty cash book is not part of the double entry accounting system. The expense accounts of postage, travel, tea and coffee, sundry along with the VAT account will be debited, the corresponding impact on the petty cash control account will be to credit it (to reduce the balance) by the amount in total that has been paid out.

Remember the account name in the general ledger should always match the analysis column headings in the petty cash-book and not the description of the expense given in the 'Details' column.

We must also record the impact of the top-up to the petty cash from the bank account. This will be shown as a credit from the bank ledger account and a debit to the petty cash control account.

Step 2 We will now make the entries required into the general ledger accounts.

VAT account

	£		£
Petty cash book (PCB)	3.20		

The entry has come from the petty cash book and this is the reference – this is now shortened to PCB.

Postage account

	£		£
PCB	16.35		

Travel account

	£		£
PCB	22.10		

Tea and coffee account

	£		£
PCB	17.53		

Sundry expenses account

	£		£
PCB	16.00		

Bank account

	£		£
		PCB	50.00

Petty cash control

	£		£
Balance b/d	100.00	PCB	75.18
Bank	50.00		

Test your understanding 8

Summary of petty cash vouchers in hand at 31 October 20X7

Date	*Description*	*Total*	*VAT included*
		£	£
1/10	Envelopes (Administration)	19.72	3.28
4/10	Cleaner (Administration)	8.75	
6/10	Food for staff lunch (Marketing)	17.13	
6/10	Taxi fares (Marketing)	16.23	
6/10	Rail fares (Marketing)	43.75	
10/10	Postage (Administration)	4.60	
15/10	Tea and coffee (Production)	4.39	
17/10	Light bulbs and refuse sacks (Distribution)	8.47	1.41
20/10	Flowers for reception (Administration)	21.23	
26/10	Cleaner (Administration)	8.75	

(a) Write up the payments side of the petty cash book for October 20X7 from the information given.

You should allocate a sequential voucher number to each entry in the petty cash book. The last voucher number to be allocated in September was 6578.

Use the blank petty cash book provided.

(b) Total each of the columns in the petty cash book and cross-cast them.

(c) Post the totals to the general ledger accounts given.

PETTY CASH BOOK – PAYMENTS							
Date	*Voucher no*	*Total*	*Production*	*Distribution*	*Marketing*	*Administration*	*VAT*
		£	£	£	£	£	£

Production expenses account

£	£

Distribution expenses account

£	£

Marketing expenses account

£	£

Administration expenses account

£	£

VAT account

£	£

6.12 Reconciling the petty cash

We saw earlier in the chapter that when an imprest system is being used for petty cash then at any point in time the amount of cash in the petty cash box plus the total of the vouchers in the petty cash box should equal the imprest amount.

At regular intervals, usually at the end of each week, this check will be carried out.

6.13 Procedure for reconciling the petty cash box

The total amount of cash in the petty cash box will be counted. The vouchers that have been paid during the week are also in the petty cash box and they must also be totalled.

When the amount of cash is added to the total of the vouchers in the box they should equal the imprest amount.

The petty cash vouchers for the week will then be removed from the box and filed. The petty cash will then be topped up by the value of the vouchers to bring the petty cash back up to the imprest level.

Example 16

The amount of cash remaining in a petty cash box at the end of a week is as follows:

Notes/coins	*Quantity*
£10	1
£5	2
£2	3
£1	7
50p	9
20p	10
10p	15
5p	7
2p	16
1p	23

The imprest amount is £100 and the vouchers in the petty cash box at the end of the week are as follows:

PETTY CASH VOUCHER			
Authorised by C Alexi	*Received by* P Trant	*No* 0467	
Date	*Description*	*Amount*	
4 May 20X3	Window cleaner	15	00
	Total	15	00

PETTY CASH VOUCHER			
Authorised by C Alexi	*Received by* F Saint	*No* 0468	
Date	*Description*	*Amount*	
5 May 20X3	Train fare	9	80
	Total	9	80

PETTY CASH VOUCHER			
Authorised by C Alexi	*Received by* A Paul	*No* 0469	
Date	*Description*	*Amount*	
5 May 20X3	Stationery	8	00
	VAT	1	60
	Total	9	60

PETTY CASH VOUCHER			
Authorised by C Alexi	*Received by* P Peters	*No* 0470	
Date	*Description*	*Amount*	
7 May 20X3	Postage	6	80
	Total	6	80

PETTY CASH VOUCHER			
Authorised by C Alexi	*Received by* C Ralph	*No* 0471	
Date	*Description*	*Amount*	
5 May 20X3	Train fare	16	90
	Total	16	90

The cash and vouchers in the petty cash box at the end of the week are to be reconciled.

Solution

The petty cash must be totalled:

Notes/coins	*Quantity*	*Amount*
		£
£10	1	10.00
£5	2	10.00
£2	3	6.00
£1	7	7.00
50p	9	4.50
20p	10	2.00
10p	15	1.50
5p	7	0.35
2p	16	0.32
1p	23	0.23
		41.90

Now the vouchers must be totalled.

	£
0467	15.00
0468	9.80
0469	9.60
0470	6.80
0471	16.90
	58.10

Finally, total the cash and the vouchers to ensure that they add back to the imprest amount.

	£
Cash	41.90
Vouchers	58.10
	100.00

6.14 Possible causes of difference

If there is more cash in the petty cash box than the balance on the petty cash control account this could be due to an error in writing up the petty cash book as more has been recorded in payments than has actually been paid out. In this case the entries in the petty cash book should be checked to the underlying petty cash vouchers to discover the error.

If there is less cash in the petty cash box than the balance on the petty cash control account this could also be due to an error in writing up the petty cash book as this time less payments have been recorded in the petty cash control account than were actually made. This may be due to a petty cash voucher having been omitted from the petty cash book and therefore again the underlying petty cash vouchers should all be checked to their entries in the petty cash book.

If no accounting errors or posting errors can be found then the cause is likely to be one of the following:

- an error has been made in paying a petty cash voucher and more money was handed out than was recorded on the voucher
- cash has been paid out of the petty cash box without a supporting voucher
- cash could have been stolen from the petty cash box.

In such cases the matter should be investigated and security of the petty cash and petty cash procedures improved.

Test your understanding 9

Your business runs a petty cash box based upon an imprest amount of £60. This morning you have emptied the petty cash box and found the following notes, coins and vouchers.

Notes

£5 × 2

Coins

£1 × 3

50p × 5

20p × 4

10p × 6

5p × 7

2p × 10

1p × 8

Vouchers	£
2143	10.56
2144	3.30
2145	9.80
2146	8.44
2147	2.62
2148	6.31
2149	1.44

You are required to reconcile the cash and the vouchers in the petty cash box.

7 Additional test your understandings

Test your understanding 10

You work in the accounts department of Farmhouse Pickles Ltd and given below are two receivables' accounts from the sales ledger.

Grant & Co SL07

		£		£
1 April	Balance b/d	337.69	12 April SRDB – 0335	38.70
4 April	SDB 32656	150.58	20 April CRB	330.94
18 April	SDB 32671	179.52	20 April DAB – discount allowed	6.75
25 April	SDB 32689	94.36	24 April SRDB – 0346	17.65

Mitchell Partners SL10

		£		£
1 April	Balance b/d	180.46	12 April SRDB – 0344	66.89
7 April	SDB 32662	441.57	21 April CRB	613.58
20 April	SDB 32669	274.57	21 April DAB – discount allowed	8.45

Required:

Prepare statements to be sent to each of these customers at the end of April 20X1 on the blank statements provided.

FARMHOUSE PICKLES LTD

To:

225 School Lane
Weymouth
Dorset
WE36 5NR
Tel: 0261 480444
Fax: 0261 480555
Date:

STATEMENT

Date	*Transaction*	*Debit* £	*Credit* £	*Balance* £

May we remind you that our credit terms are 30 days

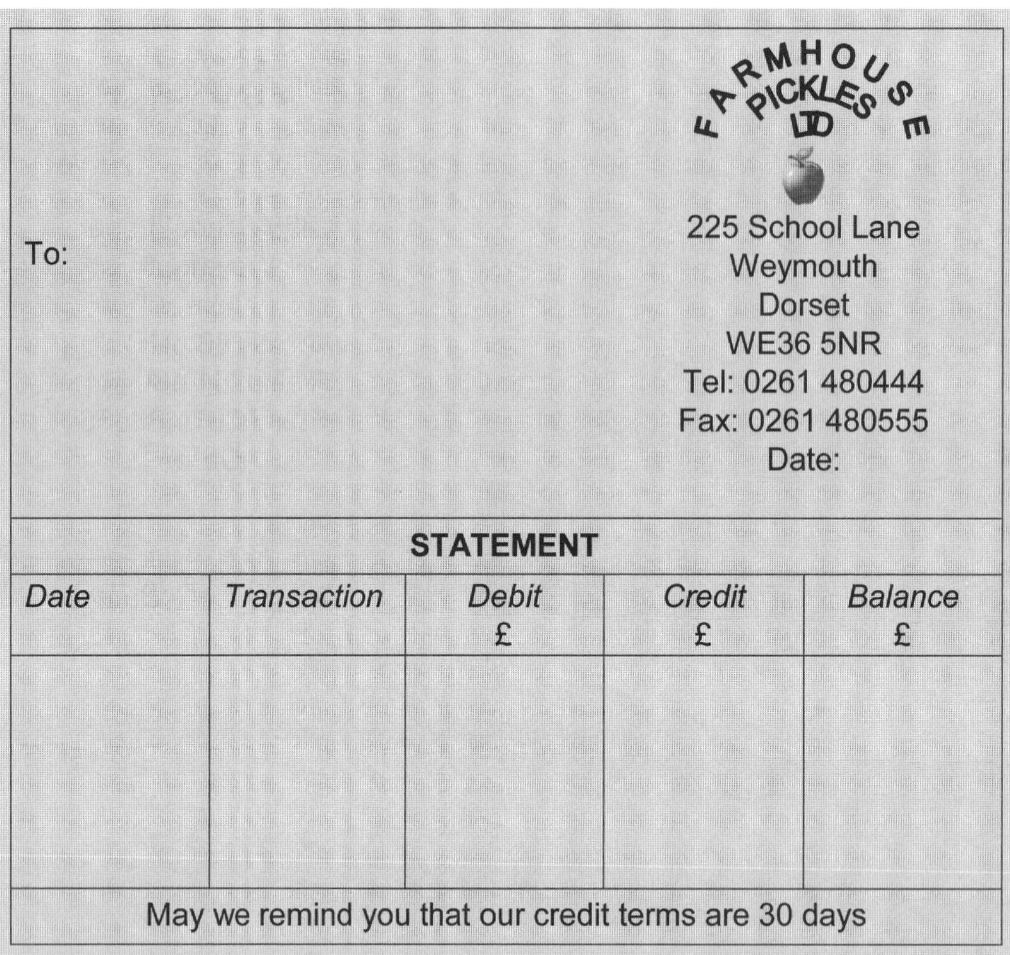

To:				FARMHOUSE PICKLES LTD 225 School Lane Weymouth Dorset WE36 5NR Tel: 0261 480444 Fax: 0261 480555 Date:
		STATEMENT		
Date	*Transaction*	*Debit* £	*Credit* £	*Balance* £
May we remind you that our credit terms are 30 days				

Test your understanding 11

Shown below is a customer's account from the sales ledger of Ryan's Toy Shop Ltd, along with a statement of account to be sent to that customer.

Arnold's Toys Ltd

Dr Cr

Date	*Transaction*	£		*Date*	*Transaction*	£	
19/11	Invoice 2195	118	08	20/11	Credit note 2198	323	60
20/11	Invoice 2198	2,201	95	22/11	Cheque	118	08
				22/11	Balance c/d	1,878	35
		2,320	03			2,320	03
23/11	Balance b/d	1,878	35				

Required:

Complete the statement of account below.

Ryan's Toy Shop LTD 125 Finchley Way Bristol BS1 4PL Tel: 01272 200299 STATEMENT OF ACCOUNT					
Customer name: Arnold's Toys Ltd **Customer address:** 14 High Street, Bristol, BS2 5FL					
Statement date 1st December		**Amount**		**Balance**	
Date	**Transaction**	£	p	£	P

Test your understanding 12

Simon Harris is a self-employed accountant who has a number of clients who all pay by cheque. Today's date is 5 May 20X1 and in the last week he has received the following cheques.

Required:

Inspect each one carefully to ensure that it is valid and make a note of any problems you find.

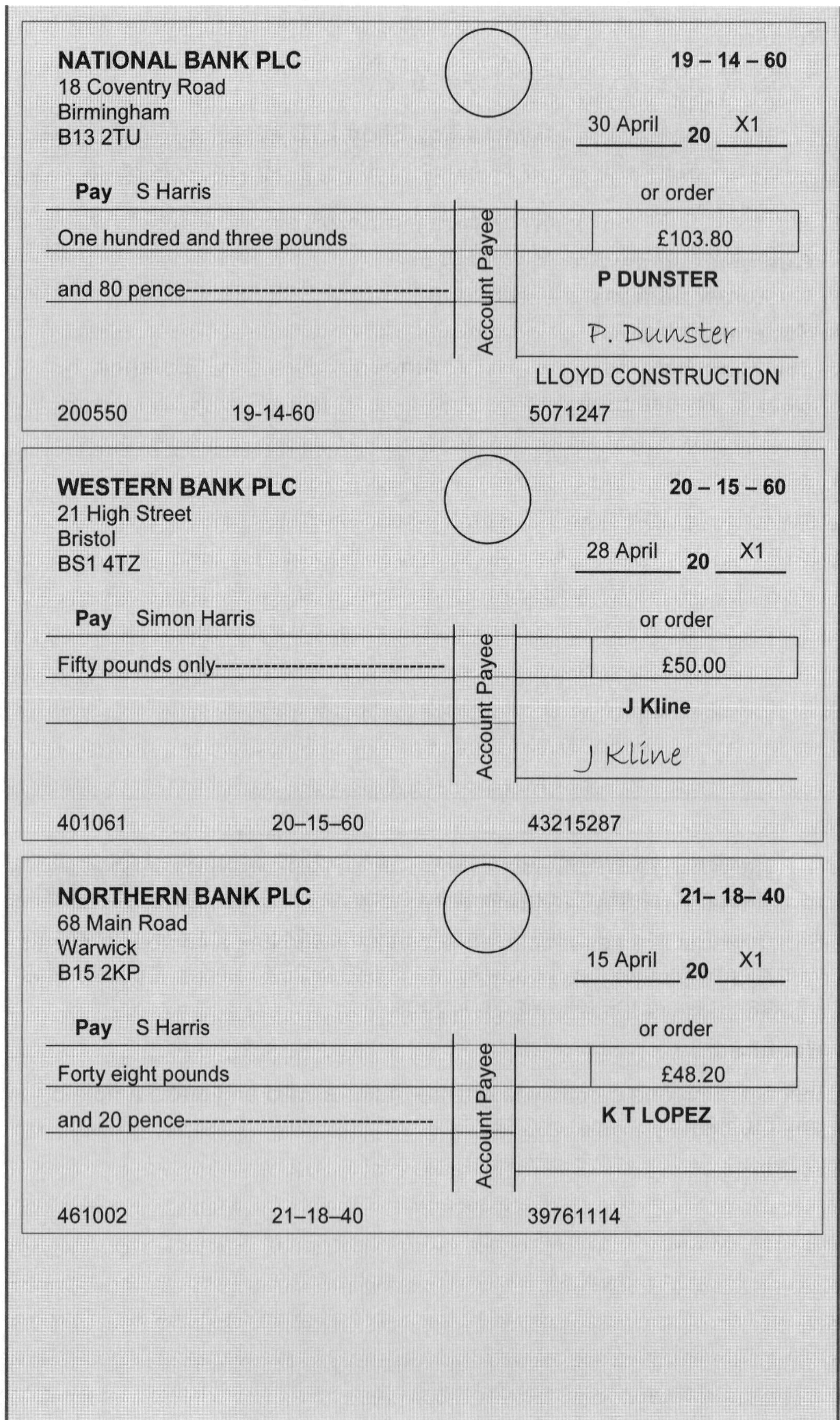

NATIONAL BANK PLC
18 Coventry Road
Birmingham
B13 2TU

19 – 14 – 60

30 April **20** X1

Pay S Harris or order

One hundred and three pounds and 80 pence------------------------------------ £103.80

Account Payee

P DUNSTER

P. Dunster

LLOYD CONSTRUCTION

200550 19-14-60 5071247

WESTERN BANK PLC
21 High Street
Bristol
BS1 4TZ

20 – 15 – 60

28 April **20** X1

Pay Simon Harris or order

Fifty pounds only------------------------------- £50.00

Account Payee

J Kline

J Kline

401061 20–15–60 43215287

NORTHERN BANK PLC
68 Main Road
Warwick
B15 2KP

21– 18– 40

15 April **20** X1

Pay S Harris or order

Forty eight pounds and 20 pence---------------------------------- £48.20

Account Payee

K T LOPEZ

461002 21–18–40 39761114

CENTRAL BANK PLC **16 – 20 – 30**
44 Warwick Road
Birmingham
B6 4LK

1 May **20** X1

Pay S Harris or order

One hundred and eighteen pounds £118.50

and 50 pence-----------------------------------

Account Payee

A RANKIN

A Rankin

610400 16–20–30 32146921

NATIONAL BANK PLC **19 – 14 – 60**
18 Coventry Road
Birmingham
B13 2TU

12 May **20** X1

Pay S Harris or order

Two hundred and one pounds £201.67

and 67 pence-------------------------------------

Account Payee

L GARRY

L Garry

201660 19-14-60 43012004

CENTRAL BANK PLC **16 – 20 – 30**
44 Warwick Road
Birmingham
B6 4LK

1 May **20** X1

Pay S Harper or order

Sixty two pounds £62.50

and 50 pence-----------------------------------

Account Payee

L BARRETT

L Barrett

100417 16–20–30 321426107

NATIONAL BANK PLC
18 Coventry Road
Birmingham
B13 2TU

19 – 14 – 60

12 April **20** X1

Pay S Harris or order

Forty eight pounds
and 60 pence-------------------------------------

Account Payee

£48.60

F DELAWARE
F Delaware

389152 19-14-60 61298432

FIRST NATIONAL BANK PLC
Trent Park
Leeds
LS4 6OL

23 – 16 – 40

21 Oct **20** X0

Pay S Harris or order

One hundred and thirty-seven pounds
and 40 pence-------------------------------------

Account Payee

£137.40

P IBBOTT
P Ibbott

001071 23-16-40 71294684

NATIONAL BANK PLC
18 Coventry Road
Birmingham
B13 2TU

19 – 14 – 60

28 April **20** X1

Pay S Harris or order

One hundred and thirty five pounds
and 80 pence-------------------------------------

Account Payee

£153.80

J LOVELL
J Lovell

041261 19-14-60 32114687

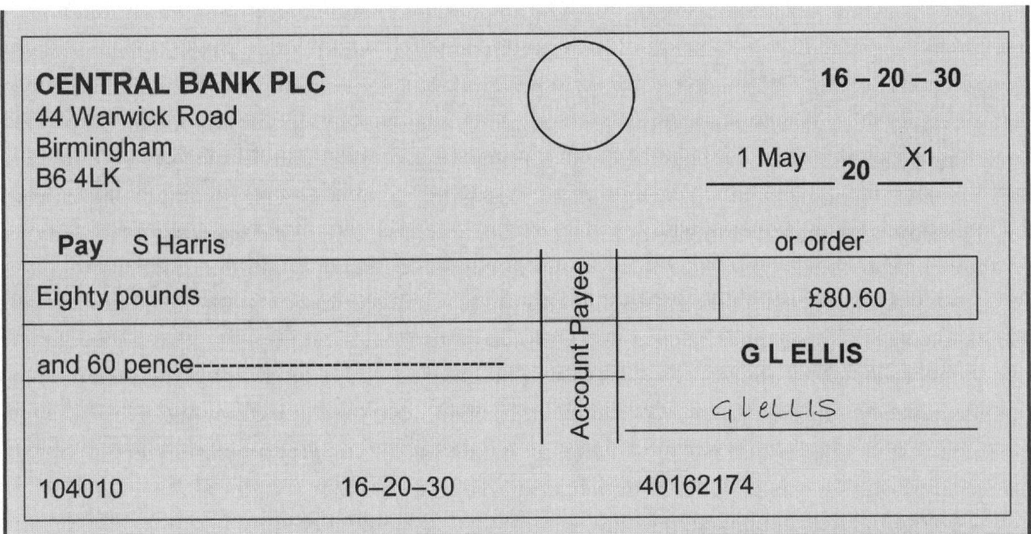
CENTRAL BANK PLC
44 Warwick Road
Birmingham
B6 4LK

16 – 20 – 30

1 May 20 X1

Pay S Harris or order

Eighty pounds
and 60 pence----------------------------------

£80.60

Account Payee

G L ELLIS

G L ELLIS

104010 16–20–30 40162174

Test your understanding 13

You work for Keyboard Supplies. Today's date is 12 May 20X1 and the following five cheques have arrived in this morning's post. You have found the invoices that these payments relate to – these are also given.

Required:

Check each receipt is correct and make a note of any problems you find.

NATIONAL BANK PLC
18 Coventry Road
Birmingham
B13 2TU

19 – 14 – 60

9/5/ 20 X1

Pay Keyboard Supplies or order

Three hundred and thirty five pounds
and 23 pence-------------------------------------

£335.23

Account Payee

J Lovell

B Z S Music

100417 19-14-60 36211412

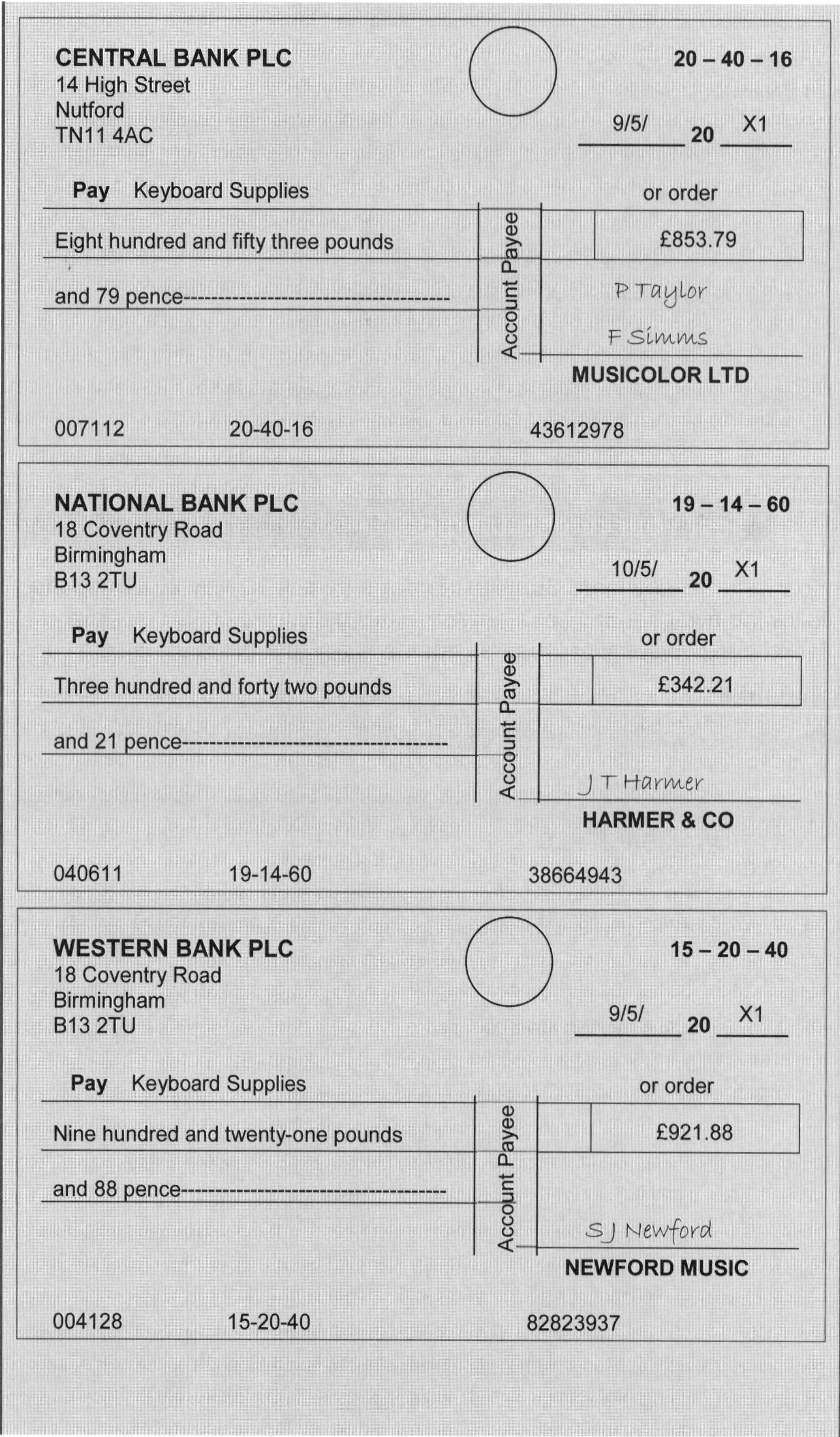

CENTRAL BANK PLC
14 High Street
Nutford
TN11 4AC

20 – 40 – 16

9/5/ 20 X1

Pay Keyboard Supplies or order

Eight hundred and fifty three pounds £853.79

and 79 pence------------------------------------

Account Payee

P Taylor

F Simms

MUSICOLOR LTD

007112 20-40-16 43612978

NATIONAL BANK PLC
18 Coventry Road
Birmingham
B13 2TU

19 – 14 – 60

10/5/ 20 X1

Pay Keyboard Supplies or order

Three hundred and forty two pounds £342.21

and 21 pence------------------------------------

Account Payee

J T Harmer

HARMER & CO

040611 19-14-60 38664943

WESTERN BANK PLC
18 Coventry Road
Birmingham
B13 2TU

15 – 20 – 40

9/5/ 20 X1

Pay Keyboard Supplies or order

Nine hundred and twenty-one pounds £921.88

and 88 pence------------------------------------

Account Payee

S J Newford

NEWFORD MUSIC

004128 15-20-40 82823937

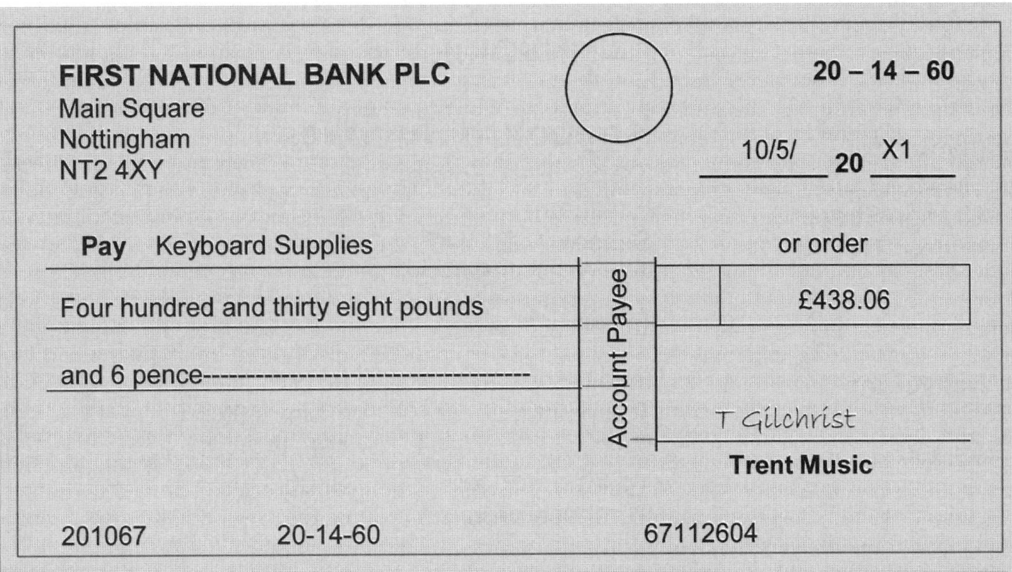
FIRST NATIONAL BANK PLC
Main Square
Nottingham
NT2 4XY

20 – 14 – 60

10/5/ **20** X1

Pay Keyboard Supplies or order

Four hundred and thirty eight pounds

and 6 pence------------------------------------

Account Payee

£438.06

T Gilchrist

Trent Music

201067 20-14-60 67112604

INVOICE

Keyboard Supplies
Trench Park Estate
Fieldham
Sussex TN21 4AF
Tel: 01829 654545
Fax: 01829 654646

Invoice to:
BZS Music
42 Westhill
Nutford TN11 3PQ

Deliver to:

Invoice no: 06180
Tax point: 3 May 20X1
VAT reg: 466 1128 30
Your reference: SL01
Purchase order no: 77147

Code	*Description*	*Quantity*	*VAT rate %*	*Unit price £*	*Amount excl of VAT £*
B4012	Bento Keyboard	2	20	180.00	360.00
					360.00
Trade discount 20%					72.00
					288.00
VAT					57.60
Total amount payable					345.60

Deduct discount of 3% if paid within 10 days, net 30 days

INVOICE

Invoice to:
Musicolor Ltd
23 High Street
Nutford TN11 4 TZ

Keyboard Supplies
Trench Park Estate
Fieldham
Sussex TN21 4AF
Tel: 01829 654545
Fax: 01829 654646

Deliver to:

As above

Invoice no: 06176
Tax point: 1 May 20X1
VAT reg: 466 1128 30
Your reference: SL06
Purchase order no: 6362

Code	*Description*	*Quantity*	*VAT rate %*	*Unit price £*	*Amount excl of VAT £*
Z4600	Zanni Keyboard	3	20	185.00	555.00
A4802	Atol Keyboard	2	20	130.00	260.00
					815.00
Trade discount 10%					81.50
					733.50
VAT					146.70
Total amount payable					880.20

Prompt payment discount of 3% if paid within 5 days, net 30 days

INVOICE

Invoice to:
Harmer & Co
1 Acre Street
Nutford TN11 0HA

Keyboard Supplies

Trench Park Estate
Fieldham
Sussex TN21 4AF
Tel: 01829 654545
Fax: 01829 654646

Deliver to:

As above

Invoice no: 06183
Tax point: 3 May 20X1
VAT reg no: 466 1128 30
Your reference: SL17
Purchase order no: 047786

Code	*Description*	*Quantity*	*VAT rate %*	*Unit price £*	*Amount excl of VAT £*
G4326	Garland Keyboard	3	20	98.00	294.00
					294.00
VAT					58.80
Total amount payable					352.80

Prompt payment discount of 3% if paid within 10 days, net 30 days

INVOICE

Invoice to:
Newford Music
32/34 Main Street
Welland
Sussex TN4 6BD

Keyboard Supplies
Trench Park Estate
Fieldham
Sussex TN21 4AF
Tel: 01829 654545
Fax: 01829 654646

Deliver to:

As above

Invoice no:	06171
Tax point:	30 April 20X1
VAT reg :	466 1128 30
Your reference:	SL18
Purchase order no:	47202

Code	*Description*	*Quantity*	*VAT rate %*	*Unit price £*	*Amount excl of VAT £*
Z4406	Zanni Keyboard	6	20	165.00	990.00
					990.00
Trade discount 20%					198.00
					792.00
VAT					158.40
Total amount payable					950.40

Prompt payment discount of 3% if paid within 5 days, net 30 days

INVOICE

Invoice to:	Keyboard Supplies
Trent Music Trent House Main Street Fieldham TN21 6ZF	Trench Park Estate Fieldham Sussex TN21 4AF Tel: 01829 654545 Fax: 01829 654646

Deliver to:

Invoice no:	06184
Tax point:	3 May 20X1
VAT reg :	466 1128 30
Your reference:	SL41
Purchase order no:	93754

Code	*Description*	*Quantity*	*VAT rate* %	*Unit price* £	*Amount excl of VAT* £
G4030	Garland Keyboard	4	20	105.00	420.00
					420.00
Trade discount 10%					42.00
					378.00
VAT					75.60
Total amount payable					453.60

Prompt payment discount of 3% if paid within 10 days, net 30 days

Test your understanding 14

Ellis Electricals makes the following credit sales to A and B giving a 20% trade discount plus a 5% prompt payment discount if customers pay their invoices within 5 days.

	Customer A	*Customer B*
	£	£
Sales value	1,000	4,000
Trade discount (20%)	200	800
Net sales value	800	3,200
VAT (calculated on the net sales value after deducting the trade discount)		
Customer A: (800 × 20%)	160	
Customer B: (3,200 × 20%)		640
Total invoice value	960	3,840

Ellis Electricals also makes a cash sale to C for £300 plus VAT at 20%.

Prompt payment discount is only deducted upon the receivable making payment within the discount period.

Customer A pays his invoice in full within 5 days and takes the prompt payment discount. Customer B pays £2,000 on account.

Task

Write up the sales day book, the cash receipts book and the discounts allowed book and post the entries to the general and sales ledgers.

Test your understanding 15

Given below is the debit side of the cash book and the discount allowed book completed for transactions that took place on 15 May:

CASH BOOK – DEBIT SIDE			
Date	*Narrative*	*SL Code*	*Bank* £
20X1			
15/5	McCaul & Partners	M04	117.60
	P Martin	M02	232.80
	F Little	L03	93.12
			443.52

DISCOUNTS ALLOWED BOOK					
Date	*Customer*	*SL Code*	*Total* £	*VAT* £	*Net* £
20X1					
15/5	McCaul & Partners	M04	2.40	0.40	2.00
	P Martin	M02	7.20	1.20	6.00
	F Little	L03	2.88	0.48	2.40
			12.48	2.08	10.40

Required:

Show what the entries in the sales ledger will be:

Account name	Amount £	Dr ✓	Cr ✓

Show what the entries in the general ledger will be:

Account name	Amount £	Dr ✓	Cr ✓

Test your understanding 16

Given below are three invoices received by Nethan Builders that are to be paid today, 18 May 20X1. It is the business policy to take advantage of any prompt payments discounts possible.

You are required to complete a remittance advice for each payment. The last cheque used was number 200549.

INVOICE

Invoice to:
Nethan Builders
Brecon House
Stamford Road
Manchester
M16 4PL

Building Contract Supplies
Unit 15
Royal Estate
Manchester
M13 2EF
Tel: 0161 562 3041
Fax: 0161 562 3042

Deliver to:
As above

Invoice no: 07742
Tax point: 8 May 20X1
VAT reg no: 776 4983 06

Code	*Description*	*Quantity*	*VAT rate %*	*Unit price £*	*Amount excl of VAT £*
SDGSL6	SDGS Softwood 47 × 225 mm	20.5 m	20	8.30	170.15
					170.15
VAT					34.03
Total amount payable					204.18
Prompt payment discount of 1½% if paid within 14 days					

INVOICE

Jenson Ltd
30 Longfield Park, Kingsway
M45 2TP
Tel: 0161 511 4666
Fax: 0161 511 4777

Invoice to:
Nethan Builders
Brecon House
Stamford Road
Manchester
M16 4PL

Deliver to:
As above

Invoice no: 47811
Tax point: 5 May 20X1
VAT reg no: 641 3229 45
Purchase order no: 7174

Code	*Description*	*Quantity*	*VAT rate %*	*Unit price £*	*Amount excl of VAT £*
PL432115	Door Lining set 32 × 115 mm	6	20	30.25	181.50
					181.50
Trade discount 15%					27.22
					154.28
VAT					30.85
Total amount payable					185.13

Prompt payment discount of 3% if paid within 10 days

INVOICE

Magnum Supplies
140/150 Park Estate
Manchester
M20 6EG
Tel: 0161 561 3202
Fax: 0161 561 3200

Invoice to:
Nethan Builders
Brecon House
Stamford Road
Manchester
M16 4PL

Deliver to:
As above

Invoice no: 077422
Tax point: 11 May 20X1
VAT reg no: 611 4337 90

Code	*Description*	*Quantity*	*VAT rate %*	*Unit price £*	*Amount excl of VAT £*
BH47732	House Bricks – Red	600	20	1.24	744.00
					744.00
Trade discount 15%					111.60
					632.40
VAT					126.48
Total amount payable					758.88

Prompt payment discount of 2% if paid within 10 days

REMITTANCE ADVICE

To:

Nethan Builders
Brecon House
Stamford House
Manchester
M16 4PL

Tel: 0161 521 6411
Fax: 0161 530 6412
VAT reg: 471 3860 42
Date:

Date	Invoice no	Amount £	Discount taken £	Paid £

Total paid £

Cheque no

REMITTANCE ADVICE

To:

Nethan Builders
Brecon House
Stamford House
Manchester
M16 4PL

Tel: 0161 521 6411
Fax: 0161 530 6412
VAT reg: 471 3860 42
Date:

Date	Invoice no	Amount £	Discount taken £	Paid £

Total paid £

Cheque no

REMITTANCE ADVICE

To:

Nethan Builders
Brecon House
Stamford House
Manchester
M16 4PL

Tel: 0161 521 6411
Fax: 0161 530 6412
VAT reg: 471 3860 42
Date:

Date	Invoice no	Amount £	Discount taken £	Paid £

Total paid £

Cheque no ____________

Test your understanding 17

Given below is a business' petty cash book for the week.

Petty cash book

Receipts			Payments								
Date	*Narrative*	*Total*	*Date*	*Details*	*Voucher no*	*Amount* £	*Postage* £	*Staff welfare* £	*Station-ery* £	*Travel expenses* £	*VAT* £
5/1/X1	Bal b/d	150.00	12/1/X1	Postage	03526	13.68	13.68				
				Staff welfare	03527	25.00		25.00			
				Stationery	03528	15.12			12.60		2.52
				Taxi fare	03529	12.25				10.21	2.04
				Staff welfare	03530	6.40		6.40			
				Postage	03531	12.57	12.57				
				Rail fare	03532	6.80				6.80	
				Stationery	03533	8.16			6.80		1.36
				Taxi fare	03534	19.20				16.00	3.20
				Bal c/d		30.82					
						150.00	26.25	31.40	19.40	33.01	9.12

Required:

NB: The petty cash book also forms part of the general ledger. Show what the entries in the general ledger will be:

Account name	Amount £	Dr ✓	Cr ✓

 Test your understanding 18

Given below is a completed petty cash book for transactions that took place on 12 April 20X1:

Petty cash book

Receipts			Payments									
Date	*Narrative*	*Total*	*Date*	*Narrative*	*Voucher no*	*Total* £	*Postage* £	*Staff welfare* £	*Stationery* £	*Travel expenses* £	*VAT* £
12/04	Bal b/d	100.00	12/04	Coffee/milk	2534	4.68		4.68			
				Postage	2535	13.26	13.26				
				Stationery	2536	10.48			8.74		1.74
				Taxi fare	2537	15.32				12.77	2.55
				Postage	2538	6.75	6.75				
				Train fare	2539	7.40				7.40	
				Stationery	2540	3.94			3.29		0.65
				Bal c/d		38.17					
						100.00	20.01	4.68	12.03	20.17	4.94

Required:

Post the required entries to the general ledger accounts:

Postage

	£		£
Balance b/d	231.67		

Staff welfare

	£		£
Balance b/d	334.78		

Stationery

	£		£
Balance b/d	53.36		

Travel expenses

	£		£
Balance b/d	579.03		

VAT account

	£		£
		Balance b/d	967.44

Test your understanding 19

A business runs its petty cash on an imprest system with an imprest amount of £100 per week.

At the end of the week ending 22 May 20X1 the vouchers in the petty cash box were:

Voucher no	£
02634	13.73
02635	8.91
02636	10.57
02637	3.21
02638	11.30
02639	14.66

The cash remaining in the petty cash box was made up as follows:

£10 note	1
£5 note	2
£2 coin	3
£1 coin	7
50p coin	5
20p coin	4
10p coin	1
5p coin	2
2p coin	3
1p coin	6

You are required to reconcile the petty cash in the box to the vouchers in the box at 22 May 20X1 and if it does not reconcile to suggest reasons for the difference.

8 Summary

This chapter has reviewed over all aspects of making and receiving payments. The previous chapters have taken us through making credit sales and credit purchases, the documents and processes involved and how to record these transactions in the general and subsidiary ledgers.

In this chapter we have completed the sales and purchases cycle by reviewing the purpose and content of statements of accounts for receivables and from payables, what a remittance advice is and how to enter transactions into the cash books and discounts day book and make entries from those day books to the general and subsidiary ledgers. Finally, the chapter reviewed the maintenance of a petty cash system.

Test your understanding answers

Test your understanding 1

Thames Traders

To: Jack Johnson

Date: 31 May 20X6:

STATEMENT

Date	*Transaction*	*Debit* £	*Credit* £	*Balance* £
03 May	Inv 1848	38.79		38.79
07 May	Inv 1863	50.70		89.49
08 May	CN 446		12.40	77.09
10 May	Inv 1870	80.52		157.61
15 May	Payment		77.09	80.52
18 May	Inv 1881	42.40		122.92
23 May	Inv 1892	61.20		184.12
24 May	CN 458		16.50	167.62
30 May	Inv 1904	27.65		195.27

May we remind you that our credit terms are 30 days

Test your understanding 2

False. A remittance advice is a slip that the customer can send back to the supplier with his payment to identify what the payment is for.

Test your understanding 3

(a) No

(b) Any two from the following:

- (i) The cheque has not been signed.
- (ii) The cheque is out of date.
- (iii) The words and figures on the cheque are not the same.

Test your understanding 4

The entries in the sales ledger will be:

Account name	Amount £	Dr ✓	Cr ✓
G Hunt	114		✓
L Tessa	110		✓
J Dent	342		✓
F Trainer	97		✓
A Winter	105		✓
G Hunt	6		✓
J Dent	18		✓

The entries in the general ledger for the cash receipts book will be:

Account name	Amount £	Dr ✓	Cr ✓
Bank	888	✓	
Sales ledger control account (receivables)	768		✓
Sales	100		✓
VAT	20		✓

The entries in the general ledger for the discounts allowed book will be:

Account name	Amount £	Dr ✓	Cr ✓
Discounts allowed	20	✓	
VAT	4	✓	
Sales ledger control account (receivables)	24		✓

Test your understanding 5

The entries in the purchases ledger will be:

Account name	Amount £	Dr ✓	Cr ✓
Homer Ltd	176.40	✓	
Forker & Co	285.18	✓	
Print Ass.	190.45	✓	
ABG Ltd	220.67	✓	
G Greg	67.89	✓	
Homer Ltd	3.60	✓	
Forker & Co	8.82	✓	

The above entries in the purchases ledger are for the cash payments made and the discounts received from the suppliers.

The entries in the general ledger for the cash payments book will be:

Account name	Amount £	Dr ✓	Cr ✓
Bank	1480.59		✓
PLCA	940.59	✓	
Purchases	450.00	✓	
VAT	90.00	✓	

The entries in the general ledger for the discounts received day book will be:

Account name	Amount £	Dr ✓	Cr ✓
Discounts received	10.35		✓
VAT	2.07		✓
PLCA	12.42	✓	

Test your understanding 6

Postings to general ledger

Account	Amount	Dr or Cr
Motor vehicle	20,000	Dr
Motor expenses	400	Dr
VAT	80	Dr
PLCA	6,500	Dr

Postings to the purchases ledger

Account	Amount	Dr or Cr
Payable B account	6,500	Dr

Test your understanding 7

Details	Amount £	Debit/Credit
Motor expenses	300	Debit
VAT	60	Debit
Wages	4,785	Debit

Test your understanding 8

(a), (b)

PETTY CASH BOOK – PAYMENTS													
Date	*Voucher no*	*Total*		*Production*		*Distribution*		*Marketing*		*Administration*		*VAT*	
		£		£		£		£		£		£	
01/10/X7	6579	19	72							16	44	3	28
04/10/X7	6580	8	75							8	75		
06/10/X7	6581	17	13					17	13				
06/10/X7	6582	16	23					16	23				
06/10/X7	6583	43	75					43	75				
10/10/X7	6584	4	60							4	60		
15/10/X7	6585	4	39	4	39								
17/10/X7	6586	8	47			7	06					1	41
20/10/X7	6587	21	23							21	23		
26/10/X7	6588	8	75							8	75		
		153	02	4	39	7	06	77	11	59	77	4	69

(c)

Production expenses account

	£		£
PCB	4.39		

Distribution expenses account

	£		£
PCB	7.06		

Marketing expenses account

	£		£
PCB	77.11		

Administration expenses account

	£		£
PCB	59.77		

VAT account

	£		£
PCB	4.69		

Test your understanding 9

Notes and coins

	£	£
£5 × 2	10.00	
£1 × 3	3.00	
50p × 5	2.50	
20p × 4	0.80	
10p × 6	0.60	
5p × 7	0.35	
2p × 10	0.20	
1p × 8	0.08	
		17.53
Vouchers		
2143	10.56	
2144	3.30	
2145	9.80	
2146	8.44	
2147	2.62	
2148	6.31	
2149	1.44	
		42.47
Imprest amount		60.00

Test your understanding 10

FARMHOUSE PICKLES LTD

To: Grant & Co

225 School Lane
Weymouth
Dorset
WE36 5NR
Tel: 0261 480444
Fax: 0261 480555
Date: 30 April 20X1

STATEMENT

Date	*Transaction*	*Debit* £	*Credit* £	*Balance* £
1 April	Opening balance			337.69
4 April	Inv 32656	150.58		488.27
12 April	Credit 0335		38.70	449.57
18 April	Inv 32671	179.52		629.09
20 April	Payment		330.94	298.15
20 April	Discount		6.75	291.40
24 April	Credit 0346		17.65	273.75
25 April	Inv 32689	94.36		368.11

May we remind you that our credit terms are 30 days

FARMHOUSE PICKLES LTD

To: Mitchell Partners

225 School Lane
Weymouth
Dorset
WE36 5NR
Tel: 0261 480444
Fax: 0261 480555
Date: 30 April 20X1

STATEMENT

Date	*Transaction*	*Debit* £	*Credit* £	*Balance* £
1 April	Opening balance			180.46
7 April	Inv 32662	441.57		622.03
12 April	Credit 0344		66.89	555.14
20 April	Inv 32669	274.57		829.71
21 April	Payment		613.58	216.13
21 April	Discount		8.45	207.68

May we remind you that our credit terms are 30 days

Test your understanding 11

Ryan's Toy Shop LTD
125 Finchley Way Bristol BS1 4PL Tel: 01272 200299

STATEMENT OF ACCOUNT

Customer name Arnold's Toys Ltd
Customer address 14 High Street, Bristol, BS2 5FL

Statement date 1st December		**Amount**		**Balance**	
Date	**Transaction**	£	p	£	p
19/11	Invoice 2195	118	08	118	08
20/11	Invoice 2198	2,201	95	2,320	03
20/11	Credit note 2198	323	60	1,996	43
22/11	Cheque	118	08	1,878	35
				1,878	35

Test your understanding 12

The following problems exist on the cheques received:

Cheque from K T Lopez – not signed

Cheque from L Garry – post dated

Cheque from L Barrett – made out to wrong name

Cheque from P Ibbott – more than six months old

Cheque from J Lovell – discrepancy between words and figures.

Test your understanding 13

Cheque from BZS Music – prompt payment discount of £10.37 has been taken – this is valid.

Cheque from Musicolor Ltd – prompt payment discount of £26.41 has been taken – but is not valid as the cheque has been received after 5 days from the invoice date. However, in the interest of good customer relations, perhaps the discount should be granted but the customer should be informed and reminded of the prompt payment discount terms.

Cheque from Harmer & Co – prompt payment discount of £10.59 has been taken – this is valid.

Cheque from Newford Music – prompt payment discount of £28.52 has been taken – this is not valid as the receipt is too late to claim the discount. Again the discount might be granted in the interest of good customer relations but the customer should be informed and reminded of the prompt payment discount terms.

Cheque from Trent Music – prompt payment discount of £15.54 has been taken – however it should have been £13.61 (3% × £453.60). Customer should be informed of the error.

Test your understanding 14

Step 1

Write up the sales day book.

SALES DAY BOOK				
Date	*Customer*	*Total* £	*VAT* £	*Sales* £
	A	960.00	160.00	800.00
	B	3,840.00	640.00	3,200.00
		4,800.00	800.00	4,000.00

Step 2

Write up the cash receipts book and the discounts allowed book.

CASH RECEIPTS BOOK					
Date	*Customer*	*Total* £	*VAT* £	*SLCA* £	*Cash sales*
	A (W)	912.00		912.00	
	B	2,000.00		2,000.00	
	C	360.00	60.00		300.00
		3,272.00	60.00	2,912.00	300.00

DISCOUNTS ALLOWED BOOK				
Date	*Customer*	*Total* £	*VAT* £	*Net* £
	A (W)	48.00	8.00	40.00
		48.00	8.00	40.00

Working:

Cash paid by A:

	£
Sale value net of VAT	800.00
Less: prompt payment discount (£800 × 5%)	(40.00)
	760.00
VAT (760 × 20%)	152.00
	912.00

The prompt payment discount is:
Net £800 × 5% = £40
VAT £160 × 5% = £8
Gross £48

Step 3

Post the totals to the general ledger. Note that for this example the source of the data (day book references have been used for the narrative), the opposite account posted to is also acceptable.

Sales

	£		£
		SDB	4,000.00
		CRB	300.00

VAT

	£		£
DAB	8.00	SDB	800.00
		CRB	60.00

SLCA

	£		£
SDB	4,800.00	CRB	2,912.00
		DAB	48.00

Discount allowed

	£		£
DAB	40.00		

Step 4

Post individual amounts for the SDB and CRB to the sales ledger.

A

	£		£
SDB	960.00	CRB	912.00
		DAB	48.00

B

	£		£
SDB	3,840.00		2,000.00

Test your understanding 15

The entries in the sales ledger will be:

Account name	Amount £	Dr ✓	Cr ✓
McCaul & Partners	117.60		✓
P Martin	232.80		✓
F Little	93.12		✓
McCaul & Partners	2.40		✓
P Martin	7.20		✓
F Little	2.88		✓

Show what the entries in the general ledger will be:

Account name	Amount £	Dr ✓	Cr ✓
Discounts allowed	10.40	✓	
VAT	2.08	✓	
Sales ledger control account	12.48		✓
Sales ledger control account	443.52		✓

Test your understanding 16

REMITTANCE ADVICE

To:

Building Contract Supplies
Unit 15 Royal Estate
Manchester
M13 2EF

Nethan Builders
Brecon House
Stamford House
Manchester
M16 4PL

Tel: 0161 521 6411
Fax: 0161 530 6412
VAT reg: 471 3860 42
Date: 18 May 20X1

Date	Invoice no	Amount £	Discount taken £	Paid £
8 May 20X1	07742	204.18	3.06	201.12

Total paid £201.12

Cheque no 200550

REMITTANCE ADVICE

To:

Jenson Ltd
30 Longfield Park
Kingsway
M45 2TP

Nethan Builders
Brecon House
Stamford House
Manchester
M16 4PL

Tel: 0161 521 6411
Fax: 0161 530 6412
VAT reg: 471 3860 42
Date: 18 May 20X1

Date	Invoice no	Amount £	Discount taken £	Paid £
5 May 20X1	47811	185.13		185.13

Total paid £185.13

Cheque no 200551

REMITTANCE ADVICE

To:

Magnum Supplies
140/150 Park Estate
Manchester
M20 6EG

Nethan Builders
Brecon House
Stamford House
Manchester
M16 4PL

Tel: 0161 521 6411
Fax: 0161 530 6412
VAT reg: 471 3860 42
Date: 18 May 20X1

Date	Invoice no	Amount £	Discount taken £	Paid £
11 May 20X1	077422	758.88	15.18	743.70

Total paid £743.70

Cheque no 200552

Test your understanding 17

The entries in the general ledger will be:

Account name	Amount £	Dr ✓	Cr ✓
Postage	26.25	✓	
Staff welfare	31.40	✓	
Stationery	19.40	✓	
Travel expenses	33.01	✓	
VAT	9.12	✓	

Test your understanding 18

Postage

	£		£
Balance b/d	231.67		
PCB	20.01		

Staff welfare

	£		£
Balance b/d	334.78		
PCB	4.68		

Stationery

	£		£
Balance b/d	53.36		
PCB	12.03		

Travel expenses

	£		£
Balance b/d	579.03		
PCB	20.17		

VAT account

	£		£
PCB	4.94	Balance b/d	967.44

Test your understanding 19

Voucher total

	£
02634	13.73
02635	8.91
02636	10.57
02637	3.21
02638	11.30
02639	14.66
	62.38

Cash total

		£
£10 note	1	10.00
£5 note	2	10.00
£2 coin	3	6.00
£1 coin	7	7.00
50p coin	5	2.50
20p coin	4	0.80
10p coin	1	0.10
5p coin	2	0.10
2p coin	3	0.06
1p coin	6	0.06
		36.62

Reconciliation of cash and vouchers at 22 May 20X1

	£
Voucher total	62.38
Cash total	36.62
	99.00

The reconciliation shows that there is £1 missing. More cash has been paid out of the petty cash box than is supported by the petty cash vouchers. This could be due to a number of reasons:

- A petty cash claim was made out for, say, £11.30 but mistakenly the amount given to the employee was £12.30.
- An employee borrowed £1 from the petty cash box for business expenses and this has not been recorded on a petty cash voucher.
- £1 has been stolen from the petty cash box.

MOCK ASSESSMENT

1 Mock Assessment Questions

Each task is independent.

You must complete all tasks.

Task 1.1 (12 marks)

A sales invoice is being prepared for goods supplied, as shown in the customer order below:

Customer order

ELA Ltd

Order number 154

Please supply: 14 June 20XX

10 units of product VC

@ £40.00 each less 5% trade discount

(a) Calculate the amounts (pounds and pence) to be included on the invoice: (4 marks)

	£
Net amount before discount	
Net amount after discount	
VAT	
Total	

(b) What will be the amounts entered in the sales day book when the invoice in (a) is prepared? (3 marks)

Sales day book

Date 20XX	**Details**	**Invoice number**	**Total £**	**VAT £**	**Net £**
14 June	ELA Ltd	314			

A cheque for £995 has been received from ELA Ltd which incorrectly states is in full settlement of their account as at 31 May 20XX. The customer's account in the sales ledger is shown below:

ELA Ltd

Date 20XX	*Details*	*Amount £*	*Date 20XX*	*Details*	*Amount £*
1 May	Bal b/f	900	4 May	Bank	900
5 May	Invoice 200	600	6 May	Credit note 34	12
10 May	Invoice 232	1,010	18 May	Credit note 39	300
12 May	Invoice 237	532			
29 May	Invoice 289	285			

(c) Show which THREE transactions are still outstanding by circling the relevant transactions shown below: (3 marks)

Transactions

Bal b/f

Credit note 39

Invoice 289

Credit note 34

Bank

Invoice 237

Invoice 232

Invoice 200

A quotation to supply goods for £2,440 plus VAT has been sent to ELA Ltd offering a prompt payment discount of 3% for payment within 5 days of the invoice date.

(d) What will be the amount ELA Ltd will pay if they purchase the goods and pay within 5 days of the invoice date? (2 marks)

£

Task 1.2 (9 marks)

The invoice and purchase order below relate to goods received from LGJ Ltd.

Invoice:

LGJ Ltd	
VAT registration 369 4577 00	
Invoice number 231	
To: T Blossom 5 May 20XX	
	£
200 product code 156CC @ £1.50 each	300
VAT @ 20%	60
Total	360
Terms: 30 days	

Purchase order:

T Blossom

Order number 756

4 May 20XX

Please supply:

200 units of product 156CC

@ £1.70 each less 5% trade discount

Terms: 30 days

(a) Identify any discrepancies on the invoice by placing a tick in the appropriate box in the table set out below: (4 marks)

	Correctly shown on invoice	Not shown on invoice	Incorrectly shown on invoice
Product code			
Unit price			
Terms of payment			
Trade discount			

The invoice below has been received from Carrera Ltd.

Invoice:

Carrera Ltd	
VAT registration 446 4482 01	
Invoice number 54879	
To: T Blossom 15 May 20XX	
	£
350 product code 546TC @ £1.25 each	437.50
VAT @ 20%	87.50
Total	525.00
Terms: Net monthly account	

(b) Record the invoice in the appropriate day book by: (5 marks)

- Inserting the correct day book title (in the first row):

Select from: sales day book, purchases day book, discounts allowed day book, discounts received day book, sales returns day book, purchases returns day book.

- Inserting the correct details:

Select from: Carrera Ltd, T Blossom

- Making the necessary entries.

Date 20XX	Details	Invoice number	Total £	VAT £	Net £
15 May		54879			

Task 1.3 (9 marks)

Shown below is a statement of account received from a credit supplier, Spence & Co and the supplier's account as shown in the purchases ledger of Alfie Electricals.

Spence & Co

42 Armour Lane, Kilwinning, KA16 7YH

To: Alfie Electricals

1 Albert Street

Edinburgh, EH1 4BH

STATEMENT OF ACCOUNT

Date 20X2	*Invoice number*	*Details*	*Invoice amount £*	*Cheque amount £*	*Balance £*
1 Oct	232	Goods	900		900
5 Nov	248	Goods	400		1,300
6 Nov	269	Goods	300		1,600
23 Nov	–	Cheque		900	700
26 Nov	299	Goods	100		800

Spence & Co

Date 20X2	*Details*	*Amount £*	*Date 20X2*	*Details*	*Amount £*
23 Nov	Bank	900	1 Oct	Purchases	900
26 Nov	Bank	700	5 Nov	Purchases	400
			6 Nov	Purchases	300

(a) Which item is missing from the statement of account from Spence & Co and which item is missing from the supplier account in Alfie Electricals? (3 marks)

Item missing from the statement of account from Spence & Co:

Select your account name from the following list: Invoice 232, Invoice 248, Invoice 269, Invoice 299, Cheque for £700, Cheque for £900

Item missing from the supplier account in Alfie Electricals purchases ledger:

Select your account name from the following list: Invoice 232, Invoice 248, Invoice 269, Invoice 299, Cheque for £700, Cheque for £900

(b) Assuming any differences between the statement of account from Spence & Co and the supplier account in Alfie Electricals purchases ledger are simply due to omission errors, what is the amount owing to Spence & Co? (1 mark)

£

This is the account of RR & Co in the purchases ledger and a credit note that has been received from the supplier but not yet entered into their account.

RR & Co

Date 20X2	*Details*	*Amount £*	*Date 20X2*	*Details*	*Amount £*
3 Nov	Bank	1,500	1 Nov	Balance b/f	1,840
3 Nov	Credit note 50	100	3 Nov	Invoice 134	550
			4 Nov	Invoice 148	700
			5 Nov	Invoice 176	860

Credit note:

RR & Co

VAT registration 432 4577 00

Credit note number 56

To: Alfie Electricals 6 November 20XX

For return of goods on invoice 132

	£
10 product code A132 @ £20 each	200
VAT @ 20%	40
Total	240

Terms: 30 days

(c) What will be the amount owed to RR & Co once the credit note has been entered into their account? (1 mark)

£

The two invoices below were received on 7 November from credit suppliers who offer prompt payment discounts.

Invoices:

Hudson & Co	
VAT registration 446 4852 01	
Invoice number 15963	
To: Alfie Electricals 6 November 20XX	
	£
10 product code 517 @ £63.50 each	635.00
VAT @ 20%	127.00
Total	762.00
Terms: 3% prompt payment discount if payment is received within 5 days of the invoice date.	

Marsh & Co	
VAT registration 446 4982 01	
Invoice number 986	
To: Alfie Electricals 6 November 20XX	
	£
32 product code 121 @ £57.25 each	1,832.00
VAT @ 20%	366.40
Total	2,198.40
Terms: 2.5% prompt payment discount if payment is received within 10 days of the invoice date.	

(d) Calculate the amount to be paid to each supplier if the prompt payment discount is taken and show the date by which the supplier should receive the payment. (4 marks)

Supplier	£	Date by which the payment should be received by the supplier
Hudson & Co		
Marsh & Co		

Task 1.4 (15 marks)

There are five payments to be entered in Adams & Son's cash-book.

Receipts

Received cash with thanks for goods bought. From Adams & Son, a customer without a credit account.	Received cash with thanks for goods bought. From Adams & Son, a customer without a credit account.	Received cash with thanks for goods bought. From Adams & Son, a customer without a credit account.
Net £400	Net £320	Net £350
VAT £80	VAT £64	(No VAT)
Total £480	Total £384	
Johnson Ltd	*A Alpha*	*Bond's*

Cheque book counterfoils

ABC Ltd (Purchase ledger account ABC006)	Twilight (Purchase ledger account TWI001)
£2,000	£240
000123	000124

(a) Enter the details from the three receipts and two cheque book stubs into the credit side of the cash-book shown below and total each column. (7 marks)

Cash-book – credit side

Details	*Cash*	*Bank*	*VAT*	*Payables*	*Cash purchases*
Balance b/f					
Johnson Ltd					
A Alpha					
Bond's					
ABC Ltd					
Twilight					
Total					

There are two cheques from credit customers to be entered in Adam & Son's cash book:

Rhoda Ring £560

Reef £210

(b) Enter the above details into the debit side of the cash-book and total each column. (6 marks)

Cash book – debit side

Details	*Cash*	*Bank*	*Receivables*
Balance b/f	1,500	11,710	
Rhoda Ring			
Reef			
Total			

(c) Using your answers to (a) and (b) above, calculate the cash balance. (1 mark)

£

Using your answers to (a) and (b) above, calculate the bank balance. Use a minus sign if your calculations indicate an overdrawn balance, e.g. –123 (1 mark)

£

Task 1.5 (15 marks)

This is an extract of the petty cash book containing transactions for the month of June made by an organisation. The organisation maintains an imprest system level of £200.00 on the last day of each month.

Date	Details	Amount £	Date	Details	Amount £	VAT £	Carriage and postage £	Travel £	Office Expenses £
1 Jun	Bal b/f	200.00	5 Jun	Mick Ltd	24.00	4.00		20.00	
			17 Jun	R Walsh	22.80	3.80	19.00		
			21 Jun	Office Supplies Ltd	26.40	4.40			22.00
			28 Jun	Stationery Stop	20.88	3.48			17.40

(a) What will be the entry in the petty cash book to restore to the imprest level on 30th June? (3 marks)

Details	Amount £	Debit ✓	Credit ✓

Details picklist: Amount, Balance b/d, Balance c/d, Cash from bank

(b) What will be the entry in the petty cash book to record the closing balance on 30th June after the imprest level has been restored? (3 marks)

Details	Amount £	Debit ✓	Credit ✓

Details picklist: Amount, Balance b/d, Balance c/d, Cash from bank

(c) What will be the total of the Office Expenses column in the petty cash book? (1 mark)

£

It is now 3rd July and the petty cash vouchers below require entry into the petty cash book:

Petty cash voucher 285	Petty cash voucher 286
3rd July	3rd July
Your Office – A4 paper 5 × 500 sheets	Speedy Delivery – Courier services
£13.50 including VAT	£27.50 plus VAT

(d) What will be the total, VAT and net amounts to be entered into the petty cash book? (6 marks)

Petty cash voucher number	Total £	VAT £	Net £
285			
286			

(e) What analysis columns in the petty cash book will be used to record the net amounts of the petty cash payments detailed in (d)? (2 marks)

Petty cash voucher number	Analysis column
285	
286	

Analysis column picklist: Amount, Carriage and postage, Office expenses, Travel, VAT

Task 1.6 (12 marks)

These are the totals of the discounts allowed day book at the end of the month.

Details	Total £	VAT £	Net £
Totals	600	100	500

(a) What will be the entries in the general ledger? (9 marks)

Account name	**Amount** £	**Debit** ✓	**Credit** ✓

Select your account name from the following list: Discounts allowed, Discounts received, Purchases, Purchases ledger control, Purchases returns, Sales, Sales ledger control, Sales returns, VAT

One of the entries in the discounts allowed day book is for a credit note sent to Johnson Cooper for £60 plus VAT.

(b) What will be the entry in the sales ledger? (3 marks)

Account name	**Amount** £	**Debit** ✓	**Credit** ✓

Select your account name from the following list: Discounts allowed, Discounts received, Johnson Cooper, Purchases, Purchases ledger control, Purchases returns, Sales, Sales ledger control, Sales returns, VAT

Task 1.7 (12 marks)

The following transactions all took place on 31 December and have been entered in the cash-book as shown below – the debit side and credit side have been shown separately. No entries have yet been made in the ledgers.

Cash-book – Debit side

Date 20X1	*Details*	*Bank* £
31 Dec	Balance b/f	3,110
31 Dec	Paul Bros (trade receivable)	500

Cash-book – Credit side

Date 20X1	*Details*	*VAT* £	*Bank* £
31 Dec	Office expenses	30	180
31 Dec	Travel expenses		48

What will be the entries in the general ledger? (12 marks)

Select your account name from the following list: Balance b/f, Bank, Entertainment, Insurance, Office expenses, Purchases ledger control, Sales ledger control, Travel expenses, VAT

Account name	**Amount** £	**Debit** ✓	**Credit** ✓

Task 1.8 (12 marks)

The following two accounts are in the general ledger of Brooklyn Boats at the close of day on 31 December.

Motor vehicles

Date 20XX	*Details*	*Amount £*	*Date 20XX*	*Details*	*Amount £*
01 Dec 12 Dec	Balance b/f Bank	12,500 7,000			

Loan from the bank

Date 20XX	*Details*	*Amount £*	*Date 20XX*	*Details*	*Amount £*
5 Dec	Bank	500	1 Dec	Bal b/f	10,000

(a) What will be the balance brought down at 1 January on each account. (4 marks)

Account name	**Balance b/d at 1 January £**	**Debit ✓**	**Credit ✓**
Motor vehicles			
Loan from the bank			

(b) The following account is in the general ledger of ABC Ltd at the close of day on 31 December.

Complete the account below by:

- Inserting the balance carried down together with date and details.
- Inserting the totals.
- Inserting the balance brought down together with date and details. (8 marks)

Electricity

Date 20XX	*Details*	*Amount £*	*Date 20XX*	*Details*	*Amount £*
01 Dec 12 Dec	Balance b/f Bank **Total**	870 350		 **Total**	

Picklist: Balance b/d, Balance c/d, Bank, Closing balance, Opening balance, Purchases ledger control

Task 1.9 (12 marks)

Below is a partially prepared trial balance as at 31st December 20XX.

(a) Insert the total of the debit and credit columns of the partially prepared trial balance. (2 marks)

Account name	**Debit** £	**Credit** £
Sales revenue		646,818
Sales returns	135,629	
Purchases	273,937	
Purchases returns		1,348
Discounts received		1,700
Discounts allowed	2,340	
Wages	152,099	
Motor expenses	2,853	
Office sundries	14,579	
Rent and rates	7,345	
Advertising	1,452	
Totals		

The remainder of the balances have now been extracted from the accounting records.

(b) Complete the trial balance by transferring the relevant amounts to the debit or credit column. Do not enter a zero in the unused cells. (10 marks)

General ledger	£
Inventory	28,814
Sales ledger control	172,696
Purchases ledger control	75,987
VAT owed to tax authorities	63,252
Capital	28,352
Hotel expenses	1,785
Motor vehicles	?
Bank loan	?

Other balances	£
Petty cash book	200
Cash book	10,222

The account balances for motor vehicles and the bank loan were missed from the general ledger accounts' listing above, however the ledger accounts have been provided below:

Motor vehicles

Date 20XX	**Details**	**Amount £**	**Date 20XX**	**Details**	**Amount £**
1 Dec 5 Dec	Bal b/f Bank	20,500 10,427	31 Dec	Bal c/d	30,927
		30,927			30,927

Bank loan

Date 20XX	**Details**	**Amount £**	**Date 20XX**	**Details**	**Amount £**
28 Dec 31 Dec	Bank Bal c/d	579 17,421	1 Dec	Bal b/f	18,000
		18,000			18,000

Account name	Debit £	Credit £
Motor vehicles		
Inventory		
Bank		
Petty cash control		
Sales ledger control		
Purchases ledger control		
VAT owed to tax authorities		
Capital		
Bank loan		
Sales revenue		646,818
Sales returns	135,629	
Purchases	273,937	
Purchases returns		1,348
Discounts received		1,700
Discounts allowed	2,340	
Wages	152,099	
Motor expenses	2,853	
Office sundries	14,579	
Rent and rates	7,345	
Advertising	1,452	
Hotel expenses		

Task 1.10 (12 marks)

Earl & Robinson, code all purchase invoices with a supplier code AND a general ledger code. A selection of the codes used is given below.

Supplier	*Supplier account code*
Alpha Ltd	ALP21
Burton Products	BUR14
Cuddington Couriers	CUD22
Farrah Ltd	FAR13
Jacob Brothers	JAC17

Item	*General ledger code*
Pasta	GL12
Tomatoes	GL14
Herbs	GL21
Cheese	GL23
Wine	GL34

This is an invoice received from a supplier.

Jacob Brothers **19 Clough Road, Sale M34 5HY** **VAT Registration No. 349 2354 13**	
Earl & Robinson 42 Maple Street Audenshaw, M11 2SQ	20 March 20X2
500 ....Tins of tomatoes @ £0.15 each	£75
VAT	£15
Total	£90

(a) Select which codes would be used to code this invoice. (2 marks)

Supplier account code	Select your account code from the following list: ALP21, BUR14, CUD22, FAR13, JAC17, GL12, GL14, GL21, GL23, GL34
General ledger code	Select your account code from the following list: ALP21, BUR14, CUD22, FAR13, JAC17, GL12, GL14, GL21, GL23, GL34

One customer has been offered a prompt payment discount for payment within 5 days.

(b) Show what TWO actions should be taken if the customer does pay within 5 days. (2 marks)

Action	✓
Issue a credit note for the discount taken plus VAT.	
Issue a new invoice for the amount paid.	
Change the amounts of the original invoice.	
Record the amount received in the appropriate day books and ledgers.	

A business has the following assets and liabilities.

Assets and liabilities	£
Land & Buildings	545,000
Cash at bank	12,547
Loan from bank	25,879
Plant & Machinery	35,489
Receivables	24,056
Payables	17,697

(c) Show the accounting equation by inserting the appropriate figures. Enter all figures as positive values. (3 marks)

Assets £	Liabilities £	Capital £

(d) Select one option in each instance below to show whether the item will be capital expenditure, revenue expenditure, capital income or revenue income. (5 marks)

Item	*Capital expenditure*	*Revenue expenditure*	*Capital income*	*Revenue income*
Purchase of stationery				
Receipts from cash sales				
Receipt from sale of machinery				
Purchase of additional machinery				
Payment of rates				

2 Mock Assessment Answers

Task 1.1 (12 marks)

(a) Calculate the amounts (pounds and pence) to be included on the invoice: (4 marks)

	£
Net amount before discount	400.00
Net amount after discount	380.00
VAT	76.00
Total	456.00

(b) What will be the amounts entered in the sales day book when the invoice in (a) is prepared? (3 marks)

Sales day book

Date 20XX	Details	Invoice number	Total £	VAT £	Net £
14 June	ELA Ltd	314	456.00	76.00	380.00

(c) Show which THREE transactions are still outstanding by circling the relevant transactions shown below: (3 marks)

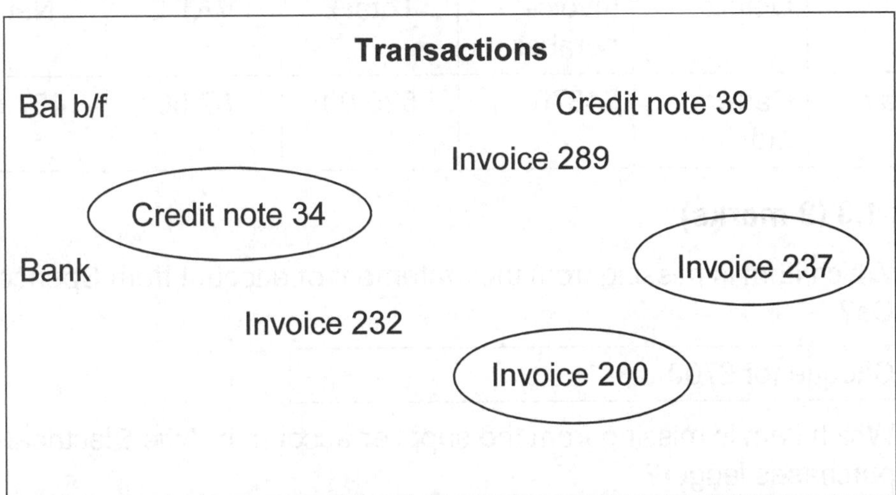

(d) What will be the amount ELA Ltd will pay if they purchase the goods and pay within 5 days of the invoice date? (2 marks)

£2,840.16

Task 1.2 (9 marks)

(a) Identify any discrepancies on the invoice by placing a tick in the appropriate box in the table set out below: (4 marks)

	Correctly shown on invoice	Not shown on invoice	Incorrectly shown on invoice
Product code	✓		
Unit price			✓
Terms of payment	✓		
Trade discount		✓	

(b) Record the invoice in the appropriate day book by: (5 marks)

- Inserting the correct day book title (in the first row):

Select from: sales day book, purchases day book, discounts allowed day book, discounts received day book, sales returns day book, purchases returns day book

- Inserting the correct details:

Select from: Carrera Ltd, T Blossom

- Making the necessary entries.

Purchases day book					
Date 20XX	Details	Invoice number	Total £	VAT £	Net £
15 May	Carrera Ltd	54879	525.00	87.50	437.50

Task 1.3 (9 marks)

(a) Which item is missing from the statement of account from Spence & Co?

Cheque for £700

Which item is missing from the supplier account in Alfie Electricals purchases ledger?

Invoice 299

(b) Assuming any differences between the statement of account from Spence & Co and the supplier account in Alfie Electricals purchases ledger are simply due to omission errors, what is the amount owing to Spence & Co?

£100

(c) What will be the amount owed to RR & Co once the credit note has been entered into their account? (1 mark)

£2,110

(d) Calculate the amount to be paid to each supplier if the prompt payment discount is taken and show the date by which the supplier should receive the payment. (4 marks)

Supplier	£	Date by which the payment should be received by the supplier
Hudson & Co	739.14	11 November 20XX
Marsh & Co	2143.44	16 November 20XX

Task 1.4 (15 marks)

(a) Enter the details from the three receipts and two cheque book stubs into the credit side of the cash-book shown below and total each column. (7 marks)

Cash-book – credit side

Details	*Cash*	*Bank*	*VAT*	*Payables*	*Cash purchases*
Balance b/f					
Johnson Ltd	480		80		400
A Alpha	384		64		320
Bond's	350		–		350
ABC Ltd		2,000		2,000	
Twilight		240		240	
Total	1,214	2,240	144	2,240	1,070

There are two cheques from credit customers to be entered in Adam & Son's cash book:

Rhoda Ring £560

Reef £210

(b) Enter the above details into the debit side of the cash-book and total each column. (6 marks)

Cash book – debit side

Details	*Cash*	*Bank*	*Receivables*
Balance b/f	1,500	11,710	
Rhoda Ring		560	560
Reef		210	210
Total	1,500	12,480	770

(c) Using your answers to (a) and (b) above, calculate the cash balance. (1 mark)

£286

Using your answers to (a) and (b) above, calculate the bank balance. Use a minus sign if your calculations indicate an overdrawn balance, e.g. –123 (1 mark)

£10,240

Task 1.5 (15 marks)

(a) What will be the entry in the petty cash book to restore to the imprest level on 30th June? (3 marks)

Details	**Amount** £	**Debit** ✓	**Credit** ✓
Cash from bank	94.08	✓	

(b) What will be the entry in the petty cash book to record the closing balance on 30th June after the imprest level has been restored? (3 marks)

Details	**Amount** £	**Debit** ✓	**Credit** ✓
Balance c/d	200.00		✓

(c) What will be the total of the Office Expenses column in the petty cash book? (1 mark)

£39.40

(d) What will be the total, VAT and net amounts to be entered into the petty cash book? (6 marks)

Petty cash voucher number	Total £	VAT £	Net £
285	13.50	2.25	11.25
286	33.00	5.50	27.50

(e) What analysis columns in the petty cash book will be used to record the net amounts of the petty cash payments detailed in (d)? (2 marks)

Petty cash voucher number	Analysis column
285	Office expenses
286	Carriage and postage

Task 1.6 (12 marks)

(a) What will be the entries in the general ledger? (9 marks)

Account name	Amount £	Debit ✓	Credit ✓
Discounts allowed	500	✓	
VAT	100	✓	
Sales ledger control	600		✓

(b) What will be the entry in the sales ledger? (3 marks)

Account name	Amount £	Debit ✓	Credit ✓
Johnson Cooper	72		✓

Task 1.7 (12 marks)

What will be the entries in the general ledger? (12 marks)

Account name	Amount £	Debit ✓	Credit ✓
Sales ledger control	500		✓
Office expenses	150	✓	
VAT	30	✓	
Travel expenses	48	✓	

Task 1.8 (12 marks)

(a) What will be the balance brought down at 1 January on each account. (4 marks)

Account name	Balance b/d at 1 January £	Debit ✓	Credit ✓
Motor vehicles	19,500	✓	
Loan from the bank	9,500		✓

(b) The following account is in the general ledger of ABC Ltd at the close of day on 31 December.

Complete the account below by:

- Inserting the balance carried down together with date and details.
- Inserting the totals.
- Inserting the balance brought down together with date and details. (8 marks)

Electricity

Date 20XX	*Details*	*Amount £*	*Date 20XX*	*Details*	*Amount £*
01 Dec	Balance b/f	870	31 Dec	Balance c/d	1,220
12 Dec	Bank	350			
	Total	1,220		**Total**	1,220
1 Jan	Balance b/d	1,220			

Task 1.9 (12 marks)

(a) Insert the total of the debit and credit columns of the partially prepared trial balance. (2 marks)

Account name	**Debit** £	**Credit** £
Sales revenue		646,818
Sales returns	135,629	
Purchases	273,937	
Purchases returns		1,348
Discounts received		1,700
Discounts allowed	2,340	
Wages	152,099	
Motor expenses	2,853	
Office sundries	14,579	
Rent and rates	7,345	
Advertising	1,452	
Totals	590,234	649,866

(b) Complete the trial balance by transferring the relevant amounts to the debit or credit column. Do not enter a zero in the unused cells. (10 marks)

Account name	Debit £	Credit £
Motor vehicles	30,927	
Inventory	28,814	
Bank	10,222	
Petty cash control	200	
Sales ledger control	172,696	
Purchases ledger control		75,987
VAT owed to tax authorities		63,252
Capital		28,352
Bank loan		17,421
Sales revenue		646,818
Sales returns	135,629	
Purchases	273,937	
Purchases returns		1,348
Discounts received		1,700
Discounts allowed	2,340	
Wages	152,099	
Motor expenses	2,853	
Office sundries	14,579	
Rent and rates	7,345	
Advertising	1,452	
Hotel expenses	1,785	

NB Although it is not a requirement of the question, the accuracy of the trial balance can be tested by ensuring both the totals of the debit and credit columns agree. In this task both the debit and credit columns total £834,878.

Task 1.10 (12 marks)

(a) Select which codes would be used to code this invoice. (2 marks)

Supplier account code – JAC 17

General ledger code – GL14

(b) Show what TWO actions should be taken if the customer does pay within 5 days. (2 marks)

Action	✓
Issue a credit note for the discount taken plus VAT.	✓
Issue a new invoice for the amount paid.	
Change the amounts of the original invoice.	
Record the amount received in the appropriate day books and ledgers.	✓

(c) Show the accounting equation by inserting the appropriate figures. Enter all figures as positive values. (3 marks)

Assets £	Liabilities £	Capital £
617,092	43,576	573,516

(d) Select one option in each instance below to show whether the item will be capital expenditure, revenue expenditure, capital income or revenue income. (5 marks)

Item	*Capital expenditure*	*Revenue expenditure*	*Capital income*	*Revenue income*
Purchase of stationery		✓		
Receipts from cash sales				✓
Receipt from sale of machinery			✓	
Purchase of additional machinery	✓			
Payment of rates		✓		

INDEX

Q

R

S

T

U

V

Z